THE SHEEP RAISER'S MANUAL

To Sarah and Ken,
Here's to your continued affection for
our favorite animal and the unexpected
events out in the sheep barn! Good luck
always!
Bill Kruesi

S^{THE}HEEP RAISER'S MANUAL

William K. Kruesi

WILLIAMSON PUBLISHING
CHARLOTTE, VERMONT 05445

Library of Congress Cataloging in Publication Data

Kruesi, William K.
  The sheepraiser's manual.

  Bibliography: p.
  Includes index.
  1. Sheep—Handbooks, manuals, etc. I. Title.
SF375.K78 1984 636.3 84-25765
ISBN 0-913589-10-1

Cover and interior design: Trezzo-Braren Studio
Typography: Villanti & Sons, Printers, Inc.
Printing: Capital City Press

Williamson Publishing Co.
Charlotte, Vermont 05445

Manufactured in the United States of America

First Printing February 1985

Contents

Continued on next page

Contents (continued)

Preface

The latest USDA Census of Agriculture reveals that 64 percent of all farmers are part-timers, with some Northeast states reporting a staggering 50 to 120 percent increase in part-time farmers from 1978 to 1982. Part-time farming is replacing large-scale, capital-intensive production with methods requiring less mechanization, less fossil energy use, and greater conservation of resources. The part-time farmers are typically well-educated, ambitious, and innovative, with a keen awareness of environmental quality.

Some of these part-time farmers have started up commercial-scale sheep operations. Many family farms throughout the country also have a moderate-sized flock as part of their farm operation. It is often a complementary enterprise. The sheep help convert crop residues into a profit, or they are part of a grazing management scheme with beef to maximize animal productivity per acre, or the sheep graze steep pastureland to maximize total farm productivity. Sheep are sometimes a supplemental enterprise: someone in the family enjoys shepherding and the area provides enough shepherding support services to make the operation worthwhile. It is to these farm flocks that I wish to address my book.

I will present the latest technical information to provide a basis for higher levels of production, and, I hope, greater profitability. Sheep farming, whether it is with 50 or 500 ewes, is a business; and for a business to survive, it must be profitable. This book fills a gap between several good beginners' books on raising sheep and the *Sheepman's Production Handbook*, a standard reference for commercial producers. My hope is that sheep farmers will continue to adopt new and alternative methods of farming to sustain agricultural productivity far into the future—with less energy, less waste, and a more skillful use of resources.

I am especially grateful to the many farmers, sheep specialists, and agricultural leaders who inspired my wife and me to be more successful in raising sheep and to extend our knowledge to others. In particular, I wish to thank Bruce Clement, director of the New England Sheep Project, for his innumerable lessons and practical advice on raising sheep; Dr. Paul Saenger, University of Vermont Extension Livestock Specialist, for giving us fresh ideas; Brian Magee of Cornell University, for his appreciation of the biology of sheep and his insight into the research needs of the producer; Henry and Cornelia Swayze, manufacturers of electric fencing and sheep farmers from Tunbridge, Vermont, for opening our eyes to the best pasture management practices; Bill and Hilda Yates, sheep farmers from Brownsville, Vermont, who challenge us to be better farmers; Roger Parrott, my school teacher from Putney, Vermont, for giving me an appreciation of agriculture and ecology; and Dave Thompson, editor and publisher of *Sheep!* magazine, for his support, encouragement, and friendship. I was extremely fortunate to have help from my wife, Katy, who spent many hours reviewing the book and clarifying important points. I would like to extend my gratitude to my sister, Kate Lincoln, and to Mary Ann Carroll for spending so many hours on the word processor preparing my manuscript. Of course, this book would not have been possible without the patience and understanding of Katy and our sons, Mitchell and Jonathan.

Bill Kruesi
Woodstock, Vermont

Chapter 1

THE SHEEP ENTERPRISE

Many sheep producers in the United States and Canada are at levels of production that are no better than what was possible with the same breeds of sheep 30 years ago. The typical lambing percentage is still about 120, or a little better than 1 lamb born per ewe per year. Our market lambs are not gaining any faster than lambs did in the 1950s, although today's lambs have more lean meat and less fat when they go to market. Pastures that supported 5 ewes per acre back then are still considered average pastures today.

But, while our levels of production have practically stayed the same, our costs of production are several times higher. Fuel, fertilizer, feed, and supplies are increasing in price at a rate of 8 to 10 percent per year, and no relief is in sight. Lamb prices, as with the price of all major farm commodities, have not kept up with the costs of production, and more farmers are leaving agriculture than are entering it.

Great improvements are possible in the areas of reproduction, pasture management, lamb nutrition, and the use of production and financial records. We do not have to resort to miracle products, chemicals, or drugs to accomplish our objectives of higher production and profitability. Good livestock management and attention to the basic requirements of the animal are the fundamentals of successful farming.

Producers have seen the good results of feeding lambs a high-concentrate ration from birth to market weight. The lambs are ready for market in 4 to 5 months instead of the 6 to 10 months required for range-fed or pasture-fed lambs. Unfortunately, the high-concentrate feed costs 2 to 3 times more than pasture and other low-cost forages, and producers have not increased the lambing percentage high enough to compensate for the higher feed costs.

Producers also have made large capital investments in housing, machinery, feed-handling equipment, and automation to take advantage of push-button farming systems. This has resulted in an unprecedented debt load for North American farmers. We need to concentrate on the resources on the farm which directly affect income — namely the land and the livestock — rather than place too much emphasis on capital items which do not increase operating receipts.

LOW-INPUT PRODUCTION SYSTEM

There are 2 main directions I think we can take towards improved profitability in our sheep operations. The first direction involves few, if any, buildings, and very little equipment. It is a low-input, low-labor system based on pasture and other low-cost feedstuffs and once a year lambing. Under this system, sheep lamb in late April or early May on pasture. Lamb losses are kept low because of the mild weather. The ewes lactate on the spring flush of pasture and do not receive grain. Ewes in early to mid gestation are fed hay or other stored feed outdoors, all winter, with little more than a windbreak or a grove of pine trees for protection. With adequate nutrition and a full fleece, they are well cared for, despite the winter cold. The lambs are born, raised, and sold off pasture. Most will be at market weight by the end of the grazing season, others can be sold as feeder lambs. The lambs are creep fed a low-cost energy supplement, such as whole corn or barley, from birth to market for the fastest gains at the least cost. Labor is kept to a minimum by flushing ewes on pasture rather than feeding grain daily during the flushing season. Ewes are selected to be easy keepers; they have good mothering ability, are able to lamb without assistance, have good milk production, and have a high rate of twinning. The low-input system is marked by the intensive use of pasture rather than the intensive use of labor and capital.

INTENSIVE PRODUCTION SYSTEM

The second direction that producers can take to increase profitability involves more intensive use of labor, facilities, crop land, and capital—as practiced in the dairy, swine, and poultry industries. Under the low-input system, we try to obtain a lambing percentage in the area of 180 to 200 percent, or 2 lambs born per ewe per year. Under the intensive production system, the emphasis is on maximizing the reproductive capacity of the ewe by lambing at shorter intervals (accelerated lambing), having multiple births and synchronized breeding, and feeding lambs high-concentrate rations and harvested forage.

Both production systems have merit, and both can be profitable. The level of production is much higher under the intensive system, but at a proportionately higher cost. Intensive production has worked extremely well for dairy farmers in terms of labor efficiency, milk production per cow, and profitability. On the other hand, the low-input system is working very well in New Zealand, where grassland farming is a model of resource efficiency.

On high-priced cropland, the intensive production system is favored. Yields of crop or animal products per acre must be very high to justify the costs of owning the land. The situation is similar to that of vegetable growers near urban areas who realize they must triple crop the same acreage in a single growing season as housing pressures force land values up.

Photo 1–1. Ewes on pasture with triplets.

CURRENT PRODUCTION SYSTEM

The production system I do *not* favor is a middle-of-the-road approach between the low-input system and intensive production. Yet this is the type of production practiced by many sheep producers. They want to lamb once a year, but build a barn that could be used for lambing every 2 months. They want to raise lambs quickly to market weight by feeding a high-concentrate ration, but they don't sell their lambs for any more than what a grass-fed lamb brings. They rent corn fields for silage, while the pasture grows up to weed trees and brush. In many cases, producers want the latest gadgets without taking care of the basic elements of production first. If you want the latest technology, you usually have to increase or intensify production to justify the technology financially. If you own pasture and forage land, and little else, then the low-input system deserves your attention.

PRODUCTION GOALS

Intensive systems of sheep production incorporate the latest technology, but production goals are difficult to arrive at. No one knows what maximum levels of production can be obtained with sheep. Production and financial goals for a low-input production system are easier to provide (Table 1-1).

Our roles as small-scale and large-scale sheep producers will grow as the world looks to grazing animals as the best converters of forage into meat, milk, and wool. There is the opportunity to develop better systems of production, which are manageable and profitable, even on the scale of 50 or 100 ewes.

Table 1-1

ANNUAL PRODUCTION GOALS	
Intensive Production	**Low-Input Production**
2.5–3.5 lambs/ewe	1.8–2 lambs/ewe
1.0–1.3 pounds gain/lamb/day	.5–.8 pounds gain/lamb/day on pasture
6–8 pounds wool/ewe	
7–8 month lambing interval	8–12 pounds wool/ewe
200 grazing days (ewes)	12 month lambing interval
7–10 hours labor/ewe	200 grazing days (ewes and lambs)
	3–5 hours labor/ewe

Table 1-1. Annual production goals for 2 systems of sheep production.

Chapter 2

FENCING, HOUSING, AND EQUIPMENT

The most important physical resource on a sheep farm is the land. Your pastures and cropland should be improved before you spend significant amounts of capital on farm machinery or buildings. An exception is the construction of reliable fences which make it possible to control grazing and to reclaim overgrown pastures. Liming, fertilizing, reseeding, and weed control are of little use if you cannot control where sheep graze and for how long. Fencing is a major capital investment on the sheep farm; but it will have immediate benefits for managing the pastures, controlling predators, and providing sheep with low-cost, high-quality forage during the grazing season.

*Parts of this chapter first appeared as an article in the *New England Farmer* magazine.

Photo 2-1. Temporary fencing made of electrified plastic netting and plastic twine is ideal for subdividing a pasture into small plots for rotational grazing.

INNOVATIVE FENCING

The trend in farm fencing is to use permanent electric fencing for all perimeter fences and to subdivide pastures into small sections or paddocks with less expensive, temporary electric fencing, allowing a more intensive use of grazing livestock to improve rough, unproductive pastureland. Permanent and temporary electric fences can be used together to carefully control livestock grazing and increase the carrying capacity of a given field. Intensive rotational grazing enables farmers to double or triple the stocking rate on pastures and provide a higher-quality, more steady supply of forage.

Electric Fencing

Electric fence—both temporary and permanent—has the advantage of being low cost and easy to erect, using lightweight line posts. It is adaptable to hill terrain, repels predators, and adapts well to intensive or rotational grazing. A typical permanent electric fence system costs 20 to 50 percent less than a conventional woven or barbed wire fence.

A permanent electric fence is good for 10 years or more. It qualifies for investment tax credit and can be depreciated the same way as other capital investments on the farm. A well-planned, properly constructed fence will last for many years, with minimum maintenance, giving you a good return on materials and labor invested.

One of the disadvantages of electric fencing is that it is ineffective when the power fails. However, the spring-loaded multi-strand fence designs provide a visual and, to some degree, a structural barrier to livestock.

Maintenance needs are much greater on an electric fence that uses a low-quality fence charger. The fenceline requires periodic maintenance in the summer; mostly you will need to trim tall weeds under the fence. If the weeds are high and thick enough to ground the fence, cut them by hand with a sharp scythe, grass whip, high-wheeled mower, or a weedeater/spin trimmer. Mowing the fenceline twice a season is usually enough to keep the weeds down and is a necessary chore with the low-cost fence chargers. A hand-held voltage meter or neon light fence tester is useful for locating spots where the fence is grounded, and for checking the charge without touching a hot wire yourself.

Photo 2–2. Permanent electric fencing can be installed for one-third the cost of a woven wire fence.

A low-impedance, high-voltage charger, however, will still deliver a strong shock on a weed-loaded fence. The New Zealanders have developed several models of high-voltage chargers which solve the problem of wet weeds grounding a fence. It is only a matter of time before an American firm will manufacture a charger that competes with the imports from New Zealand and Australia.

An electric fence will contain only livestock that are trained to it. They have to learn that it hurts when they touch the fence. You can train animals to respect the fence by offering some grain, just inside the fence. While eating the grain, they will bring their heads up and touch the wire. A wet nose makes a good contact with the charged wire, and retraining will not be needed usually. Of course, the fence must always be "on" to be effective. A second way to train animals to respect fencing is to tie ear corn onto the fence with baling wire and let the animals investigate the corn. Sheep in full fleece will be well-insulated against a shock, unless they touch their noses to the wire.

Spacing of Fence Wires

The spacing of the fence wires should be determined by the size and type of livestock and predators, and if the fence is to be temporary or permanent. For sheep and lambs, there should be 5 strands of wire, spaced at 5 inches, 10 inches, 17 inches, 27 inches, and 38 inches above the soil.

Existing woven wire fences can be made predator-proof by adding a single strand of electric wire. The wire should be placed 8 inches above the ground, and 8 inches away from the fence on the "outside" of the woven wire fence. An animal will get a shock attempting to go under the wire, or a shock across the stomach attempting to climb the fence. With low fences, add an electric wire just high enough to meet whatever animals might jump the fence. Other designs for anti-coyote fences are available as a result of research done by the USDA and fence manufacturers. The high tensile wire is adaptable for use as a coyote trip wire fence.

Permanent Electric Fence Systems

With a permanent electric fence system, the entire system must be used: high tensile wire, springs, insulators, pressure-treated battens and posts, and special charger. Some manufacturers are using fiberglass posts, others a pressure-treated wood post that is self-insulating. While creosote pressure-treated posts may cost 25 percent more than untreated posts, they extend fence post life by 20 years and eliminate the need for insulators. These innovative fence designs work as a system, so follow the manufacturer's installation guidelines.

Temporary Fencing

Further improvements in electric fence systems are coming from England and New Zealand in the form of electrified plastic netting and plastic twine. Fine stainless steel wire is braided into bright-colored plastic twine. The flexible wire can be cut with a knife and spliced together with a simple knot. It is useful for temporary electric fence because it is very lightweight, quick to erect and take down, low cost, and flexible. It is ideal for subdividing a pasture into small plots for rotational grazing or for subdividing an annual crop for strip grazing to increase total productivity per acre.

HOUSING AND EQUIPMENT

Animals perform better and require less feed when they are raised under ideal environmental conditions. For many areas of the country, some winter housing is necessary for lambing because of extreme cold. With thorough planning, the sheep housing also can be used for shearing, artificial rearing, routine sheep handling, and for storing bedding, feed, or wool.

There is no "best" set-up for a sheep flock. It depends on the degree of confinement, how much you want to trade labor for facilities and equipment, and the amount of capital investment that you are willing to make. Similarly, it is difficult to generalize about old or existing buildings to be modified or used for sheep. If you own facilities for dairy cattle or other livestock and want to use the buildings for sheep, request an on-site visit from your state Extension Agricultural Engineer to discuss how to modify the barn for sheep.

In general, housing costs should be about 10 percent of income. The annual housing cost includes depreciation, repairs, interest, taxes, and insurance. As the flock size increases, housing and other fixed costs generally decrease.

A small flock of sheep can be housed with other livestock without sacrificing labor efficiency or reducing their production. As the flock size increases above 50 ewes, more specialized facilities may reduce the labor involved in feeding, handling, or loading sheep. In addition, intensive sheep production can be more efficient when the facilities are designed for feeding groups of sheep according to their production, rearing orphan lambs, lambing more than once a year, and handling ewes and lambs more often.

The general specifications for sheep housing are to allow 15 to 20 square feet of floor space per ewe, and 8 square feet per lamb on a solid floor or bedding. Provide at least 10 to 14 square feet per ewe and 4 to 6 feet per lamb on slatted floors. The lower figures are for small ewes (120 to 140 pounds) and small lambs (up to 50 pounds).

The shelter or barn should be built on a well-drained site. Its open side should face away from the prevailing winter winds to avoid drafts and drifting snow. There should be wide access areas for hay wagons, trucks, tractors, and other equipment that load and unload around the barn.

Barns to be used for a flock under accelerated lambing should have multiple areas for feeding ewes according to their stage of production (late pregnancy, nursing, ready to breed, etc.). There should be a lamb creep for young lambs and a separate feeding area for weaned lambs.

If you usually have some lambs that have to be reared on milk replacer, an artificial rearing pen is useful. Details on the size of the pen and the self-feeders are covered in Chapter 13.

CONFINEMENT REARING

Confinement sheep production requires a high level of management and a high level of production to justify the housing costs. Under total confinement, all environmental factors, including light, temperature, nutrition, and atmosphere, are the shepherd's responsibility. The objective is to maintain the animal's good health by providing the optimum environment.

The comfort zone for shorn sheep is between 45 and 75 degrees F., and 30 to 40 degrees F. for ewes in full fleece. The optimum temperature for young lambs in cold housing is approximately 45 degrees F. The relative humidity in confinement housing should be 50 to 75 percent. Temperature and humidity can be controlled by forced air ventilation that provides 20 to 25 cubic feet per minute (CFM) of air movement or fan capacity per ewe, and 15 CFM per lamb, year-round. The minimum window area or translucent roof-panel area should be 3 to 5 percent of total floor area. For night lighting, provide one 100-watt lamp for each 400 to 500 square feet of floor area.

Where land, labor, and interest costs are relatively high, confinement rearing and intensive production are more cost effective. Confinement rearing can lower the amount of feed required to maintain

Photo 2–3. Confinement sheep barn at the Ohio Agricultural Research and Development Center, Wooster.

mature ewes by approximately 38 percent. Decreasing the total nutrient requirements by 38 percent during the maintenance period and early gestation may result in 20 percent annual savings in feed. However, there are few flocks which have shown that total or year-round confinement is profitable. Profitability depends on a high rate of reproductive efficiency, having sources of inexpensive feedstuffs, using labor efficiently, and making maximum use of new and/or existing facilities.

Barns

Many sheep operations use an open front, 3-sided shed or pole barn. It is the most flexible and least expensive sheep housing. If the barn is intended to be used as winter housing, the open front should face south, and the eave should be high enough to allow sunlight to reach the back or north side of the shed. A continuous ridge vent and/or eave vents along the long side of the barn help to remove warm, moist air.

In general, the total cost of the building is insignificant if it gets used year-round, reduces labor that could be put to better use, and improves production efficiency. The least expensive new housing usually is built with your own hands and with used or salvaged materials. It should incorporate a sloped dirt floor and straw bedding or have a slatted floor. Old barns with concrete floors are suitable for sheep, but new concrete floors are cost-prohibitive in new housing. Concrete or asphalt has a place in feed alleys, clean-out areas, and other high-traffic areas. Otherwise, there doesn't seem to be much advantage to concrete over a packed dirt floor, especially if a bedding pack is allowed to accumulate for several months at a time. Concrete floors are useful for manure storage facilities and bunker silos, which are loaded and unloaded with heavy equipment.

Slatted Floors

Manure handling is one of those necessary tasks that gives farmers little or no return for their work. Sheep housing can be designed to minimize the time and effort spent in feeding, watering, and cleaning out manure. Any time saved with these chores can be put to better use in work that generates income.

One way to reduce manure handling is to house sheep on slatted floors, thereby eliminating daily or weekly cleaning and the cost

Photo 2–4. Low-cost wooden slatted floors work well to reduce labor, bedding costs, space requirements, and exposure to parasites and foot rot.

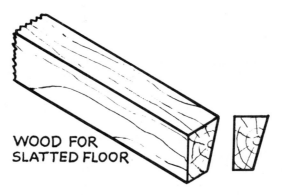

WOOD FOR
SLATTED FLOOR

*Figure 2–1. The diagonal cut of the wooden slats
for sheep flooring makes them self-cleaning.*

of bedding materials. Slatted floors can reduce exposure to internal parasites, labor, bedding costs, space requirements, and foot rot. They also can increase the level of environmental control, rate of gain, summer comfort, and wool quality.

The flooring can be concrete, wood, plastic, or fiberglass (used for confinement swine housing) or expanded metal. It should support a 200-pound load at the center, be self-cleaning, provide good footing, and be rot-resistant.

Low-cost wood slats have worked very well. They can be cut from local lumber, including oak, hemlock, southern yellow pine, and other rot-resistant woods. Each slat should be 2 inches wide with a ¾-inch to ⅞-inch spacing between slats. A diagonal cut should be made along one of the long verticle sides of each slat (see Figure 2–1) to allow the manure to drop through easily without sticking.

Floor panels should be light enough to be moved by 1 or 2 people. The maximum size of each floor panel should be 6 feet by 7 feet with 2×4 supports and nailers. Each floor section should be supported by 2×12 stringers bolted to 8×8 (pressure treated) posts. Other practical panel sizes for slatted wood flooring are 4 feet by 8 feet, 5 feet by 8 feet, 4 feet by 10 feet, and 4 feet by 12 feet. These are small and light enough to be removed for cleaning out the manure that accumulates under the floor. Slatted floors should be at least 3 feet off the ground to allow for manure storage and air circulation. The livestock waste will be practically 100 percent manure since little or no bedding is used with slatted floors. To clean it out, remove the floor panels and scoop out the manure with a front-end loader or shovel. Wood floors built with 2-inch lumber should last 8 to 10 years in a total confinement barn.

The most popular material for metal slatted floors is ¾-inch No. 9 flattened expanded metal or "safety mesh." Metal floors are more expensive than wood slats and also have a life expectancy of 8 to 10 years in a total confinement barn. Metal floors are not suitable in cold barns during lambing, as the newborns can freeze to the floor. There have been reports of injured teats and metal splinters from new sheets of expanded metal. New sheets can be buffed to remove any sharp splinters at the time they are installed. Expanded metal flooring is also noisy compared to wood slats.

Support 4-foot by 8-foot sheets of expanded metal on 2×6 wood stringers (which run lengthwise) and 2×4 wood nailers (which run widthwise), 18 inches on center and 12 inches on center near feeders. Mobile home trailer frames work very well as a base for metal flooring and have the advantage of making the entire unit movable. When manure accumulates, the trailer can be moved to a new site. The manure can then be picked up and spread with conventional equipment. Thus, the floor sections do not have to be removed.

Do not weld sheets of metal flooring together; welding changes the crystalline structure of the steel and weakens it at the welds. Instead, staple the metal sheets to wood stringers and nailers, slightly overlapping each sheet as you go along. The slatted floor barn or trailer unit can be skirted with bales of straw or sheets of plywood to block any drafts during winter.

Photo 2-5. Steel mesh flooring using wood shavings for bedding in the lamb barn. (Courtesy US Sheep Experimental Station, DuBois, Idaho)

Photo 2–6. Polyethylene greenhouses can be used for temporary sheep housing.

TEMPORARY HOUSING

When temporary housing is needed for lambing, a double-layer polyethylene greenhouse can be adapted for sheep. The greenhouse is especially good for lambing in cold weather since it can warm up inside on a sunny day. Greenhouse grade plastic has a life expectancy of 3 years; improved materials are introduced all the time. The greenhouse structures are made of aluminum or steel pipe, bent in a Quonset shape to withstand some snow load, deflect wind and rain, and allow the plastic covering to be stretched smoothly. They are easy to erect, warm, bright inside, and may be property-tax exempt as a "temporary structure." The bottom 4 feet of the polyethylene walls should be sheathed in plywood or left open to prevent the sheep from puncturing the plastic. Good forced-air ventilation is necessary if these houses are enclosed at both ends.

HAY AND GRAIN FEEDERS

A good hay feeder keeps the fleeces clean, conserves fine, leafy material, will not allow lambs to jump in, and prevents the sheep from pulling the hay out while they eat and wasting it. A straight-sided, flat-bottomed bunk (Figure 2–2) built in portable 8-foot sections has worked very well for hay, silage, and grain. It should allow 10 to 15 inches linear space per ewe. The base should be 10 to 12 inches deep for sufficient feed capacity and to keep sheep from pulling hay out.

Vertical slats, spaced 8 inches apart, can be added to keep the sheep from putting their front feet in. Fenceline feeders or bunks are easy to fill from an alleyway and give visitors/buyers a good view of the sheep. The only drawback is that a long perimeter or fenceline is needed to give 10 to 15 inches of linear space per ewe.

Self-feeders are recommended for feeding grain to lambs. They reduce labor and waste, and may increase average daily gains by approximately 0.1 pound per head over hand-feeding. Lambs with free-choice access to grain are less likely to overeat than lambs fed a large amount of grain once or twice a day. With adequate feeder space, even the timid and weak lambs get their share.

Hanging poultry feeders are great for creep feeding lambs up to 8 weeks of age. After 8 weeks, a stronger and larger feeder is needed, such as a turkey or hog feeder. These can be used to creep feed lambs on pasture also.

Photo 2–7. Fenceline feeders allow the shepherd to feed grain to the sheep without getting trampled.

Photo 2–8. Hog feeders are used for self-feeding lambs in a drylot.

Photo 2–10. Angus cattle self-feed from the front of a bag of silage placed in a movable feed panel. (Photograph by Chuck Savage, courtesy Ag-Bag Corporation)

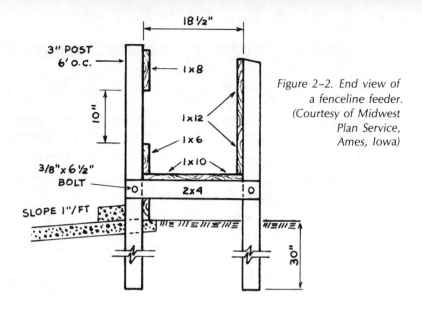

Figure 2-2. End view of a fenceline feeder. (Courtesy of Midwest Plan Service, Ames, Iowa)

BARNYARDS AND FEEDLOTS

Muddy barnyards present a special problem for sheep farmers. Feeding sheep in ankle deep mud is no fun, but it is a common sight on a lot of farms in the spring. Here are several options that can be used to avoid having a sloppy feedlot or barnyard.

- **Keep sheep in confinement under a roof until pasture is available for grazing and loafing (an expensive option).**

- **Feed hay on pasture all winter. Hay can be stacked or hauled out to the pasture or left in the field in round bales for winter grazing. Manure handling is kept to a minimum, the sheep get plenty of exercise, and their health overall is probably better than in confinement.**

- **Cover the lot with asphalt, concrete, or stone chips and scrape daily or every few days to keep the surface relatively clean and dry. The cost may be $1.50 to $2.00 per square foot, just for materials.**

- **Grade the area to permit fast runoff of water. A south-facing hill with an 8-degree to 12-degree slope will be drier than a lot with a 2-degree to 5-degree slope.**

- **Build a series of 5-foot high mounds running the length of the barnyard or feedlot. Runoff, manure, and mud tend to collect at the base of the mound while the sheep stay cleaner on top of the mounds. The mounds must be far enough apart and shaped so that manure-handling equipment can be used easily between the mounds.**

HANDLING FACILITIES

A handling facility can be used to gather, hold, sort, and treat sheep in groups or as individuals. A good handling facility encourages sheep to flow through with a minimum of effort for both the sheep and the shepherd, reducing operator fatigue and animal stress. They do not have to be expensive. Here are the basic components:

- **A crowding area to collect and funnel the sheep**
- **A long chute or race that funnels the sheep through and will hold 4 to 5 sheep (single file)**
- **Scales for weighing the sheep**
- **A sorting gate**
- **Holding pens**

Footbaths, dip tanks, turning cradles, and loading ramps can be added to the basic handling facility.

Sheep by nature are followers. Lambs will follow a ewe within hours of birth. Sheep will instinctively flock and move together. Animal behavioral trials have provided more specific answers as to how sheep will move in a given situation. Here are the main concepts.

- **Sheep are inclined to start moving and move faster through a straight chute than in any other chute configuration. Once sheep are moving, they move faster through chutes with corner angles of 45 degrees.**
- **Sheep move faster through a level chute; if there is no alternative but to build on a slope, build the chute so the sheep flow up instead of down. Sheep prefer to move uphill.**
- **Sheep flow better through yards or sheds if the same paths are always followed. A trained "leader" sheep can be used to lead sheep through an established facility.**
- **Avoid contrasts of light and darkness where sheep are to be moved. Sheep prefer to move towards light and towards other sheep.**
- **Wide chutes (60 inches) allow faster movement than narrow chutes (20 inches).**

A chute designed for moving sheep in single-file can be built with tapered sides to permit ewes and lambs to move through without giving the lambs enough room to turn around and reverse their flow. The single-file chute should be narrow enough (20 to 24 inches) so that ewes cannot turn around in the chute, no matter if it is straight-sided or tapered. It should have solid sides so the sheep are not distracted by seeing sheep to either side and will keep moving forward. A 3-inch gap at the bottom of the chute walls will provide air to an animal if it falls down.

Sorting gates at the end of the chute are useful for separating groups of sheep, such as ewes and lambs at weaning, fat and thin ewes, breeding groups by the ram to be used, and finished lambs from light lambs.

Footbaths should be at least 20 feet long to soak the feet thoroughly if they are used for a single treatment. A 2-inch layer of wool on the bottom of the bath will act as a sponge, keeping the chemical solution from splashing out. Footbaths placed in pastures or in the barn where sheep move daily through the bath do not have to be 20 feet long but only long enough to prevent sheep from jumping over the bath (about 4 feet).

If a loading ramp is used, it should be cleated for traction or have steps built in with as gradual an incline as possible. The ramp or loading chute should be set at a 45-degree angle from the handling facility so that sheep will flow around the blind turn into the truck or trailer. Access to both sides of a chute is desirable, as is a roof to keep the floors dry. The facilities should be located on a well-drained site.

More Information

See Appendix G for sources of information on designs for barns, equipment, and handling facilities.

Chapter 3

GRAZING
MANAGEMENT

Many producers began raising sheep because they had pasture that was not being used, or was not being used efficiently. Grazing management is an important part of profitable sheep production. Grazing management attempts to maximize animal production while maintaining or improving the quality of the pasture. The crop in this case is forage, and the sheep are just a convenient way of harvesting the grass and converting it into food and fiber. Permanent and temporary electric fencing are the tools that have made it possible to intensively manage pastures and to reclaim overgrown pasture in a low-capital system. Pasture reclamation and renovation using sheep are covered in Chapter 4.

BASIC MANAGEMENT SYSTEMS

We currently follow 2 basic grazing management systems in the United States: continuous grazing and various forms of rotational grazing. Both systems can be improved by fertilizing for early spring, summer, and fall growth; reseeding to legumes; and by holding some pasture in reserve for use during drought periods.

Pastures must be managed carefully to provide maximum yields of high-quality forage. Throughout the growing season, grazing can be controlled to keep pasture plants vigorous and in a palatable stage of growth. Livestock, especially sheep, tend to pick the desirable plants and graze them preferentially. It is up to you to control where, when, and how long the livestock will graze on a particular piece of land.

Much of the pasture in the United States has been poorly managed. These areas are no longer productive because of low soil fertility, shading, competition from weeds, and the effects of overgrazing. Abandoned acres, which once furnished grass and clover to livestock, reflect a traditional system of grazing that has failed.

PASTURE FALLACIES

The traditional grazing system is one of continuous grazing of a pasture over an entire season. Animals are moved to a pasture when growth starts in the spring and are not rotated or removed until the pasture stops growing, sometime in the fall. This grazing system is based on several misconceptions; but many landowners still rely on these ideas to manage their pastures.

First, the landholders believe that open land starting to grow up to weed trees and brush should continue to be grazed by livestock to keep the brush "chewed down." What really happens is the good forage gets overgrazed, and the brush grows better due to the lack of competition. Livestock will not chew or eat juniper, hemlock, and the like, unless they are desperate. Overgrown pastures need more help than simply releasing some ewes or heifers to run wild over the summer.

A second misconception involves claims about manure. Some people believe that grazing a pasture is beneficial since manure is left behind by the livestock. Actually, grazing allows a net removal of minerals from the soil in the form of milk, meat, bone, and hide that is shipped off the farm. Manure recycles about three-fourths of the nutrients from the plant material eaten by livestock; but when you sell farm products, some of the soil's fertility is leaving the farm. Shipping livestock off the farm for several decades results in a significant loss of minerals from the fields and pastures.

Pastures need periodic liming and fertilizing if they are to remain productive. It has been clearly demonstrated that grass yields increase with applications of nitrogen fertilizer up to a level of over 264 pounds/acre (300 kg N/ha), be it in the form of manure or commercial fertilizer. However, only about 10 to 20 percent of the pasture and rangeland in the United States is fertilized on an annual basis. Pastures rarely even receive the barn manure accumulated over winter.

Low soil pH and the associated toxic effect of high iron, aluminum, and manganese on forage plants also limits pasture productivity. Nearly 60 percent of the soil samples submitted to the University of Vermont Soil Testing Laboratory come back with lime recommendations, most of them requiring 3 tons of lime per acre or more. Low levels of soil acidity are especially critical to the establishment and growth of legumes in the pasture. You can expect up to a 300 percent return on every dollar you spend on lime and fertilizer in short-term benefits alone.

Third, there is a false notion that legumes cannot be established in particular areas. However, there is at least 1 species of forage legume that will grow in your pastures. Soils ranging from poorly drained clays to droughty gravels can support either alfalfa, trefoil, lupines, vetch, or one of the clovers. Without a legume to fix atmospheric nitrogen, the pasture will require supplemental commercial nitrogen fertilizer to stimulate growth. The added cost of the nitrogen fertilizer versus relying on legumes to fix free nitrogen will be at least $20 per acre every year.

Finally, we have to stop thinking that pasture reclamation is impossible and that pasture is low-value, unproductive farmland. Pastures can be improved with a fairly low budget and with a quick return on investment.

CONTINUOUS GRAZING

The simplest form of grazing management is to do nothing, to set livestock on a pasture for the entire season, and let them pick and choose their grazing areas. The disadvantages of this system, called **continuous grazing**, is that there is a wide fluctuation in quality and quantity of feed available throughout the season. Livestock soon start to graze selectively, leaving some areas overgrazed and some undergrazed in the same pasture at the same time. Plants in the undergrazed areas become overmature, tough, dry, and unpalatable.

ROTATIONAL GRAZING

In **rotational grazing**, livestock are moved to different areas at more or less predetermined intervals. It involves more fencing and labor compared to continuous grazing. The grazed areas may accommodate a higher stocking rate (number of sheep and lambs per acre), perhaps 2, 5, or 10 times that of continuous grazing, but the plots are rested in between grazings for a period of regrowth. Size of the plots and duration of the regrowth period will vary depending on seasonal precipitation, average temperatures, and so on.

There are many advantages to rotational grazing, the most significant being an increase in dry matter (DM) production per acre. Dry matter is the total amount of matter in a feedstuff, less the moisture it contains. Forages, such as pasture grasses and legumes, contain about 85 percent water and about 15 percent dry matter. Carrying capacity also is increased and the quality of the forage over the entire season is higher and more uniform than under continuous grazing. Carrying capacity is the ability of pasture land to provide feed for a certain number of livestock at a given level of production. (Ewes that are not bred and not lactating are at a different level of production than ewes nursing lambs.)

Sod density also increases when the pasture grasses and legumes are kept in a vigorous vegetative stage of growth. Close grazing followed by a regrowth period encourages side branching (tillering) in grasses, which thickens the stand. The effect of rotational grazing is similar to a multicut hay or silage system, but it requires less energy, less investment, and it is without the expense of feeding animals mechanically harvested forage.

ALTERNATE GRAZING

Alternate grazing is partway between continuous and rotational grazing, since livestock use 2 paddocks during the grazing season. This results in slightly better use of the pasture compared to continuous grazing, but does not allow adequate rest periods. Each grazing period is long, usually 2 to 3 weeks per paddock. This is enough time for regrowth in the spring, but not enough rest for the 2 paddocks during a long dry spell.

When the livestock are moved to the "rested" pasture, they tend to eat the shortest grass for a few days, then turn to whatever is left, which is usually tall, stemmy growth. With only 2 paddocks, it is nearly impossible to keep animals from grazing the short grass before it has fully recovered. As a result, pasture growth becomes uneven and livestock nutrition rises up and down over the long 2-week to 3-week grazing periods.

As with continuous grazing, the alternate grazing system forces the animals to cover more area in search of the best pasture, rather than limiting their grazing area and the amount of energy they have to expend.

STRIP GRAZING

Strip grazing is a more intense form of rotational grazing. In this system, animals are given an area adequate for a single day (or a few hours) of grazing and no more. Alternatively, a temporary fence, such as electrified plastic netting, can be erected around an annual crop, and the animals allowed to progressively graze the crop. Standing crops of corn, rape, turnip, millet, sudangrass, and other annual crops can be fed out daily by allowing strip grazing in a few rows at a time. The animals eventually graze down all of the forage, but are not allowed to trample down unused feed.

Both rotational and strip grazing have the advantage that tall, high-yielding forages, such as millet or sudangrass, can be rationed out depending on the sheep's nutritional needs, with a minimum of crop losses due to trampling. Small grains, such as wheat, oats, and rye, also can provide some temporary grazing in the vegetative stage.

The main drawback with annual forage crops is the additional expense of plowing, harrowing, and reseeding that must be done, whereas permanent pasture remains undisturbed for years. Any use of annual forage crops should be weighed against making improvements in the permanent pastures.

STOCKING RATES

Continuous, alternate, and rotational grazing can be carried out under *light* or *heavy* stocking rates — purely relative terms that refer to the number of livestock placed on a particular area.

Under light stocking rates, there are not enough animals to consume all of the available forage. The animals selectively graze the forage plants which are in the highly palatable vegetative stage of growth. Some of the plants accumulate a considerable amount of top growth, become overmature, and less palatable. The tall grass species become dominant and the low-growing clovers get shaded out. Without a legume to fix nitrogen, the grasses become increasingly nitrogen-deficient and productivity declines. Light grazing tends to produce an open sod, made up of the tall, bunch-type grasses, such as timothy and orchardgrass. An open sod is more susceptible to weed invasion than a well-managed pasture, which has short, dense growth.

Light grazing yields the highest weight gains or production per animal since the animals can selectively graze the most nutritious forage. However, the production per acre, whether in the form of meat, wool, or forage dry matter, is generally lower under light grazing (particularly light, continuous grazing) because some forage gets overmature and is wasted.

Continuous grazing under high stocking rates can defoliate the pasture plants so much that it forces them to draw on root reserves. This weakens the plant, slows the rate of regrowth, and reduces plant vigor. Heavy stocking rates with rotational grazing, on the other hand, result in the periodic "harvest" of each paddock with rest periods for regrowth. The animals cannot be as selective so there is more complete utilization of the available forage. Pasture growth (or regrowth) is more uniform than under light, "selective" grazing, and legumes can increase due to the lack of shade competition from tall grasses.

INTENSIVE ROTATIONAL GRAZING

We are fortunate to have an excellent model of intensive grazing management practiced in New Zealand, Australia, and the United Kingdom. Progress under intensive grazing is measured by increases in pasture carrying capacity, higher rates of gain in the animals, a reduced need for nitrogen fertilizer, a denser sod, lower fluctuations in grass growth and, ultimately, higher farm profits. With a reasonable commitment from the farmer, rotational grazing can be expected to

- **Provide top-quality feed all season**
- **Extend the grazing season at both ends of the year**
- **Increase total dry matter production per acre**
- **Reduce costs for fuel, nitrogen fertilizer, machinery repair, and concentrates**
- **Shift the pasture to low-growing grasses and legumes**
- **Distribute manure more evenly**
- **Increase the outlay for fencing**
- **Ease sheep handling by regular movements**

Getting Started

In its simplest form, intensive rotational grazing involves little more than moving animals on and off an improved piece of land. The trick is to have enough paddocks to provide a sufficient regrowth period for the pasture during hot, dry periods. Without the regrowth periods, rotational grazing has no advantage over continuous grazing.

Under intensive rotational grazing all but 1 paddock are rested, while the livestock graze on it for 2 days. The livestock is moved on to the next freshest paddock and so on, until they are returned to the first paddock, and the rotation starts all over. Some dairy farmers have progressed to a daily rotation, using as many as 30 to 50 paddocks to ensure a steady supply of pasture for their cows. In general, the more paddocks there are, the more control you have over where the animals graze and for how long.

Rest periods are lengthened in hot, dry weather and are shortest when growing conditions are favorable. In the Northern states, you may need a rest period of 15 days around Memorial Day before putting livestock back into an area, 24 days by the 4th of July, and 36 days by Labor Day. Provide more paddocks than are required in the spring because they will be needed during the dry season when the regrowth is slower.

Number of Paddocks Needed

Start with 10 to 12 paddocks to provide enough forage for 1 to 3 days of grazing from each paddock. Some paddocks will have to be mown or cut for hay during the usual spring flush of growth to keep forage from becoming overmature (and less palatable).

Wth 12 or more paddocks, there should be satisfactory control of grazing, and your pasture will provide twice the carrying capacity over continuous grazing. Each paddock should provide 1 to 3 days of grazing and should have a 12-day to 36-day period for regrowth. This will be adequate except in an unusually dry year.

Continue to subdivide as time and resources allow, until there are close to 30 paddocks. The goal is to have this many paddocks, each with permanent fencing and watering facilities. This goal is achieved only after many years of capital improvements, building up soil fertility, and sheep numbers.

Fencing Lay-out

When laying out the fencelines, give careful attention to the location of watering facilities and gates. Try to avoid having all the pastures funnel down or radiate from a single watering facility, which would cause heavy traffic around the watering area and turn this part of the pasture into a mudhole. Instead, using a series of gates, have each paddock open into a main corridor. A truck can travel down the main corridor to service watertanks in each paddock, or the livestock can use the corridor to reach a central watering facility without damaging any part of the pasture. Paddock gates should open into the corridor. Locate the gates in the corner of the paddocks to have as straight a line to the barn as possible. Otherwise, when the lead cow or sheep goes out the gate to head back to the barn, the stragglers will walk alongside the leaders, but *inside* the fence, and get stuck in the corner, and you have to herd them back up the fenceline to the gate.

Stocking Rates

The stocking rate depends largely on soil fertility. Fair quality pasture consisting of native grasses and weeds only provides enough forage for 3 ewes per acre under continuous grazing. Typically this kind of land has low soil fertility, low pH, and poor summer regrowth.

Good pasture might consist of short grasses with up to 20 percent legumes, moderate soil fertility, and moderate fluctuations in grass production. A reasonable stocking rate is 5 ewes per acre under continuous grazing.

Excellent pasture has high soil fertility, a pH above 6.0, and at least a third of the stand is in legumes. It is characterized by rapid regrowth and high summer productivity. This pasture can be stocked with up to 8 ewes per acre for the entire season.

What is a reasonable stocking rate under intensive rotational grazing? My recommendation is to start the first year of this system with the same stocking rate that you normally use for continuous grazing. If you are not sure what the stocking rate is, use the guidelines mentioned above. Now, instead of giving the entire pasture to these animals, confine them to an area one-tenth as large. The stocking rate will now be ten times the conventional rate, but the animals will only graze this paddock for a few days before they are moved to a fresh paddock.

Often the use of intensive rotational grazing can double or triple the conventional stocking rate in the first year or two. A paddock may contain up to 100 ewes per acre at a time, though the season-long stocking rate may average 8 ewes per acre. At high stocking rates, slight delays (even hours) before moving the sheep to the next paddock can result in severe overgrazing, so management must be excellent.

Sheep will almost never graze tall growth if there is shorter, more tender grass nearby. As a general rule, when the pasture has been grazed down to a height of 1 to 2 inches, it is time to rotate. Conversely there should be 2 to 4 inches of regrowth before the paddock is grazed again. This only applies to low-growing, perennial forage.

DRY MATTER YIELDS

The quantity of forage available — dry matter yields — in a pasture is a function of plant height and density. Each inch of height of ryegrass-clover or bluegrass-clover pasture provides approximately 200 to 300 pounds of forage dry matter per acre. Thus, a pasture with 6 inches of growth has about 1000 to 1500 pounds of dry matter per acre. (The bottom inch of pasture doesn't count as you should try to avoid grazing that close.) A medium-sized ewe on a maintenance ration requires about 2.6 pounds of dry matter per day. The pasture with 5 inches of growth has enough dry matter to support up to 250 dry ewes per acre for 2 days. A ewe nursing twins requires about 5.5 pounds of dry matter per day. The same pasture would support approximately 100 ewes for a 2-day period (not including the grass consumed by her lambs).

Assuming the average regrowth period for the pasture to accumulate 5 inches of growth is 4 weeks, there is a *total production* of about 3.5 to 5.0 tons of dry matter per acre per year! This level of production is possible under intensive rotational grazing and compares very favorably with mechanical forage harvesting.

SEASONAL GROWTH

The biggest challenge to successful grazing management is to balance the supply and quality of pasture with the nutritional needs of the livestock. Most parts of the country have a highly seasonal pattern of grass growth based on either a period of cold dormancy, drought, or both (Figures 3–1 and 3–2).

Some of the options to utilize seasonal flushes of grass are:

- **Conserve the surplus by harvesting it as hay or silage**
- **Buy feeder lambs or feeder cattle**
- **Rent the pasture**
- **Mow or clip the pastures to maintain them in a vegetative stage of growth**

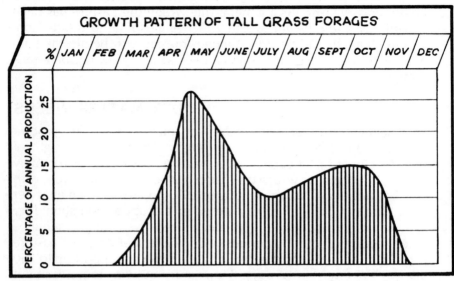

Figure 3-1. Seasonal pattern of grass growth in Ohio.

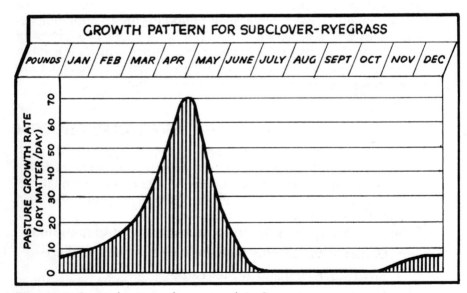

Figure 3-2. Seasonal pattern of grass growth in Oregon.

12-MONTH GRAZING SYSTEM

A 12-month grazing system is ideal for producers who utilize hay fields for sheep pasture. The tall, hay-type grasses and legumes can be harvested by the sheep or made into hay for a low-cost feeding system. It is less practical on farms with permanent pasture that cannot be cut for hay or that does not contain hay-type species.

An efficient year-round pasture system was developed by the Ohio State University in the late 1960s. The system is based on round-baling surplus summer forage and feeding the round bales on pasture over winter. Originally the system used an Allis Chalmers round baler which produced 60-pound to 80-pound bales. Unfortunately, these balers are no longer manufactured, and larger capacity round balers capable of packaging a 450-pound up to 2,000-pound bale are used today. Essential to the system are hay-type grasses and legumes, rather than the low-growing grasses found in most sheep pastures. The system outlined below proved to be a labor-saving, low-cost way of feeding the ewe flock.

- **Select a well-drained field with some protection from winter winds. A windbreak can be built from lumber, snowfence, or plastic mesh (such as Netlon), if necessary.**

- **Graze in April and May and harvest surplus forage in May or early June as hay or silage.**

- **Round bale the regrowth in late July or early August leaving weather-resistant round hay bales in the field.**

- **Fertilize the grass fields after each cutting of hay with 60 pounds of nitrogen per acre. An application in August is important to increase the amount of grass available for fall grazing.**

- **Graze the field in the fall using at least 4 to 6 paddocks to control the amount of grazing and to permit some fall regrowth. Inexpensive electric fencing can be used for the subdivisions.**

- **Forage quality of the grass still standing declines rapidly with colder midwinter temperatures. When snow falls, the sheep will start to rely more on the round bales. With small round bales (average 60 pounds), snow up to 18 inches deep was not a problem for the sheep, which were able to find all the hay and consume it.**

Photo 3-1. *Sheep grazing round bales of tall fescue in December. (Courtesy Dr. Charles F. Parker)*

- **Bring ewes into a lambing barn if they are due in January and keep them there through March. The 12-month grazing system works best, however, when ewes are bred for April lambing.**
- **In early April, fertilize the fields again with the equivalent of 60 pounds of nitrogen per acre (for example, 200 pounds of ammonium nitrate fertilizer).**

Many of the trials on the 12-month grazing system were on fields of tall fescue. This tough, hardy perennial grass made a weather-resistant hay bale, developed a tough sod, and stayed green late into the fall. However, its palatability was low and it was found to be an unsatisfactory forage for weaned lambs. The chemical analysis of fescue proved it was high in nutrients, more than adequate for ewes in early to mid gestation. Recent research has discovered a reason for poor animal performance on tall fescue pastures and hay (see Toxic Fescue, Chapter 5).

EXTENDING THE GRAZING SEASON

Good pasture is *the* lowest cost feed on the farm. It costs less than half the cost of the same forage harvested as hay and is often of better quality. Extending the grazing season provides more days of inexpensive feed, thus helping to lower the annual costs of the sheep enterprise. Increasing the total yield and availability of pasture should be your first priority before considering the use of annual crops or purchasing supplemental feed.

There are wide differences in the availability of forage throughout the year, depending on the intensity of pasture management (Figure 3-3). In an unimproved pasture, there will probably be a period of little or no midsummer growth. This is usually due to poor regrowth from cool season grasses and/or low soil fertility. The midsummer slump also occurs under continuous grazing where the pastures never have a rest period.

Renovating a pasture with legumes improves the midsummer growth as legumes are typically deep rooting and resist drought. Legumes with creeping stems (such as white clover) spread through the grasses, covering the bare spots and reducing evaporation of soil moisture. Fine-stemmed legumes, such as white clover and trefoil, remain palatable all summer, even when setting seed. Furthermore,

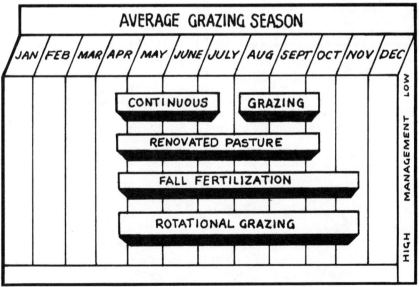

Figure 3-3. Availability of pasture with increasing levels of management.

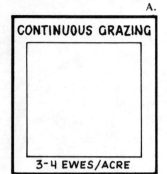

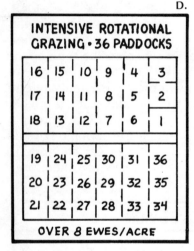

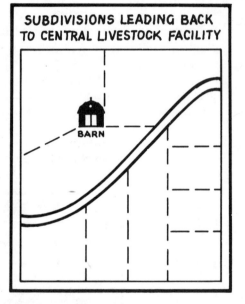

Figure 3-4. Grazing Systems.
A. Under continuous grazing, pasture carrying capacity and forage yield are low, although production per animal may be high.
B. With alternate grazing, carrying capacity and forage yield are improved.
C. Concentrate all the sheep onto 1 small paddock for 2 to 3 days of grazing before moving them onto a fresh paddock. By using 10 to 12 paddocks, the same pasture is expected to have a higher carrying capacity and forage yield than under continuous or alternate grazing.
D. Intensive rotational grazing maximizes carrying capacity and forage yield by providing up to a five-fold increase in dry matter production per acre over continuous grazing. Long-term pasture development should provide for permanent water facilities and roadways to move feed and sheep.
E. Under this arrangement, the paddocks open onto a roadway and collect at a central livestock facility or barn.

a slow but steady release of nitrogen from the nitrogen-fixing bacteria on the legume roots stimulates grass growth throughout the season. For these reasons, pastures renovated with legumes outperform grass pastures supplemented with nitrogen fertilizer.

Fall fertilization can extend the growth of cool season grasses and legumes for an additional 3 weeks over nonfertilized pasture and will initiate growth earlier in the spring. Straight nitrogen or a complete fertilizer supplying 60 pounds of nitrogen per acre should be applied 3 weeks before the first frost is expected. Using tall or red fescue as the dominant grass will provide good fall and early winter grazing due to their hardiness and tough leaves, which remain green longer than other perennial grasses.

JOINT BEEF AND SHEEP OPERATIONS

Many commercial livestock producers have joint beef and sheep operations, which take advantage of the complementary grazing habits of cattle and sheep. Some internal parasites are shared, specifically the liver fluke, tapeworms, and at least 1 species of *Haemonchus*, *Ostertagia*, and *Trichostrongylus*. However, the improved utilization of the pasture and greater production per acre offset the problem of common internal parasites. The level of parasitism probably is related more to the health and condition of the animals, use of worming medications, and environmental stress.

Sheep should follow beef cattle in a rotation or be grazed together. The cattle will make use of coarse or tall grass, and the sheep will make use of the short grasses and about 90 percent of the broadleaf weed species found in permanent pastures, resulting in more complete utilization of the available forage. More trampling of feed is possible with cattle, but only if stocking rates are not matched to the size and quality of the pasture. Sheep are probably more efficient at bringing clover into a pasture by reducing shade competition near the ground.

With a beef herd, 1 ewe can be added for every cow to take care of some of the weeds that the cattle will not browse on. You will hardly detect any extra consumption of the forage at this 1:1 mix. Later, the number of sheep can be increased until there is an equal stocking of sheep and beef by weight. At this stage, there will be approximately 6 ewes for every 1000-pound beef animal unit (such as a cow). The goal is to maximize pounds of meat produced per acre by fully utilizing the available forage.

PASTURE COSTS

Grazing sheep or other livestock isn't without some problems, the main one being an inconsistent supply of forage over the pasture season. As the season progresses there are also changes in forage quality, pasture carrying capacity, and number of internal parasite larvae. But that is the challenge of the good grass farmer. The high cost of forage harvesting equipment, automatic feeding, and push-button manure handling are traded for additional fencing, labor, and water distribution facilities.

It is a fact that pastures are providing less of the energy consumed by sheep, beef, and dairy cattle today than 20 years ago; but we now find different production costs for fuel and machinery. Despite the trend toward increased capital expenditures for forage-harvesting equipment and confinement feeding, pasture continues to be the most economical source of nutrients required by sheep.

Table 3-1

ANNUAL FORAGE PRODUCTION COSTS (PER ACRE)		
Item	Pasture	Hay
Seed	$ 1.50	$ 4.50
Lime	15.50	15.50
Fertilizer*	31.00	70.00
Machinery**	4.50	71.25
Fencing***	22.00	0.00
Taxes	17.00	22.00
Interest (at 12 percent)	11.00	19.00
TOTAL	$102.50	$202.00****

*Fertilizer includes 0–45–90 lbs. NPK on pasture and 150–45–90 lbs. NPK on hay field.
**Machinery includes fuel, repairs, and operator.
***Fencing includes materials for permanent electric fencing and labor @ $.38/foot plus temporary electric subdivision fencing @ $.08/foot.
****Storage cost could be added to hay production costs.

Table 3-1. Comparing the annual production costs of pasture and hay.

Table 3-2

FORAGE CROP COMPARISONS

	Pasture	Hay
Yield, DM	4950 lbs.	6000 lbs.
Average Quality	60–65% TDN*	45–55% TDN
Annual Cost	$102.50	$202.00
Cost/lb., DM	$ .02	$ .03
Cost/ewe/month	$ 2.40	$ 3.60

*Total digestible nutrients.

Table 3–2. Comparison of pasture and hay yields per acre.
The difference in the cost of feed per ewe per month is $.80.

To prove the point, assume there is a 30-acre field that could be used for grass-legume hay (if the slopes were gentle enough) or for pasture. Set an arbitrary yield goal of 3 to 4 tons of dry matter per acre, which requires 10 to 20 tons of sheep manure per acre or 1000 pounds of 15–5–9 fertilizer per acre per year. Figure that lime will be applied to the hay field or pasture every 3 years at 2 or 3 tons per acre. To harvest the grass as hay or silage, we have to calculate all the annual costs such as depreciation, fuel, repairs, operator's labor, storage, and so on, of the machinery. To graze the same field, we have to calculate the costs of fencing, labor, and possibly water distribution for the livestock. Labor and equipment costs involved in feeding the harvested forage and handling manure are not included in this example since there are too many different ways of carrying out these tasks.

Using typical costs in the Northeast for these inputs, you can estimate an "annual forage production cost per acre" for the 2 forage systems (Table 3-1). The annual production cost per acre of mixed hay is over $200, while the cost of maintaining the pasture is about half that figure.

Assuming that there are some inefficiencies in animal harvest versus mechanical harvest, the yield of the pasture can be set at 80 to 85 percent of the hay field, or about 4950 pounds of dry matter per acre. Using conservative figures, the cost per pound of dry matter from pasture was about $.02, while the cost of mixed hay is closer to $.03 to $.04 per pound of dry matter, or more (Table 3-2). There may be significant differences in the energy and protein levels of pasture dry matter compared to hay, due to the stage of harvest, storage losses, and so on. Use some of your figures to compare the cost of pasture against hay and silage for your levels of inputs and production.

Chapter 4

PASTURE RENOVATION

The sheep industry is a forage-based industry, and we are really grass farmers. Despite the trend to support higher levels of production by feeding more concentrates, we are working with an animal that is ideally suited to utilizing forages. Land that otherwise would yield no edible product can be utilized by a grazing animal to produce food.

Sheep producers can play an increasingly important role in soil and water conservation by carefully managing pastures and rangelands which have no alternative use. Soil erosion on a well-developed sod, as found on many sheep farms, is 100 to 300 times less than that which occurs on land under cultivation. In addition, a sod reduces soil compaction; reduces leaching of soluble plant nutrients; shades the soil, thus minimizing moisture deficiencies in midsummer; and builds the level of organic matter in the soil. In turn, a well-managed pasture increases land value and ultimately results in greater profits.

PASTURE CONDITIONS

Unfortunately, much of the pasture land in this country is reverting to brush and low-value woodland. These pastures never received enough manure, lime, or fertilizer to prevent the gradual depletion of available nutrients. Poor grazing management has left thousands of acres in desperate condition, and it is only a matter of time before these acres cease to be agriculturally productive.

In the Northeast, pasture may have a market value of $300 to $1000 per acre for nonfarm uses. It is relatively expensive farmland; and if present market trends in farmland continue, it will be worthwhile to maintain pastures just for their value as "open space." Sheep producers should then consider some kind of pasture reclamation program for short-term and long-term economic benefits.

Photo 4-1. Sheep can be used to reclaim overgrown pasture by limiting the area that they can graze. They will consume almost all of the tall grasses, weeds, and brush, leaving the ground bare and ready for frost seeding.

Before embarking on a pasture reclamation program, improve your best cropland to the point that it produces maximum economic yields. Then you can start to improve lower quality land as time, labor, and capital resources allow. There will be no limit to how much money you can invest in pasture improvement. Plowing, reseeding, fencing, liming, and fertilizing are all expensive inputs. Still, pasture reclamation and pasture improvement are cheaper than clearing trees and creating open land.

An ideal system of pasture reclamation would be relatively inexpensive, protect the soil, produce rapid results, and require a minimum of labor. Fortunately for sheep producers there is a low-capital, soil-conserving method of improving pastures without expensive tillage or chemical herbicides. The method involves a combination of "frost seeding" and grazing management.

FROST SEEDING

Frost seeding involves broadcasting seed onto frozen ground in early spring when the alternate freezing and thawing of the soil surface plants the seeds naturally. Researchers in Kentucky, Missouri, and Iowa have reported successful legume establishment with frost seeding. Farmers, highway crews, and landscapers also have used this method successfully. In some cases, livestock were used to control or subdue competing vegetation while the new seedlings got established. In other cases, timely mowing and/or discing was used to weaken the existing grasses and weeds.

The main limitation to frost seeding is that it can only be done in late winter or early spring. At this time in most parts of the northern United States and Canada, there is a 2-week or 3-week period when the snow has melted, allowing the soil to thaw; but nights are still cold enough to cause the soil surface to freeze. As it freezes, cracks develop and the seed falls into these spaces. When the soil surface thaws during the day it seals over the seed, effectively planting it, and provides moisture for germination. Frost seedings can be made on almost any site where the soil is bare or the existing vegetation is sparse. Soils with a high clay content will have a more vigorous frost action than sandy soils. However, the most important factor for seed establishment is having a minimum of competition from other plants.

Photo 4-2. *White clover is established by frost seeding.*

RECLAMATION AND RENOVATION

Pasture reclamation differs from pasture renovation only by the amount of work to be done before a mixed grass/legume stand is restored. Pastures to be reclaimed are comprised mainly of tall grasses, weeds, brush, and some low-value weed trees. Hopefully, the woody growth is not so extensive as to require a bulldozer. It will take an average of 3 years to reclaim this type of pasture using sheep.

Pastures that only need renovating are mostly old grass stands that have become sod-bound. In other pastures, the tall grass has shaded out the companion legume species, and nitrogen has become the limiting factor to plant and animal performance. Old grass pastures can be renovated with legumes in 1 year or less.

Regardless of the condition of the worn-out pasture, the objective of pasture improvement is to establish desirable forage plants, with or without plowing. Usually legumes, such as alfalfa, birdsfoot trefoil, or one of the several clovers (red, white, or ladino), are used to improve the forage stand. Legumes have many advantages over grasses, including the ability to fix atmospheric nitrogen, tolerate drought with deep roots, and provide a higher level of protein and minerals for livestock. The disadvantage of a stand with legumes in it is the extra degree of management that is required. For a mixed grass/legume stand, you will have to manage the pasture in favor of the legume.

Pasture Reclamation

Sheep can be used to graze tall weeds and grasses and even to eliminate brush by repeatedly stripping the foliage. We know that sheep will consume 90 percent of the weeds commonly found in pastures and will browse on many species that are common to waste places.

There are potential hazards during a 2-year or 3-year reclamation project. Sheep may die from being forced to eat toxic plants. Tough perennial weeds may get a head start on the desirable grasses and legumes. Or a severe rainstorm may erode newly cleared land, leaving little chance that the pasture will ever be reclaimed.

In the transition from an overgrown thicket to a green sod-covered pasture, the land is particularly susceptible to poor management. The following program has worked successfully in pasture reclamation projects around the United States.

Spring, Year 1. First, take a soil test to determine lime and fertilizer requirements. Then, fence the perimeter with permanent electric fence. The area will have to be subdivided further to control grazing.

Plan a system for watering the livestock. There are several ways to distribute water to sheep. Haul water in a tank or plastic jugs; develop a spring, well, or pond; orient the subdivision fences to a central water supply; or herd the sheep to water every other day. In some areas, federal cost sharing is available for developing water sources for improved grazing through the Agricultural Stabilization and Conservation Service.

Remove low-value trees that are not needed for shelter, shade, or conservation.

Select mature, crossbred ewes that have not been bred and which only require a maintenance ration. Treat for internal parasites before turning sheep into a pasture which has not been grazed for the previous 2 or more years.

Summer, Year 1. In midsummer, begin grazing at 5 to 15 times the conventional stocking rate (called mob stocking). In other words, if the pasture supports 4 ewes per acre in the summer, add enough sheep, or subdivide the pasture to allow the equivalent of 20 to 60 ewes per acre. There should be enough sheep on a paddock (a grazing area) to clear it of any suitable feed in 2 to 3 days. Under a higher stocking rate, some of the feed is wasted due to trampling, or sheep are forced early on to consume toxic plants. During a hot, dry period in the summer, there will be very little regrowth in the pasture. This is desirable for eliminating many low-value, weedy species. Similarly, no fertilizer should be applied until the following year to discourage regrowth.

Check the body condition of the ewes once a month and permit them to graze on improved pasture if necessary to maintain them in average condition.

Fall, Year 1. Continue to graze the pasture as late into the fall as possible to set back perennial weeds and woody species.

Apply lime as recommended by a soil test, to a pH of 6.0 to 6.8. Limit each application to 3 tons per acre, several months apart. Lime moves slowly through the soil, especially when top-dressed onto a grass sod. Little crop response would be expected from a larger application and an alkaline soil surface may result. If lime cannot be custom spread or if the pasture is not accessible to a spreader truck, rent or borrow a 4-wheel drive tractor and apply lime with a drop spreader (for a minimum of dust). Lime purchased in bulk and dumped at the farm is the least expensive. Apply lime to whatever areas you can drive on; the sheep will gradually move the calcium-rich forage to remote areas of the pasture through their manure and your grazing management. Some bulk fertilizer dealers carry pelleted lime which is used as a filler. Pelleted lime may cost twice as much as crushed lime but can be applied with a farm tractor or by air, saving time, and distributing the material more evenly. It's worth checking with your dealer for availability and price of different liming materials.

Winter, Year 1. Order legume seed, to be sown at a conventional rate per acre. Order fertilizer, taking advantage of winter price discounts and early delivery.

Early Spring, Year 2. Frost-seed freshly inoculated legume seed and grass seed at a conventional rate. Sow at daybreak, while the ground is still frozen.

After the grass resumes growth and whenever the soil is dry enough to avoid damage to the sod, graze the pasture with enough animals to keep the grass short. Remove the animals when the grass is grazed down to about 2 inches high; or add more stock to control the tall grass which is shading the legume seedlings. You should eventually have enough grazing pasture to graze down the paddocks in 3 to 7 days.

Late Spring, Year 2. Even at high stocking rates, sheep will fail to eradicate tough perennial weeds, such as burdock or thistles. These and other unpalatable or toxic weeds will have to be cut at early flowering and several times thereafter to deplete the root systems. Use a grass whip, mower, or systemic herbicide to selectively treat these weeds. The weeds will be easier to treat once the sheep clear away the other vegetation.

Summer, Year 2. Piles of woody brush or small trees should be bulldozed away or burned. If they are not removed, weeds may grow up through the pile, flower, and set seed — and the sheep will not be able to reach through and eat the plants. Be sure to check with the local fire department and county forester about local and state regulations.

If you are late with frost seeding and there are no more freezing nights, sheep and/or cattle may have to be put on the pasture in very high numbers for a week or 2 to trample the seed into the moist soil. Should erosion start, immediately sow a cover crop of oats, annual ryegrass, or winter rye depending on the season (spring, summer, fall). Cover any water channels that are starting to cut into the soil with thick layers of spoiled hay. Fence out the sheep if necessary. Consult with the local Soil Conservation Service.

Plant poisoning is a problem during pasture reclamation because livestock are forced to eat practically all of the vegetation. A comprehensive reference on this subject is *Poisonous Plants of the Midwest and Their Effects on Livestock* by Robert Evers and Roger Link (see Appendix G). It gives the description, occurrence, conditions of poisoning, toxic principle, clinical signs, necropsy, and treatment for 75 poisonous plants.

Once the legume seedlings start to grow, add phosphorus, potash, boron, and other nutrients if the soil test recommends them. Continue to graze and fertilize in favor of the legume, so it can stimulate the grass by fixing nitrogen.

Most of the physical work will be done in the first 2 years of a pasture reclamation project. If you can continue to manage the new area, it will provide more and better quality forage. When problems occur, seek help from the Soil Conservation Service or Extension Agent in your county. You will be surprised at the effectiveness of grazing sheep for land improvement.

Photo 5-1. Alfalfa is a high-yielding, high-protein forage that requires a well drained, fertile soil.

Chapter 5

PASTURE
PLANTS

The overall performance of a sheep flock and the number of sheep that can be fed depends largely on the amount and quality of forage available. Many producers use pasture as the only feed for their sheep for 6 months of the year or more. Thus, it is important to manage pastures to provide about 50 percent of the annual nutrient requirements of the sheep flock.

Ideal permanent pasture for sheep contains a dense sod of short-growing, pasture-type grasses and legumes, such as a mix of Kentucky bluegrass and white clover, or perennial ryegrass and white clover. In some soil conditions, birdsfoot trefoil, alfalfa, or other species might be the most productive legume. Soil drainage is the main limiting factor that is considered when selecting grasses and legumes to grow in a pasture. Your County Extension Agent or the Soil Conservation Service can help you identify the legumes and grasses that should grow well in your area, and what seed mix to use if you are establishing a new pasture.

PASTURE PLANTS: GRASSES, LEGUMES AND BROADLEAF WEEDS

The pasture grasses described in this section are widely adapted to grow in the northern half of the United States and Canada where there is at least 35 inches of rainfall annually. They are often called cool-season grasses because they make most of their growth during cool, wet months. These grasses are particularly useful for spring and fall grazing; but due to their shallow root systems, they tend to produce little growth in hot, dry weather.

Grasses initiate growth earlier in the spring than legumes do because of fundamental differences in the location of reserve carbohydrates. Grasses store carbohydrates in the leaves and stem bases for survival over the winter and to initiate growth in the spring. The carbohydrates are at or near the site of new leaves and are used as soon as temperatures are warm enough for growth.

Some grasses (Kentucky bluegrass, for example) retain green leaves all winter and can resume growth immediately without having to translocate stored carbohydrates. Legumes must translocate stored carbohydrates from the roots in order to develop their first leaves in the spring, a relatively slower process.

Pasture legumes combine well with grasses because they are deep rooting (compared to grasses) and continue to grow well in hot, dry weather. At the same stages of growth, legumes will have a higher mineral and protein content than grasses. One of the most important reasons to incorporate legumes into pastures is to take advantage of their symbiotic relationship with nitrogen-fixing bacteria. These bacteria invade the root, utilize the plant's carbohydrates, and convert atmospheric nitrogen into nitrogen compounds which the plant can use. The fixed nitrogen contributes to soil fertility when legume plants die and decay, when root nodules are sloughed off, or by direct transfer of nitrogenous compounds from the nodules into the soil. Legumes can contribute about 60 to 180 pounds of nitrogen per acre annually, depending on the species. There is at least 1 forage legume species adapted for every soil type, from poorly drained to droughty conditions.

Broadleaf and grassy weeds (annuals and perennials) are important pasture plants because, if for no other reason, they are always present in pastures and many of them are grazed. Many are adapted to poor soil. They may or may not be palatable to livestock and often compete with more desirable forage species. We have little information on the nutritional quality, digestibility, and potential yield of these plants. Some examples of useful broadleaf weeds are dandelion, vetch, daisy, cress, wild kale, and chicory. In general, annual grasses, such as red top and annual bluegrass, are low yielding and do not tolerate continuous grazing. Their presence is a sign that the soil was recently disturbed.

Noxious weeds may have thorns, toxins, unpalatable woody stems, or bitter substances that make them unfit for livestock. Some examples of noxious weeds are burdock, milkweed, thistles, goldenrod, spirea, nightshade, sedges, multiflora rose, juniper, and wild cherry.

GRASSES

The perennial grasses that can tolerate close and continuous grazing are ideal for sheep pasture. There are 2 types, bunch grasses and sod-formers. Bunch-type grasses produce a relatively open sod. New plants arise from seeds, then spread out, thicken by forming more side shoots or tillers, and form small clumps. Examples of bunch grasses are the fescues, orchardgrass, ryegrass, and timothy.

Sod-forming grasses spread by rhizomes, underground stems that send up shoots along their length. These shoots also can increase in size by tillering, like the bunch grasses. Sod-forming grasses spread to form a large mat of roots and shoots that resists weed invasions and shades the soil. Examples are Kentucky bluegrass, bromegrass, and quackgrass (*Agropyron repens*).

Tall grasses, both sod-formers and bunch-types, are suitable for hay or rotational grazing. They do not tolerate close and continuous grazing as this takes away too much of their leaf area. Short grasses, especially the sod-formers, are useful for continuously grazed or rotationally grazed pasture (see Table 5-1). Their leaves lie flat to the ground, so even the closest grazing does not remove all the leaf area.

Table 5-1

FORAGE GRASSES			
Perennial Grasses	Hay or Silage	Rotational Grazing	Continuous Grazing
Tall Fescue	X	X	
Red Fescue		X	X
Orchardgrass	X	X	
Perennial Ryegrass	X	X	X
Timothy	X	X	
Bluegrass		X	X
Bromegrass	X	X	
Reed Canarygrass	X		

Table 5-1. Suitability of different forage grasses for pastures.

Table 5-2

FORAGE LEGUMES

Perennial Legumes	Hay or Silage	Rotational Grazing	Continuous Grazing
Alfalfa	X	X	
Alsike Clover	X		
Ladino Clover	X	X	
Red Clover	X	X	
Subterranean Clover		X	
Trefoil, Upright	X		
Trefoil, Prostrate		X	X
White Clover		X	X

Table 5-2. Suitability of different forage legumes for pasture.

LEGUMES

The forage legumes fall into 2 groups depending on their growth habit. There are the upright types—such as alfalfa, red clover, and alsike clover—and the low-growing, creeping types—such as ladino clover, white clover, and subterranean clover. Trefoil has both upright and low creeping varieties. The upright types are suitable for hay or light rotational grazing, and the low-growing types are suitable for continuous and rotational grazing, as shown in Table 5-2.

MANAGE IN FAVOR OF CLOVER

Pastures should be managed in favor of clover, with the ideal balance of grass to clover between 2 to 1 and 3 to 1. White clover and low, creeping varieties of trefoil provide excellent summer grazing in a mixed grass/legume pasture for several reasons:

- **The creeping legumes fill in bare areas around the grasses, shading the soil and improving the density of the sod.**

- **The fine stems of white clover and trefoil remain tender and palatable throughout the summer, even during flowering and seed formation. This greatly increases feed intake and digestibility.**

- **The legumes fix nitrogen, which stimulates the grass to grow.**

- **Legumes contain more crude protein and have a higher mineral content than grasses at the same stage of growth, thus improving weight gains.**

FALL FORAGE CROPS

Sheep producers in northern parts of the country have a short grazing season to work with, generally only 6 or 7 months. This compares with a 9-month grazing season in many sheep-raising areas, including England, New Zealand, and Australia. During the winter, sheep consume stored hay or silage which often costs twice as much as the same forage harvested in the field by the animals. While we cannot eliminate the expense of making and feeding hay or silage, we can extend the grazing season at both ends, with earlier spring grazing and later fall grazing.

Fall Annual Crops

Fall annual crops can be used to extend the grazing season, thus lowering annual feed costs. The crops include winter grains (rye, wheat) and many of the brassicas, such as kale, rape, and turnip. These are easy to grow, are frost tolerant, and have a high carrying capacity (up to 1200 ewe grazing days per acre). Average daily gains for ewes and lambs on some of these crops have been comparable to gains on late summer bluegrass pasture. Typically, the fall crops are grazed from late October to late November, before a hard freeze causes deterioriation of the crop. Feed value generally remains high throughout the feed period, although dry matter levels increase with plant maturity. Tilling prior to seeding the crop may help to destroy infective parasite eggs and larvae, although some research is being done on no-till or sod seeding. Most researchers have found that no supplementary feed is needed for breeding ewes or those in early gestation other than water and a salt/mineral mix.

Nutrient Values of Fall Forage Crops

Nutrient values for fall forage crops are difficult to compare between research studies since some analyses are on a whole plant basis, some are on tops only, roots only, dry matter basis, or stage of development (Table 5–3). The brassicas are quite similar in digestibility and mineral content although protein values differ significantly, perhaps due to the relative leafiness of rape and kale compared to turnip. The National Research Council published data on the protein level of turnip tops on a moisture-free basis of 15.8 percent compared to roots at 11.9 percent.

The important results from the nutrient analyses are that all of the brassica forage crops used for sheep are about 85 percent moisture in the field. When fed alone, they provide an adequate flushing or maintenance ration for ewes in early gestation. In several studies (Tables 5–4 and 5–5), the average daily gain of ewes on unsupplemented fall forage crops ranged from 0.13 to 0.68 pounds per day.

Table 5-3

NUTRIENT VALUES OF FALL FORAGE CROPS

Crop	% Dry Matter*	October % Dry Matter	% Rumen Digestibility	% Total Protein	% P	% CA
Purple Top Turnip	10	10	78	13	.39	1.56
Essex Rape	8	17	85	17	.42	1.86
Kale	9	16	83	12	.38	2.11

* 60 days from planting

Table 5–3. A comparison of nutrient values of turnip, rape, and kale.

From: Ladd A. Mitchell, Area Extension Agent, Washington State University.

Sheep on fall forage crops should be limited to subdivisions of the field (strip grazing) to avoid trampling and soiling the crop. Flexible electric netting or temporary electric fence can be used to control access to the crop and to set stocking rates within a range of 10–20 ewes per acre of turnips, for 35–45 days. October and November are ideal months to take advantage of frost-hardy annual forages.

If lambs are turned out to turnips or other brassicas, an "experienced ewe" should be placed with them to start eating the new crop. Research by D. W. Evans of Washington State University showed significant differences in grazing efficiency of lambs compared to ewes on purple top turnip. Evans found the lambs did not consume the roots as efficiently, leaving 16.2 percent of the roots in the field, compared to 8.6 percent of the roots left by older sheep. Some leaves of turnips are wasted due to trampling, but the combined losses of leaves and remaining roots are small when we consider the high carrying capacity and high yields of the brassicas compared to bluegrass or fescue pasture (Table 5-4).

Establishing Fall Forage Crops

Establishing fall forage crops is inexpensive due to low-cost seed, low fertilizer requirements, and minimal use of pesticides (see Estimated Added Production Costs, page 64). Commercial vegetable production recommendations can be used to plan a crop of turnip, rape, or kale to use as a forage. For rye or winter wheat, refer to the field crop recommendations from the Extension Service for general information. Generally, the lime and fertilizer requirements stay the same or are reduced to take advantage of any residual nutrients from the previous crop. Of course, a major portion of the nutrients in the fall forage crop will be recycled through sheep manure. Planting dates may be different since the crops will be "harvested" out of season, in late October and November. The forage crops discussed here should be planted between 60 and 90 days prior to the fall grazing period; they will have little or no yield after being grazed.

Fall forage crops are short-season plants with good growth in cool soils. However, they have to be seeded in early August when it is hot and dry. No-till planting has been used to seed turnips into an existing sod that was killed or set back with an herbicide. This method has several problems, including poor seedling emergence through the sod, insect damage, and poor herbicide results.

Dr. Gerald Jung, a research agronomist with the U.S. Regional Pasture Research Laboratory at Pennsylvania State University, has been

Table 5-4

ANNUAL PRODUCTION GOALS

Crop	Parts Grazed	Soil Protection	Approximate* Dry Matter Yields (tons/acre)	Suffolk*** Ewes ADG (lb/day)	Stocking rate (ewes/acre)	Total weight gain per acre
Purple Top Turnip	Whole plant, once	Poor	1.8 (tops only)	0.57	11.0	149
Essex Rape	Top grazable	Excellent	3.8	0.68	17.3	245
Kale	Top grazable	Excellent	3.8**	NA	NA	NA
Winter Rye	Top grazable	Excellent	2.8	0.50	14.1	158
Tall Fescue	Top grazable	Excellent	1.5***	0.25	10.9	59

*From: J. J. Faix, et al, *Sheep Research Expo-80*, Dixon Springs Agricultural Center, Simpson, Illinois (1980).
**From: D. W. Evans, *Sheep Harvested Feeds of the Intermountain West*, Proceedings Nov. 6–8, 1979. Colorado State. Univ.
***Grazing period started November 8 and ended December 6. J. J. Faix, et al, *Sheep Research Expo-80*, Dixon Springs Agricultural Center, Simpson, Illinois (1980).

Table 5–4. Comparing various fall forage crops.

comparing no-till and conventional seeding methods to establish brassica forage crops. Jung grew over 30 cultivars and was able to substantiate that the brassicas are high-yielding, fast-growing forage crops. He emphasizes that an herbicide treatment for no-till seeding should be adequate to control sod growth but not kill it. Dr. Jung feels the advantages for no-till establishment of brassicas include reduced soil erosion; less soil moisture loss because the sod acts as a mulch; more time saved over conventional planting; the sod permits livestock grazing in inclement weather with little crop loss due to trampling; and no-till seeding is available in many areas on a custom basis.

In a study at Dixon Springs Agricultural Center, rape was found to be more reliable than turnip for no-till seeding because of superior seedling vigor. The rape also seemed to have more resistance to leaf insect pest injury. Most crops in a no-till field are subject to soil insect pests, particularly wireworms, which turn from the roots of the killed sod to any living plant roots. This is particularly damaging to turnips which have most of their yield and feed value in the root.

Early regrowth of orchardgrass, tall fescue, and other perennial grasses is common after a contact herbicide is used to kill back the leaves. Better herbicides, such as glyphosate, with a systemic action but short residual life, are being used for nonselective control of grasses prior to a no-till seeding. Better planters that minimize problems with

Table 5-5

CARRYING CAPACITY OF FALL FORAGE CROPS

Crop	Stocking Rate (Ewes/Acre)	ADG Per Ewe (lbs.)	Grazing Days Per Acre
Purple Top Turnip (1977)	20	.17	1180
Fescue and Shell Corn (1977)	10	.03	590
Purple Top Turnip (1979)	13.5	.13	472.5
Bluegrass and Shelled Corn (1979)	4	.26	143.5

Table 5–5. From: J. B. Outhouse, et al., Turnip Pasture For Ewes, Indiana Sheep Day Proceedings, April 19, 1980.

ESTIMATED ADDED PRODUCTION COSTS PER ACRE
OF FALL FORAGE TURNIPS

Cash Costs	Total Per Acre
Plow*	$ 12.00
Harrow	6.50
Plant & Fertilize	4.25
Seed: Purple Top Turnip 2 lbs. @ $2.10	4.20
Kale 1 lb. @ $1.50	1.50
Fertilizer: 350 lbs. 15–8–12	34.00
Weed Control**	
Spraying	4.50
Herbicide: Dacthal 75 WP @ 10 lbs./acre or	45.00
Herbicide: Roundup @ 1½ qts./acre	

Cash Overhead	
Miscellaneous expenses @ 2%	2.25
Interest on operating capital: 3 months @ 5%	5.70
Total Added Costs.	$119.90

Reduced Costs	
Stored feed: Hay @ $80/ton	
20 Ewes @ 4.5 lbs. hay per day × 35 days	$126.00
Net Change in Farm Income***.	$ 6.10

*Machinery rates include labor and fuel.
**This study assumes that the previous crop was a grass or grass/legume sod. If the previous crop was cultivated or treated for weeds, the cash costs would be reduced by substituting a second discing for conventional plowing and eliminating the herbicide (approximately $55). The net change in farm income would then approach (+) $60.
***Turnips are suggested as a "break" crop, used during the fall before reseeding a hayfield or planting the field to corn the following spring.

TOXIC FESCUE

Tall fescue (*Festuca arundinacea* Schreb.) is grown on 35 million acres in the United States for good reasons: it produces high forage yields, has a long growing season, has excellent seed production, and tolerates a wide range of management. However, livestock do poorly on fescue pasture and hay. Recently, researchers at the USDA Russell Research Laboratory in Athens, Georgia, identified a fungus, *Epichloe typhina* (later classified as *Acremonium coenophalium*), as responsible for the widespread problem of "fescue toxicosis," the condition afflicting livestock on fescue forages. The syndrome is characterized by rough hair coats, excessive nervousness, salivation, lameness, low tolerance for hot weather, and a constant low-grade fever.

In a 4-year trial at the Agricultural Experiment Station in Alabama, fungus-infected fescue pastures produced only 71 percent as much beef gain per acre, 60 percent as much average daily gain, and 58 percent less weight gain per head compared to noninfected fescue pasture. It was found that the animal days per acre was higher in the infected pastures, an indication that the cattle were not consuming as much feed.

In another experiment with steers, feeding fungus-infected tall fescue hay or seed resulted in as much reduction in animal performance as having animals graze fungus-infected pastures. The fungus is apparently transmitted by seed and dies out in seed stored over a year or 2 (depending on storage conditions). Surveys in Alabama and Kentucky show that over 95 percent of the tall fescue pastures are infested heavily with the fungus. Research at the University of Kentucky has shown the presence of the fungus is correlated with increased levels of naturally occurring alkaloids, which may be the toxic principle.

W. D. Stidham and colleagues at the University of Arkansas confirmed that fescue produced a severe decrease in ewes' milk production, but the effect was short-lived once the sheep were switched to another feed source. Fescue also has been implicated as a cause of reproductive problems, abortions, and stillbirths. Seed of cultivars Kenhy, Johnstone, and Triumph tall fescue is being increased from certified fungus-free seed fields. It is not known whether red fescue also develops alkaloids or is host to the *Acremonium* fungus.

PRODUCTION RECOMMENDATIONS FOR FALL FORAGE CROPS

Varieties. Turnip (*Brassica rapa*), **Kale** (*B. oleracea var. acephala*), **and Rape** (*B. napus*).

Soil Preparation. Choose a sunny, well-drained site. Add lime if necessary to increase the soil pH to 6.0 to 6.8. Plow any previous crop residue or sod at least 2 weeks before planting. Harrow to obtain a surface free from clods and trash.

Fertilizers. Broadcast a complete fertilizer to provide 40 to 75 lbs. nitrogen, 40 to 100 lbs. phosphate, and 40 to 100 lbs. potash per acre, depending on soil test levels. Apply 1 to 2 pounds boron (B) per acre with the broadcast fertilizer. Nitrogen can be side-dressed at a rate of 30 lbs. N per acre, 4 to 6 weeks after seeding, when rainfall has been heavy or soils are low in organic matter.

Planting. Broadcast seed by hand or with the fertilizer at the following rates:
- **Turnip: 2.5 lbs./acre**
- **Kale: 3 lbs./acre**
- **Rape: 3 lbs./acre**
- **Turnip/Rape: 2 lbs. turnip + 1 lb. rape/acre**
- **Turnip/Kale: 2 lbs. turnip + 1 lb. kale/acre**

Sow fall forage crops during the last week in July to first week in August, or 75 to 90 days before the crop is expected to be grazed. The seed can be dragged in with a chain harrow or spike-tooth harrow or rolled into the soil to a depth of ½ inch.

Weed Control. DCPA (Dacthal 75WP) can be applied as a pre-emergence herbicide at 10 lbs./acre. Or, apply glyphosate (Roundup) to annual and perennial weeds before plowing.

An alternative to using herbicides is to plant a companion crop of oats or annual ryegrass at 1 to 2 bushels of oats/acre or 20 lbs. of ryegrass/acre. These grasses will establish quickly, helping to shade out weeds while the turnips are getting established.

Varieties. Purple top turnip and kale seeds are available from commercial vegetable seed catalogs, such as Agway, Harris, and Stokes. Rape, oat, and annual ryegrass seeds are available from feed and farm supply outlets.

Fencing. Temporary electric fencing should be installed before the ground freezes. Fresh water, salt, and minerals should be available free choice. Use the same mineral mix as for sheep on a high legume ration.

seeds being placed too deeply or not in contact with the soil are available. Whether conventional or no-till planting methods are used, the August seeded crop has to catch, because there will not be an opportunity to replant later in the season.

A low seeding rate should be used on fall brassica crops to allow each plant to develop adequate roots and stems before grazing begins. Too much seed causes more leaf area in relation to the root in the case of turnips. A 6-inch to 8-inch turnip root is utilized well by sheep and gives a higher yield per acre. Swedes or rutabaga should not be used for sheep as the root develops below ground. Turnip roots swell at the soil surface, then heave up, protruding out of the soil after a freeze. Heinemann at the Irrigated Agricultural Research and Extension Center, Washington State University, found ewes on purple top turnip would obtain 68 percent of their digestible dry matter intake from the root portion.

More work is needed to evaluate vegetable cultivars for their suitability as fall forage crops. Currently, the Essex rape variety seems to be widely adapted and is frost hardy. Marrow stem kale is a popular forage; its succulent stem is readily consumed by livestock. Some work is being carried out on hybrids intended for forage, including Tyfon, a Chinese cabbage x turnip cross and Radicole, a forage radish x marrow stem kale hybrid. Grazer 2000 is a winter rye being evaluated for use as a fall pasture crop, with excellent early growth.

More Advantages and Disadvantages of Fall Forage Crops

The benefits of high carrying capacity and high yield in these crops is not without some drawbacks. Perhaps the most significant problem is due to the lack of a sod to support hoof traffic. Without a dense root structure, a turnip, rape, or kale field turns to mud, increasing the chances for foot scald or foot rot to occur. These crops are marginally competitive with weeds, and annual grasses, such as crabgrass or foxtails, get started, causing problems in next year's crops. Finally, mob stocking in the fall leaves the field without adequate soil protection over winter.

One solution to all of these problems is to sow a companion grass with the brassica crops. Annual ryegrass with its rapid growth and abundance of fine roots, might work. However, a sod-forming perennial, such as bluegrass or bromegrass, would be better, if the field is oversown with a companion legume the following spring. Obviously the mud, weeds, and soil compaction problems would be minimal in a no-till situation, but drawbacks from that method have already been discussed. Areas with a sandy soil probably would have the least difficulty with erosion and foot rot on temporary fall pastures.

The best opportunity to use a fall forage crop is probably in a rotation from hay to a row crop, such as corn. This has a number of advantages:

- **The cost of tillage is split between the fall crop and corn the next year.**
- **The sod has up to a year to decompose due to midsummer seedbed preparation.**
- **Fall weed control materials applied to the forage crop help reduce weed problems in corn the next year (especially if annual grasses are controlled).**
- **A fall forage crop could be double-cropped after a spring grain, such as oats or barley, which would be harvested by mid-August.**

Various fodder crops, such as turnip, beets, Swedes, and the like, have been utilized by sheep for many years. There are many other aftermath forages, summer annuals, and crop residues than those discussed here that can serve as low-cost sheep feeds. Further information on this subject is available from the proceedings of a symposium on "Sheep Harvested Feeds for the Intermountain West." Copies are available for a nominal fee from the Sheep Industry Development Program, 200 Clayton Street, Denver, Colorado 80206.

Chapter 6

INTERNAL
PARASITES

Internal parasites are a major cause of disease and death in sheep. Worming medications (anthelmintics) provide only a short-term control of parasite populations because sheep are exposed almost constantly to infective eggs and/or larvae. Wormers should not be a substitute for sound management practices that reduce the exposure of sheep and lambs to parasites.

Sheep apparently are more susceptible to internal parasites than cattle because of their close grazing habit and the pelleted form of their manure. Sheep and goats can graze right over their fresh feces, whereas cattle cannot because their manure blocks out any access to the grass beneath it. For many years sheep were not wormed as they are now, and they seemed to survive in spite of it. Under a traditional system of moving sheep with the seasons, sheep were allowed to graze in 1 area, then moved to a new grazing area every few days. The sheep would not retrace their steps until their return trek, many months later. They had little opportunity to regraze an area and pick up parasite eggs or larvae from their own manure. However, under more intensive grazing, the risk of parasite buildup on the pasture is greatly increased.

PARASITES AT LAMBING

The parasite burden fluctuates with climatic factors, intensity of grazing, and the sheep's production cycle. There is a sharp rise in fecal parasite egg counts in most classes of sheep which occurs in ewes anytime from 2 weeks before to 8 weeks after lambing, irrespective of the season. The rise is associated with lactation and may be due to changes in the hormone level of the ewe. If a ewe aborts or if her lambs are removed within 12 hours of birth, the rise in the number of parasite eggs does not occur, and the ewe is capable of rejecting newly acquired and established worms. The rise also appears to be the result of a general reduction in immune response to worms. The worm egg count rise comes at a time when the ewe is already stressed from lambing and has the greatest nutritional needs. Thus, the pre-lambing rise ensures a heavy parasite contamination of pastures with spring lambing flocks.

Pre-lambing treatments with levamisole (8 mg/kg) or fenbendazole (15 mg/kg) are effective in eliminating the pre-lambing rise of fecal worm eggs. With ewes housed over the winter, the optimum time to treat for worms is the day they come off pasture. Ewes lambing on pasture need a second treatment at the time of lambing.

CLEAN PASTURE

A clean pasture is land with parasite contamination so low that infection in the animals does not have time to build up to cause economic losses. Parasite contamination begins when sheep and lambs graze on the pasture. Contamination is usually high under warm, moist conditions which favor survival of parasite eggs and larvae. Young sheep and lambs must be kept off a pasture for 12 months to reduce parasite contamination to the point that the pasture is considered clean. During this time the pasture may be grazed by species that are not hosts for sheep parasites or may be cultivated for row crops or harvested as a hay crop. Sheep producers in the United Kingdom have used a system of rotation of pasture between cattle, sheep, and hay or row crops to reduce the parasite burden on sheep and lambs.

Some producers have thought that rotational grazing would help to control internal parasites by preventing continuous exposure of the sheep to a contaminated pasture. Although sunlight, drying winds, and high temperatures can kill parasite eggs and larvae on the grass, infective larvae and fecal worm eggs persist in the pasture to significantly contaminate the sheep. Cold winter temperatures and snow cannot eliminate all of the infective stages of sheep parasites.

Three-Field, Three-Year Grazing System

One way to benefit from clean pasture is to lamb on pasture early in the season, move the lambs to a clean summer pasture (such as a new seeding or after row cropping), and cut the lambing pasture for hay or silage. Lambs and young sheep are the most susceptible to worms and need the cleanest pasture. The ewes can graze the lambing pasture in the fall because they are resistant to worms at this time. Then it should be plowed and planted to row crops or returned to hay for 1 year before being grazed again. The summer grazing field becomes the lambing field the next year. Lambs utilize a third clean pasture in the second year for summer grazing and a 3-field, 3-year clean grazing system is established.

On permanent pasture, haying or row cropping is not possible. The best option is to alternate beef with sheep on a 12-month rotation. Dairy cows and heifers also can be a part of a clean grazing system with sheep.

DRUG-RESISTANT PARASITES

New strains of bacteria are developing resistance to commercial antibiotics, and new worms are becoming resistant to our widely used anthelmintics. For some farmers, the problem of drug resistance is so severe that they have become dependent on always using new and different compounds, often having to resort to the use of nonapproved drugs. It is worth repeating that a good flock health program is based on disease prevention, not rescue therapy.

When resistance does occur, the following steps may have to be taken to control internal parasites.

- **Increase the dosage, but only if it is relatively nontoxic to the sheep.**

- **Spread treatment over several days. This may result in better control than a high level of the drug given in a single dose.**

- **Use a wormer of a completely different class or effect on the parasite.**

PARASITE PREVENTION

The following points on preventing parasite infections are recommended by Dr. James R. Wadsworth, V.M.D., Extension Animal Pathologist at the University of Vermont.

- **Worm all new arrivals of sheep. Hold them in a drylot for 1 or 2 days following treatment before moving them to pasture.**

- **Do not overstock pastures. Pasture transmission rates increase exponentially as the stocking rates increase.**

- **Wean lambs early and separate them from ewes as soon as possible; older animals are sources of infection. Pasture lambs on fresh, clean pasture which has been free of sheep for a year or more.**

- **Avoid poorly drained pastures. Parasite eggs and larvae survive longer under moist conditions.**

- **Feed sheep in a drylot if possible. Parasite spread is minimal here because there are no live plants for the noninfective larvae to feed on.**

- **Prevent contamination of feed and water with manure.**

- **If sheep are in a barn, clean the barn often. Compost the manure or spread it on ground that will not be used for pasture within the next 12 months.**

- **Provide clean quarters or clean, noninfected pastures for lambing.**

- **Strategic wormer treatments (following fecal studies) may be as follows:**

  1. **Treat ewes, rams, and replacement ewe lambs in late fall just after removal from pasture.**

  2. **Treat all sheep in midwinter, 1 to 1½ months before lambing to prevent a pre-lambing rise in fecal egg counts.**

  3. **Treat all animals when winter-born lambs are 2½ to 3 months old.**

  4. **Treat all sheep in the spring just before pasturing.**

5. Treat all animals 3 weeks after they are placed on spring pasture to eliminate parasites which were picked up during the first weeks of grazing.

6. Treat all breeding ewes and rams just before the flushing period.

7. For feeder lambs, treat immediately upon arrival. Keep them in drylot for 3 to 4 weeks and treat before placing them on pasture. Treat feeder lambs again in midsummer. Re-treat in the fall when they are taken off pasture, if lambs will be held beyond the pasture season.

• Feed ample, well-balanced rations to increase resistance to parasites.

• If possible, select for parasite resistance; cull extremely susceptible individuals.

See Appendix G for recommended books that deal with sheep health.

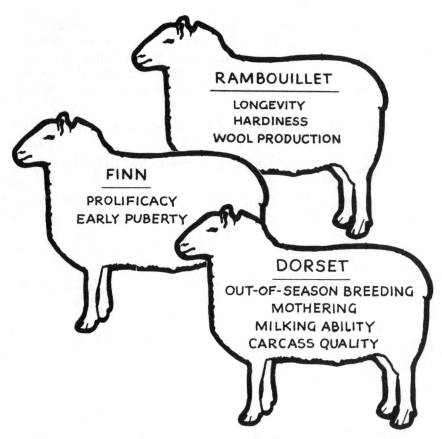

RAMBOUILLET

LONGEVITY
HARDINESS
WOOL PRODUCTION

FINN

PROLIFICACY
EARLY PUBERTY

DORSET

OUT-OF-SEASON BREEDING
MOTHERING
MILKING ABILITY
CARCASS QUALITY

Figure 7–1. The complementary traits of a Finn X Dorset X Rambouillet ewe.

Chapter 7

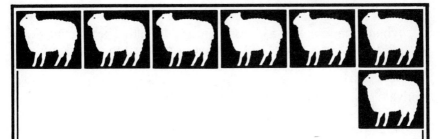

SELECTING
NEW AND
REPLACEMENT EWES

A common mistake that many new sheepbreeders make is to purchase a mixed group of ewes to begin their flocks. When you select several different kinds of sheep, you resign yourself to several years of mixed lamb crops, and rapid genetic selection becomes difficult, if not impossible.

If only a few sheep are in your plans, then by all means proceed with whatever odd ewes meet your fancy. But if you expect to compete in large-scale lamb markets, look for the most uniform group of replacement ewes available. Usually these are born within a few weeks of each other and are all half-sisters or out of no more than 3 rams for every 100 ewes.

This "family" of ewes can be mated to a superior ram with a good idea of the outcome. Repeatability in the ewe line is very important to purebred and commercial sheepbreeders. Furthermore, the most rapid genetic progress can be made by selecting for a few traits out of a uniform group of ewes, rather than selecting for many traits out of an already diverse group.

PURCHASING EWES

Where does one find a uniform group of healthy, productive ewes to start or expand a flock? Not at a livestock auction or commission sales ring—these are terminal markets for cull and meat animals and should not be considered as a source for breeding stock. In most cases, a private sale is preferred over an auction because there is less stress on the animals.

Flock dispersal sales offer another means to purchase replacements at a low cost. If the sale is by private treaty, a price discount of 10 to 15 percent may be possible if you purchase the entire lot. A flock without health and production records will be an aggravation at any price. Do not take the seller's word on registration papers either. Make sure they are in order and signed for transfer when the payment is made.

Some sheep cooperatives and state associations make group purchases of "certified" replacement ewes, usually from the Western states. Group purchases provide a savings in transportation and purchase price. A group may hire a livestock broker or agent to select the ewes, rather than purchase sheep over the telephone.

The disadvantages of a cooperative purchase are mainly at the receiving end. In sorting sheep to different farmers, someone inevitably complains about the animals they received and confidence is lost.

Some states or their local associations publish a breeder's directory that can help you identify sources for commercial or purebred ewes. Ideally, you may want to go to a breeder who usually markets all of his or her ewe lambs so you can have the pick of the entire lamb crop. A down payment of 25 to 50 percent usually is required to seal the commitment between the buyer and seller. You also may want to contract for a group of ewe lambs in advance of the breeding season, specifying the cross or sire to be used.

COMMERCIAL EWES

There are many commercial breeders who specialize in raising replacement ewe lambs. Some breeders raise a flock of ½ Finn and ½ Rambouillet ewes, which are bred to a Dorset ram to produce ¼ Finn × ½ Dorset × ¼ Rambouillet ewe lambs. Each breed contributes a different economic trait, resulting in an ideal commercial ewe with crossbred vigor (Figure 7–1). The same breeder also may maintain a small flock of purebred Finn or purebred Rambouillets to produce the ½ Finn dam. Alternatively, the breeder may have all purebred Rambouillets and use a ½ Finn ram to produce ¼ Finn offspring. The ideal system of raising ¼ Finn replacements depends on how many multiple births the producer is capable of managing.

Sheepbreeder associations hold commercial ewe sales that offer a guarantee that the sale sheep are healthy and meet certain production requirements. Production records such as birth type, birthweight, weaning weight, and weaning date are commonly listed in a commercial ewe sale catalog, whereas the purebred sales emphasize show ring placings and pedigree.

The characteristics of the commercial sheep breeds found in the United States are discussed in the *Sheepman's Production Handbook* by the Sheep Industry Development Council. Minor breeds and breeds that are commercially important in other parts of the world are discussed and illustrated in the book, *Sheep of the World in Color* by Kenneth Pointing (Bladford Press Ltd., Poole, Dorset, England).

Photo 7-1. A commercial ewe with fairly open face, long and deep body, correct feet and legs, and heavy fleece.

REGISTERED EWES

When selecting registered, purebred ewes, take advantage of the major shows and sales to find reputable sources for breeding stock. Look for the breeders who consistently place well, then talk to them. What is in their 5-year plans? In what direction would they like the breed to go as far as performance, economic traits, and its long-term role in the commercial sheep industry? What selection criteria are emphasized in their flock to obtain the best quality animals? What are the weak points in their flock (no one's sheep are perfect), and so on.

Talk to the judge to see how this year's classes compare with those from the previous year. Try to record the sale price on every animal sold in the ring, because promotional materials and advertisements often report just the top-selling sheep.

Use whatever data is available in the sale catalog to compare the performance of ewes and rams within breed and age groups. For example, all sales of purebreds require birthdates and, in some cases, birthtype; most animals will have been weighed the day before the show or sale. This gives you enough information to rank animals according to their weight per day-of-age (WDA). The WDA is simply a measurement of the animal's weight gain between 2 points in time, such as between birth and weaning.

PRICES

How much should you pay for a commercial ewe? The rule is to avoid a ewe or ewe lamb without production records at any cost. This background information is essential to a breeder to develop goals for better production. In the dairy industry, grade cows or heifers with Dairy Herd Improvement Association (DHIA) records consistently sell for 10 to 15 percent more than cows without them and the same principle should apply to sheep.

Commercial ewe lambs can be realistically priced against prevailing market lamb prices. For nondescript, crossbred ewe lambs, count on a 15 to 25 percent premium (liveweight) above the meat price. This assumes the lamb is structurally sound, healthy, and has records.

Sheepbreeders who specialize in producing replacement ewe lambs or who have a uniform group for sale expect a 20 to 30 percent premium over the market lamb price. Commercial ewe lambs currently sell for $60 to $120 per head depending on their breeding, weight, and the number sold.

Well-grown yearlings who have reached 80 to 90 percent of their mature body weight may be less expensive than ewe lambs in the long run, as they will have gained most of their skeletal and muscle tissue and therefore will have less gain to make on your farm than lighter lambs. The conception rate of yearlings will be higher than lambs.

A popular time to purchase ewe lambs is in April or May, from producers who lamb in January or February. Lambs are purchased before the summer heat and internal parasites slow their growth. They should have gained steadily from birth until the sale date, weigh at least 70 pounds, and have been weaned at least a week before being transported.

The long-term costs for a replacement ewe depend on her initial purchase price, years of useful life, current interest rate on borrowed capital, and her value as mutton. Breeds such as Rambouillet and Merino, which are noted for longevity, may have a lower annual cost than the medium wool or down breeds. Sheep are considered to have a useful life of 5 years for income tax purposes.

Photo 7–2. Purebred Finnsheep ewes.

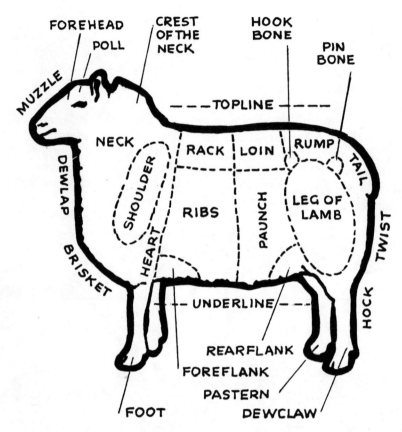

Figure 7–2. Parts of a sheep.

Photo 7-3. Wooly face on a Rambouillet X Suffolk lamb.

CONFORMATION

Conformation refers to the type, form, and shape of a live animal, usually with reference to some performance characteristic. For example, good conformation on a market lamb implies that it is well-muscled.

Regardless of the specific breed, select ewes that are correct in their mouth, feet, legs, eyes and udder. The term "correct" means free of defects, functional, and intact.

A correct mouth has the incisor teeth hitting squarely on the dental pad, not extending beyond the pad. While examining the mouth for proper bite, check the age of the ewe by counting the pairs of permanent incisors. The first pair occurs once a ewe is a year old or so, with subsequent pairs developing for each year thereafter until there are 4 pairs and the age is approximately 4 years plus. Sheep with a severely overshot or undershot jaw should not be kept for breeding as this defect is highly heritable (likely to be passed on to the next generation).

Some of the other common and highly heritable, conformational defects include inverted eyelids (entropion), excessive skin folds, wooly face cover, black fibers, excessive hairy fibers (kemp), and horns (in polled breeds).

Select a ewe or lamb with short, strong pasterns and straight legs. The legs should have a good width between them, with a slight end at the hock. Turned-out or turned-in toes can be seen from a front view. Sometimes it can be detected as uneven wear on the hooves.

The eyes should be clear and bright without evidence of scarring due to pinkeye. There should be no tears as a result of inverted eyelids or wool cover.

Set the ewe on her rump and be sure there are 2 teats, without sore mouth scabs, shearing cuts, and so on. On a mature ewe, check the udder for lumps (scar tissue) indicative of a previous mastitis infection.

A ewe lamb (or group of lambs) that is correct, grown out quickly, and out of a prolific ewe has the potential to be as good, if not better than, her parents. She should have good body capacity or depth of body for carrying lambs and utilizing forage. The back should be fairly level, straight, long, and wide over the loin and over the rump. She should not have excessive fat around the chest, ribs, back, or dock. With over 0.3 inches of backfat, the ewe lamb is becoming too fat.

In a commercial operation, the value of the sheep should be equal to or slightly greater than the value of all the other equipment and buildings combined (excluding land). Don't be afraid to pay a good price for high-quality replacement ewe lambs; and by the same logic, don't buy problem sheep at any price.

Chapter 8

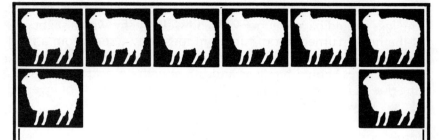

SELECTING RAMS

A great stud ram produces more than just a few exceptional lambs; he sires offspring who are all above average for the flock. In doing so he becomes more than "half the flock" since many of our economic traits have a multiplier effect down through the generations.

Let's assume you average a 160 percent lamb crop. If a ram sires offspring who are all above average for the flock, you have made progress for many more lambs than you have ewes. When this performance or trait is passed on to succeeding generations via the daughters, there is even more to gain from that superior ram. Many breeders remark that the best ram you can find will turn out to be the cheapest, due to the increased performance of his offspring.

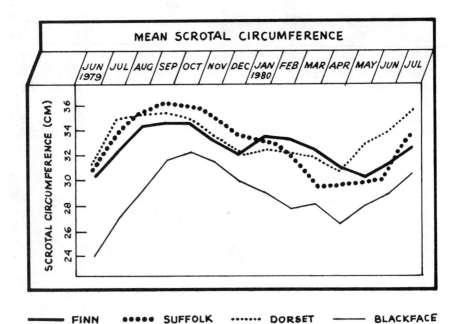

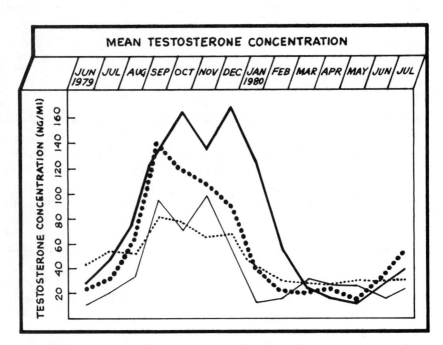

Figure 8–1. The seasonal increase in testicular size and testosterone concentration in 4 ram breeds.

As you get ready to select a new ram, keep in mind the importance of heritable defects. In a flock lambing at 12-month intervals, a bad ram will set a good breeding program back about 2 years. All of the major breed associations have outlined certain heritable defects which they discriminate against when animals are shown. Each breed association also has a "standard of excellence" by which a judge can evaluate an individual or group against an ideal type for that breed. You should familiarize yourself with these standards.

When evaluating a ram, check the reproductive parts by setting the ram on his rump. When palpating the testicles, you should feel 2 testicles, both descended and about equal in size. They should be firm and you should be able to slip them freely up and down in the scrotum; there should be no adhesions or swellings in the sac. Look for shearing cuts on the scrotum or other lesions that may result in an infection. The sheath around the penis should be free of ulceration or swelling.

Measure the scrotal circumference to get an indication of the size of the testicles and, hence, their capacity to produce sperm. The base of the scrotal sac contains the reserve of semen needed to serve a group of ewes in a short period of time. A large volume here usually means an adequate reserve of semen. Always look for rams with large, firm testicles who maintain the size of the testes throughout the year. This last point is especially important for out-of-season breeding. As you will see in Chapter 18, out-of-season breeding in an accelerated lambing program can significantly improve farm productivity.

SEASONAL EFFECTS

Special consideration must be given to rams used for breeding in the spring and summer months. In temperate regions, rams of most breeds show a seasonal variation in important reproductive characteristics such as percent normal sperm, libido, serving capacity (number of ewes he is able to breed), and scrotal circumference. The seasonal change in breeding ability or behavior is influenced partly by the genetic makeup of the ram, but the social environment (exposure to ewes) and climatic conditions (primarily photoperiod) also have an effect.

At the University of Manitoba, 4 ram breeds were used to investigate the influence of these factors on the seasonality in sexual function of rams. Breeds chosen were Finnish Landrace (Finn), Suffolk, Dorset, and Scottish Blackface.

The study showed that a seasonal increase in testicular size was maintained longer for the Dorset rams than for the other rams. Finn rams had less pronounced seasonal variations in scrotal circumference and had higher levels of testosterone than the other rams. According to the researchers, K. A. Dickson and L. M. Sanford, increased testosterone secretion in the fall further stimulates the areas of the brain that regulate sex drive. During the breeding season, testicular size and testosterone levels increased, as did the production of spermatozoa. The authors concluded that within the 4 breeds studied, there was not a single breed that excelled in all reproductive characteristics year-round.

In an earlier study at the University of Manitoba, L. M. Sanford and T. A. Varney placed rams in close proximity to ewes in estrus to determine if sexually stimulated rams had better breeding performance. The results of the study indicated that penning mature rams with or in close contact to ewes in heat slightly enhanced testicular development out of the normal breeding season. The benefits of bringing rams in close contact with ewes in heat may be greater for breeds that are highly seasonal in their breeding performance.

DAYLENGTH

Most breeds initiate their annual sexual cycle as a result of hormonal changes, brought on in response to a gradually decreasing daylength. Dr. Bruce Schanbacher at the U.S. Meat Animal Research Center in Clay Center, Nebraska, placed Suffolk rams under a photoperiod of 8 hours of light, 16 hours of darkness from late February to late May. Rams under this treatment sired 1.31 lambs per ewe compared to control rams under natural daylength conditions which sired .55 lambs per ewe. Of the ewes exposed to the experimental rams, 67 percent lambed, in contrast to 32 percent of those exposed to the control rams. This is comparable to out-of-season matings by ram breeds whose breeding performance is less affected by season (Dorset or Finnsheep, for example).

CROSSBRED RAMS

Dr. Charles Parker, at the Ohio Agricultural Research and Development Center, evaluated the merits of crossbred (F_1) rams on reproductive performance and total productivity of purebred and crossbred Columbia and Targhee ewes. His results indicate that ewes bred to crossbred rams are superior in performance to those bred to purebred rams for all traits studied, including lambing percentage, lamb vigor, number of lambs weaned at 90 days, and total pounds of lamb weaned per ewe.

The most important difference was a nearly 10 percent increase in the number of lambs born per ewe (1.34 vs. 1.22) as a result of breeding with crossbred rams. Crossbred ewes mated to crossbred rams had a significantly higher lambing and weaning percentage than if they had been bred to purebred rams. The combined effect of mating crossbred ewes and crossbred rams was a 21.5 percent increase in ewe productivity at weaning time. On the average, 17 more lambs were weaned per 100 crossbred ewes mated to first generation (F_1) crossbred rams. Many producers are using crossbred rams because of the positive effect of heterosis (hybrid vigor) on lamb survival and lamb growth rate.

LEASING RAMS

Leasing a ram has several advantages over ownership. First, there is the opportunity to deduct the cost of leasing for income tax purposes; you minimize the risks involved in owning and caring for a ram all year; and you gain the opportunity to use a new sire every year.

COST OF MAINTAINING A RAM

Initial Cost		$700.00
Annual depreciation (3 to 5 year life)		154.00
Interest on investment @ 10%		54.60
Death loss @ 5%		35.00
Maintenance Costs		
Feed and pasture	$ 75.00	
Veterinary and health care	10.00	
Labor	5.00	
Housing, insurance, misc.	5.00	
Total Maintenance	$100.00	$100.00
Total Annual Expense		$343.60

Ram:Ewes	Breeding Fee/Ewe*
1:15	$ 22.88
1:30	11.44
1:50	6.87

*Total annual expense for 1 ram divided by number of ewes bred by him annually.

Many sheep breeders lambing once a year could permit their rams to be used more often than during a 3-week to 6-week breeding period every year and generate income by leasing their rams. Leasing ram lambs helps to prove them through their offspring and can be a form of advertisement if the ram is used on a farm with high visibility to other sheepbreeders.

Terms for leasing a ram (or ewes) should be in writing and should specify his identification, delivery date, return date, feed, number of ewes to be bred, responsibility for veterinary treatment and costs, a guarantee that the ram is fertile, the breeding fee, and rights to advertise or promote. The fee depends on the value of the ram (cost or purchase price less depreciation) and number of ewes to be bred. Usually the ewes are moved to the ram, since he is considered to have a higher value than the ewes. There should be a 1-week adjustment period for new arrivals to the farm.

BRINGING HOME A NEW RAM

After bringing home a new ram, isolate him from the rest of the flock for 2 or 3 weeks and observe him daily for any illness. Introduce him to the rest of the rams by enclosing them in a pen with just a bit more than standing room, for about a day. After being in close quarters for a day, the rams will have established a close bond and rank and fighting will be less likely. Provide adequate shade, ventilation, and water, especially if it is hot. Some producers will use a dozen old tires hung from the ceiling down to the rams' shoulders to keep them from getting a running start in a fight. The tires keep the rams from being very successful at butting. Also, avoid scratching rams on the head and face as this sometimes causes them to lower their head and may lead to butting.

Chapter 9

NUTRITIONAL REQUIREMENTS OF SHEEP

Forages, such as pasture and hay, typically make up 85 to 90 percent of the sheep's diet—a higher proportion than with any other class of livestock. Concentrates, the bulk of the rest of the diet, include grain, grain by-products, plant products (molasses, oils, and so on), and animal products (blood meal, fish meal, fats, and so on), which are relatively concentrated sources of energy and/or protein. In most sheep enterprises, feed represents approximately 50 to 60 percent of the total annual variable costs, making it essential that sheep producers meet the ewe's nutritional needs at the lowest cost. This requires using low-cost feedstuffs in the most efficient manner: feeding according to production and reducing the amount of feed wasted. The essential nutrients for sheep fall into 5 general categories: energy, protein, water, vitamins, and minerals.

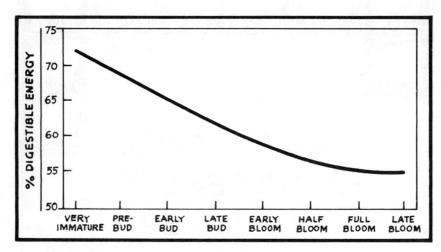

Figure 9-1. Changes in digestible energy in alfalfa with increasing maturity.

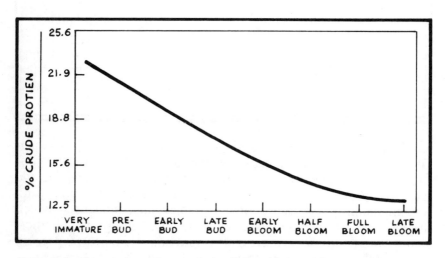

Figure 9-2. Changes in crude protein in alfalfa with increasing maturity.

ENERGY

Forages contribute most of the energy in the sheep's diet and vary widely in energy content. The energy content is primarily affected by the growth stage at which the forage is harvested and by the losses which occur at harvest and in storage. Figures 9-1 and 9-2 show the changing energy and protein content of alfalfa with advancing maturity. A similar relationship between digestible energy and plant maturity exists for other forage grasses and legumes.

Digestible energy and protein of the whole plant decrease from the very immature stage to the early bloom stage and then level off. The digestible energy and protein of the stems decline very rapidly from the immature stage to early bloom, then also level off. A greater proportion of energy and protein is found in the leaves than in the stems. Alfalfa leaves, for example, range from 74 to 72 percent total digestible nutrients (TDN) and 30 to 23 percent protein between the very immature and late bloom stage, respectively. In comparison, alfalfa stems drop from about 70 to 48 percent TDN and 18 to 8 percent protein from very immature to late bloom stage. This emphasizes the importance of harvesting forages in the early growth stages and using harvesting methods that preserve plant leaves.

Energy losses can occur at harvest by leaf shattering, when leaves (which are high in energy) are shaken off the stems during raking and baling. Rain can lower the energy value in a hay crop by leaching soluble sugars. Energy losses in storage are due to seepage of soluble sugars and other carbohydrates in high-moisture silages or by mold growth and spoilage (in hay and silages).

Feedstuffs contain readily available water-soluble carbohydrates, such as sugars and starches, and not so readily available carbohydrates, such as cellulose (plant fiber), lignin, and pectins. Microorganisms in the sheep's rumen (the first compartment of the stomach) are able to utilize cellulose and other roughage for energy, producing volatile fatty acids as waste products. The volatile fatty acids are absorbed through the rumen wall where they enter the bloodstream and are utilized for energy by the animal. Sugars, starches, alcohols, and other readily available carbohydrates are digested by enzymes in the abomasum, the fourth compartment, or so-called "true stomach." Readily available carbohydrates are further broken down and absorbed in the small intestines. Excess energy consumed is stored as fat.

PROTEIN

Sheep require protein, or more specifically the amino acids from protein, for tissue formation, wool growth, and body maintenance. In general, the quantity of protein is more important than the quality of protein, except during times of peak nutritional needs, as in late pregnancy or lactation.

There is a tendency for some portion of the protein to be dissolved in the rumen fluids. The protein fraction that goes into solution in the rumen is rapidly broken down into its nonprotein nitrogen components and may escape (get belched) as ammonia before it can be utilized by the rumen microorganisms and the animal. Some soluble protein or nonprotein nitrogen in the ration is needed, however, to maintain the rumen microorganism population. Urea, a common feed additive is 100 percent soluble and an example of nonprotein nitrogen.

The microorganisms convert simple nitrogen compounds into microbial protein for their own structure and metabolism—a process referred to as the nonprotein nitrogen activity of the rumen. With the normal turnover in the microbe population, inevitably some of this microbial protein, now in a more insoluble form, will be passed through to the lower digestive tract. Microbial protein is a relatively small portion of the insoluble protein used by the animal; a much larger contribution comes from the feedstuffs.

Insoluble protein as found in fish meal, blood meal, or heat-treated soybean meal is (more or less) passed through the rumen and broken down into amino acids in the lower digestive tract. Feeds with low protein solubility vary in the rate at which they are broken down in the lower digestive tract. (Some proteins may be readily "soluble" but poorly degraded by rumen bacteria, thus are not broken down until they reach the intestines.) These are considered high-quality protein sources because the amino acids from these proteins can be used directly for milk production or growth. The soluble protein and nonprotein nitrogen must first be converted into microbial protein before it can be utilized by the animal. Excess soluble protein is often lost as gas or excreted in the urine. In general, hay is usually low in protein solubility but hay silage, corn silage, and high-moisture corn have high protein solubilities.

WATER

Clean, fresh water must be provided almost daily at a rate of 2 to 3 pounds (or about 1 quart) of water for every pound of dry matter ingested. By the last month of gestation (pregnancy) and during lactation, this rate can double. Similarly, when the ambient air temperatures rise above 70 degrees F., water consumption increases. In winter, water should be maintained at a temperature of 45 to 50 degrees F. Water near the freezing point has an adverse affect on the microbial activity of fermentation in the rumen with the result that feed digestibility and utilization is decreased. Snow is *not* an adequate source of water, especially if it is the icy, granular type. Assume that ewes in early gestation will drink ¾ to 1½ gallons of water per day in cold weather.

VITAMINS

Vitamins are categorized into a fat-soluble group consisting of vitamins A, D, E, and K; and a water-soluble group, consisting of the various B vitamins, including thiamine, riboflavin, niacin, pantothenic acid, B6, inositol, biotin, choline, p-aminobenzoic acid, folic acid, B12, and vitamin C or absorbic acid.

All of the essential water-soluble vitamins can be synthesized in the rumen, but the fat-soluble vitamins must be provided in the ration. Vitamin A is derived from a precursor called beta-carotene, which is found in green plants and sun-cured hay. Ensiled feeds do not have active beta-carotene, and sheep on high silage rations may need a vitamin A supplement. However, sheep can store vitamin A in the liver for up to 200 days. Vitamin D is also found in sun-cured hay and can be manufactured by the animal if exposed to sunlight. Sheep in confinement and on a low forage/high concentrate ration may need to be supplemented with A and D in the feed.

Vitamin E prevents the oxidation of unsaturated fatty acids, aids intestinal absorption of fatty acids, maintains normal muscle metabolism, maintains the integrity of the vascular and central nervous system, maintains genital structures, and is important for fertility. Suckling lambs have a high demand for this vitamin due to their high fat intake. Vitamin E deficiency often is seen as a muscular dystrophy (white muscle disease) in young lambs. Fresh green forage and sun-cured hay is a good source of this vitamin.

Young lambs without a functional rumen have a dietary need for the water-soluble vitamins, specifically thiamine, riboflavin, folic acid, and possibly niacin. As more lambs are raised on high concentrate rations, deficiencies of the B vitamins may become more common than under pasture-rearing systems.

MINERALS

Minerals are the least expensive nutrient to provide in the ration, yet are often neglected because only small amounts are required. Forage should be the principal source of minerals and should be analyzed for mineral content in order to balance the ration. The total amount of each mineral provided is as important as the ratio or balance of one mineral with another, as with calcium and phosphorus, nitrogen and sulfur. Soil analyses can be used with forage analyses to determine any relationship between fertilizer needs and mineral content in the plant.

Once the mineral content of the feed is known, supplemental minerals can be provided free choice, with or without loose salt. Usually salt is used as a carrier to get other, less palatable minerals into the animals. Do not use a salt block, as sheep will have difficulty obtaining enough salt because their tongues are so small. Molasses-based salt/mineral blocks are readily consumed by sheep and do not require a special feeder. Use 1 block for every 25 head of sheep and record the date every time a new block is set out or every time the mineral feeder is filled. This will allow you to monitor the salt/mineral intake when these are provided free choice.

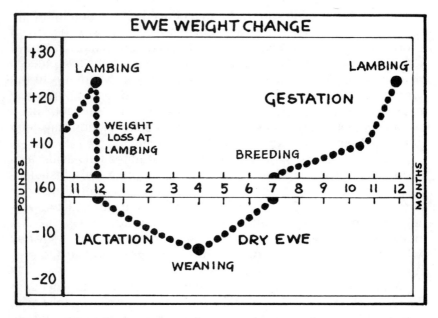

Figure 9–3. Weight changes normally expected in a year for a 160-pound ewe giving birth to and rearing twin lambs.

EWE PRODUCTION CYCLE

In discussing ewe nutrition, we must define the requirements for each of the 6 stages of the production cycle: dry, flushing and breeding, first 15 weeks of gestation, last 6 weeks of gestation, first 8 weeks of lactation, and last 8 weeks of lactation.

The stage of the production cycle is only one of the factors affecting the ewe's nutritional requirements. The total management system—including average size or body weight; rate of growth; number of lambs; amount of exercise, parasitism, or disease; and environment—also affects the nutritional requirements of the ewe.

The weight changes normally expected in a year for a 160-pound ewe giving birth to and rearing twin lambs is shown in Figure 9-3. After weaning, the ewe normally gains back body condition (fat and other tissue) lost during pregnancy and lactation. In this example, the ewe gains about 0.1 pound per day or 10 pounds over a 90-day dry period. On an accelerated lambing scheme with a much shorter dry period, the ewe might be expected to regain the 10 pounds in a month. The important point here is that a dry ewe has nutritional requirements above maintenance which depend on how soon she is to rebreed again.

Prior to and during the breeding period, keep the ewe on a rising plane of nutrition to improve fertility and conception. Note that the ewe should reach her average body weight and condition just before breeding.

After breeding, ewes should maintain a constant weight or show a slight increase during the first month of gestation. A slight weight loss (3 to 4 percent) has little effect on embryo mortality during this period. It is important to avoid any severe weight loss or change of feed during this period.

The fetus grows very slowly between the first and third months of pregnancy; at 90 days, the fetus is just 15 percent of the weight of a newborn lamb. The placenta completes its growth at this time, which places certain limits on the subsequent nutrition and growth of the lambs. A ewe that suffers a significant weight loss (5 percent or more) during early to mid-pregnancy often will have lighter lambs at birth with less chance of survival than a properly fed ewe.

In the fourth and fifth months of pregnancy, there is a dramatic increase in the growth rate of the fetuses, with a corresponding increase in the energy and protein requirements of the ewe. Over the years, the ewe has been selected to produce twins and triplets at an early age but without a corresponding increase in her rumen capacity to hold bulky forage. Thus, it becomes necessary to feed more concentrates in late gestation.

Table 9-1

SUGGESTED RATIONS BASED ON CONDITION SCORES

Stage of Production	Condition Scores			
	2.5	3.0	3.5	4.0
Flushing and Breeding	1. Excellent pasture, ½–1 lb. grain	1. Excellent pasture	1. Good pasture	1. Good pasture
	2. Free choice hay, ½–1 lb. grain	2. Free choice hay, 0–½ lb. grain	2. Free choice hay	2. Free choice hay
Early Gestation	Same as breeding	1. Fair to good pasture	1. Fair pasture	1. Fair pasture
		2. 3–4 lbs. hay	2. 3–3½ lbs. hay, plus exercise	2. 3 lbs. hay, plus exercise
Late Gestation	1. Excellent pasture, 1–1½ lb. grain	1. Good pasture, ¼ lb. grain	1. Good pasture, ¼ lb. grain	1. Good pasture
	2. Free choice hay, 1–1½ lb. grain	2. 3–4 lbs. hay, ½–1 lb. grain	2. 3–4 lbs. hay, ½ lb. grain	2. 3–4 lbs. hay, ½ lb. grain
Lactation	Same as late gestation	1. Excellent pasture	1. Good pasture	1. Good pasture
		2. 4–5 lbs. hay, 1–2 lbs. grain	2. 4–5 lbs. hay, 1–1½ lb. grain	2. 4–5 lbs. hay, ½ lb. grain

Table 9–1. Suggested rations for different condition scores and stages of production.

Fat ewes in late gestation have not been fed according to their needs and are inclined to have lambing difficulty due to excess fat in the pelvic area. Fat ewes have dull appetites after lambing which cause more problems. As feed intake decreases, her protein and energy intake are reduced. While energy intake is reduced, it is made up for by a rapid mobilization of body fat. This results in the excessive production of ketone bodies formed by the oxidation of fatty acids in the liver. An accumulation of ketones in the tissues, blood, and urine causes a disease state called ketosis, or pregnancy toxemia. In sheep, ketosis produces dehydration, weakness, starvation (due to depressed appetite), and death. It is treated with oral drenches of propylene glycol, an energy source. However, the solution to feeding the fat ewe after lambing may be to increase the protein content of the diet.

In short, a moderate amount of body fat is desirable at the time of lambing to supplement the energy intake from feed and, in turn, to support milk production. However, the ewe should not be so fat as to reduce feed consumption during lactation.

Additional protein during lactation improves the efficiency of the conversion of energy stored in body fat into usable energy for milk production. With the proper amount and quality of protein, up to half of the energy needed for lactation can be mobilized from body fat. During the first 6 weeks of lactation, when milk production is greatest, the protein supplementation should be high in insoluble protein (for example, fish meal or heat-treated soybean meal).

Research by Dr. J. Robinson and others at the Rowett Research Institute in Aberdeen, Scotland, evaluated the effect of level and type of protein fed on ewe milk yield, body condition, and utilization of body tissue for milk production. At 4 to 6 weeks of lactation, ewes fed a high protein (14.3 percent) ration produced approximately 1.3 pounds more milk per ewe per day than those fed a low protein (11.6 percent) ration. Ewes on the high protein ration reached their peak daily milk production of 8.4 pounds per head 9 days later than ewes fed a low protein ration. Lambs nursing from ewes on the high protein ration had higher average daily gains and consumed less creep feed.

Dr. Robinson recommends that supplemental protein be fed to ewes starting approximately 6 weeks before lambing and that a majority of the protein be from an insoluble source not degraded in the rumen, such as fish meal or soybean meal. By feeding the high-quality sources of protein, there is more direct utilization of the protein by the animal and less concentrate is needed to obtain high levels of production.

CONDITION SCORING

Condition scoring is a subjective way to evaluate the fat cover on mature sheep in order to adjust their feed for optimum health and economical production. This is done by feeling the sharpness or roundness of the backbone and of the bones in the loin area. The procedure is simple.

First, crowd the sheep into a pen or chute so they can't run away from you as you feel their backs. To score each sheep, put your thumb on the backbone (over the loin area) and your 4 fingers along the transverse processes (bumps, bones) of the loin, which run on each side parallel to the backbone. Press through the fleece to feel the

Photo 9–1. Ewe with a condition score of 1.5.

sharpness or roundness of these bones (Figure 9–4). Assign a condition score based on the standards as they are defined in Figure 9–5.

The range of condition scores from 1 to 5 represents a difference of approximately 30 to 50 pounds or 6 to 10 pounds between condition scores, depending on the breed. Ewes with chronic weight loss and consistently scoring below "2" should be examined for loose or missing teeth, parasites, or disease complications. If the ewe has no overriding disease problems or a physiological disorder, she can be placed on a ration of 30 to 50 percent concentrates until she recovers. Other suggested rations for different condition scores and stages of production are listed in Table 9–1.

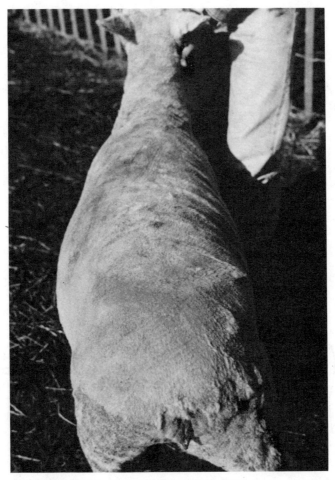

Photo 9–2. Ewe with a condition score of 5.

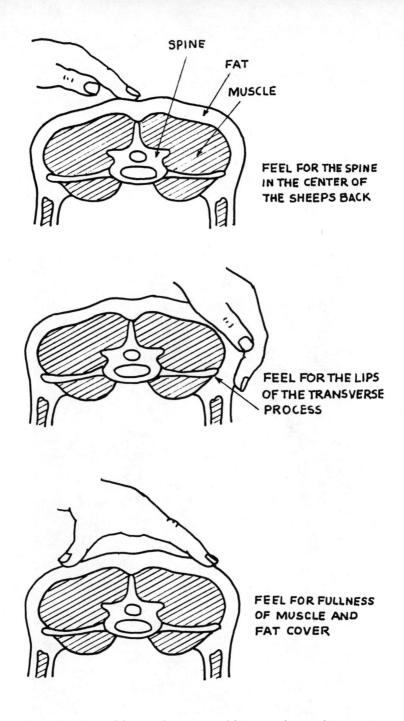

SPINE

FAT

MUSCLE

FEEL FOR THE SPINE
IN THE CENTER OF
THE SHEEPS BACK

FEEL FOR THE LIPS
OF THE TRANSVERSE
PROCESS

FEEL FOR FULLNESS
OF MUSCLE AND
FAT COVER

Figure 9–4. Fat is felt over the spine and loin area for condition scoring.

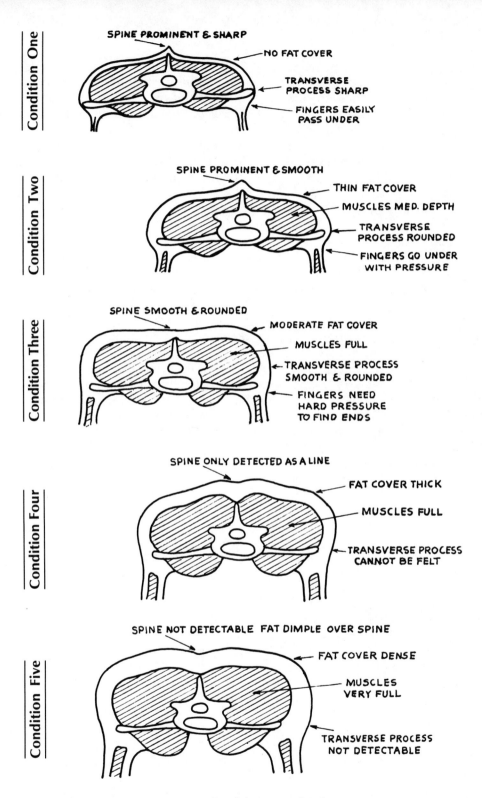

Figure 9–5. Condition scores for sheep.

Ewes on accelerated lambing should be maintained in average or above average body condition throughout the year for optimum fertility and conception rates. They should have a condition score of 2.5 at the end of lactation and 3.5 at breeding. As lambing, weaning, and breeding dates move closer together, there is less time to replace body fat lost during lactation. Accelerated lambing requires more constant attention to body condition and nutrition of the ewes, compared to once a year lambing.

Condition scores for pure Finnsheep lambing once a year or on an accelerated lambing scheme should be adjusted for internal fat. Finnsheep and their crosses tend to accumulate more internal fat (around the heart and kidneys) than other breeds. Pure Finns that score 2.5 based on your estimation of backfat are equivalent to a 3.5 on other breeds. For ¼ Finn ewes add .25 to their condition score to reflect their higher amount of internal fat. Similarly, the condition score for a ½ Finn ewe should automatically be increased by .50 point.

Condition scoring will allow you to separate ewes for supplemental feeding, flushing prior to breeding, or (for overly fat sheep) to exercise them. Excess fat constitutes wasted energy which you have to pay for in one way or another. Greater efficiency in feeding can be obtained by condition scoring at flushing, early gestation, late gestation, and at the start of lactation. I have a system of marking ewes based on their body condition using different colored livestock-marking crayons. This makes it easy to sort ewes by eye after they have been condition scored and to see how many fat or thin ewes there are.

Chapter 10

FEEDING
THE EWE

Ruminant animals are capable of consuming 5 to 6 times their maintenance requirement on concentrated feeds. On forages, their maximum consumption is about 3 times their maintenance requirement. Thus, it is important to provide high-quality forage in sufficient amounts to support optimum levels of production.

PASTURE

In New Zealand, pasture is the most important feed for sheep, beef, and dairy cows, which in turn furnish 80 percent of that country's export earnings. Good pasture is so important there that all other feeds are considered supplements to it. In this country, the farmer's objective has been deemed to be the production of more lamb, not grass. But really the 2 are completely compatible, even for operations that confine the lambs to drylot, since the nutrition of most ewe flocks is still heavily dependent on pasture.

Table 10-1 lists the percent dry matter, energy, protein, and relative energy values for pasture and other forages. All feeds in this table are ranked by energy content (on a dry basis) against a ryegrass/white clover pasture, which is used as the standard feed for sheep.

Grains have relative energy values, which are 6 to 30 percent higher than the ryegrass/white clover pasture *on a dry basis*. The energy value of hay is usually 10 to 15 percent lower than the energy value of the pasture from which it was made. The energy loss is due to plant maturity, leaf shattering, plant respiration, and weathering of the hay. Fall forage crops, such as turnip and kale, have high relative energy values, comparable with the grains (again, on a dry basis).

Pastures have different energy values mainly due to maturity of the plants. High moisture content of the fresh pasture limits the amount of forage and thus energy that can be consumed. When plenty of pasture is available, a dry ewe will graze for about 7 hours per day and consume grass at a rate of about 1.2 to 1.4 pounds of green material per hour. Lactating ewes or those deprived of feed for a while may graze for 10 or 11 hours no matter how small or large the feed supply is. The other factors affecting animal intake of pasture are obviously the amount offered, palatability, and digestibility or rate of passage of the forage through the rumen.

Table 10-1 helps to illustrate that pasture is indeed high quality feed worthy of better utilization, particularly since its cost is so low. The main limiting factor of high moisture content is more of a problem with lambs, which have small rumen capacity and high energy requirements, than with ewes. Pasture quality can be improved by maintaining the plants in a vegetative stage of growth and by incorporating legumes into the stand.

Animal production per acre is dependent upon the output per animal (pounds of bodyweight) and number of animals per acre. The relationship between grazing pressure (animals per acre), gains per animal, and gains per acre are shown in Figure 10-1. Note that the maximum gain per animal is achieved under the lowest grazing pressure when selectivity for the best forage is greatest. The maximum gain per unit area is achieved in the upper segment of the optimum range of grazing pressure. Optimum grazing pressure, then, is a compromise between gains per animal and gains per unit area. Overgrazing lowers productivity per animal and per unit area.

Balancing a potential loss in individual animal gains against the gains per acre is a primary responsibility of the sheep producer. Don't be too concerned about having the sheep graze everything in sight, since some feed selectivity is acceptable at all stages of the ewe production cycle—except when you are using sheep to reclaim pasture and temporarily force them to eat everything.

During the spring flush of pasture growth, the sheep may not be able to consume all the forage that is available. To maintain the pasture in a vegetative stage, harvest surplus forage as hay or clip the pasture.

In the fall, you may want to maximize gains per animal during the flushing and breeding period. It takes both a high intake and greater selectivity (light grazing pressure) to realize an average daily gain on ewes of 0.15 and 0.25 pounds per day. Keeping the sheep on a paddock that little bit longer to have them "clean up" any coarse growth can only hurt them at this time of year. High grazing pressures will restrict intake both in terms of quality and quantity of the forage.

SILAGE FERMENTATION

Supplying high-quality forages for sheep substantially reduces feed costs and increases the level of output, whether it is wool, lamb, or milk. Because of the harvest efficiency and high feed quality, silage production has increased substantially for corn, grasses, and legumes during the past 20 years. Many crops are ensiled and all undergo a similar chemical process of fermentation.

The quality of the silage can be no better than the quality of the forage going into the silo. During growth, the chemical composition

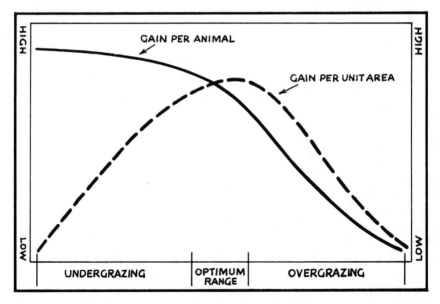

Figure 10-1. The optimum range of grazing pressure results in a reasonable gain per animal and near maximum gains per unit of area.

Table 10-1

COMPARISON OF FEED VALUES OF PASTURE AND OTHER FORAGES

Pastures	% DM	Energy Mj/kg DM*	CP (% DM)	Relative Energy
Ryegrass/White Clover				
Autumn	15	10.8	25	1.00
Spring: Short	15	12.0	22	1.11
Mixed height	15	11.2	20	1.03
Rank (overgrown)	18	10.3	15	0.95
Summer: Leafy	18	10.3	15	0.95
Dry, stalky	30	8.0	10	0.74
Hays				
Meadow Hay (Pasture Surplus)				
Young, leafy	85	9.0	12	0.83
Mature	85	8.0	10	0.74
Weathered	85	7.0	8	0.65
Alfalfa Hay (First Cutting)				
Early Bloom	85	9.8	18	0.91
Mid-bloom	85	9.0	17	0.83
Full Bloom	85	8.5	15	0.79
Weathered	85	8.0	12	0.74
Straws				
Wheat, Barley, or Oat	85	7.0	4	0.65
Corn Stover	85	7.0	5	0.65
Tree Branches (Browse, etc.)				
Willow	40	8.0	10	0.75
Poplar	80	6.0	8	0.56
Silages				
Pasture (From Rank Growth)				
High Moisture	20	10.0	15	0.93
Alfalfa (High Moisture)	23	10.5	16	0.97
Corn (Mature)	35	10.5	8	0.97

Table 10-1 (continued)

COMPARISON OF FEED VALUES OF
PASTURE AND OTHER FORAGES

Horticultural Crops	% DM	Energy Mj/kg DM*	CP (% DM)	Relative Energy
Cabbage	9	13.2	19	1.22
Pumpkins	9	12.9	16	1.19
Carrots	13	12.8	10	1.19
Potatoes	23	12.3	10	1.14
Process Crop Residues				
Apples	18	11.1	3	1.03
Corn Husks	90	9.0	4	0.83
Grape Pomace	38	5.2	14	0.48
Grains				
Barley	85	12.5	12	1.16
Wheat	85	12.5	12	1.16
Oats	85	11.5	12	1.06
Corn	85	14.0	10	1.30
Peas	85	13.0	30	1.20
Fall Forage Crops				
Turnips (Whole Plant)	9	13.0	20	1.20
Kale	15	12.5	20	1.16
Rape	17	12.0	16	1.11
Protein Concentrates				
Fish Meal	92	11.5	75	1.06
Brewer's Grains (Wet)	35	9.6	25	0.93
Other Feeds				
Bran	86	9.6	17	0.89
Molasses	75	12.0	5	1.11

*Energy is expressed in megajoules metabolizable energy per kg. of dry matter.
From: *The New Zealand Farmer*, Vol. 104, No. 12 (June 23, 1983).

Table 10-1. Approximate values for dry matter (DM), energy, crude protein (CP) and the energy content of feeds relating to good pasture.

of plants (energy and protein) changes rapidly with advancing maturity. For maximum yield of digestible nutrients, grasses and legumes should be harvested at the early bloom stage. At this point, water-soluble carbohydrates are high and crude fiber is low. Corn should be near full maturity or the hard dent stage (30 to 36 percent dry matter) at harvest.

Forage crops usually are cut, wilted, and chopped before filling the silo but direct-cut hay silage is also made. Corn is direct chopped prior to filling the silo or storage area. During the filling of the

Photo 10–1. Corn silage is eaten right to the bare floor of the feed bunkers on the Arlen Gangwish Ranch, Shelton, Nebraska. (Photograph by Chuck Savage, courtesy Ag-Bag Corporation)

silo, oxygen is trapped in the silage mass. Plant cells (which are still living) and aerobic microorganisms use this oxygen to change water-soluble carbohydrates to carbon dioxide and water, and in the process give off heat. This process is called respiration and continues until all of the oxygen is utilized.

The presence of a large amount of oxygen within the silage mass has several harmful effects on silage quality. Fewer water-soluble carbohydrates are available for fermentation and fewer carbohydrates are available to the livestock. The onset of fermentation is delayed, excessive heating lowers the protein digestibility, and molding or spoilage may occur due to the growth of harmful aerobic organisms.

Fermentation begins once the oxygen is depleted from the silage mass. Aerobic organisms die off and anaerobic microorganisms (which do not require oxygen) begin to increase, converting water-soluble carbohydrates to lactic acid and other acid products. As the acid production increases, the pH (degree of acidity) decreases in the silage mass. Fermentation continues until the pH of the silage decreases to 4.0 to 4.5. At the low pH, all microorganisms are killed and the plant material is effectively preserved in acid (pickled). The resulting silage, if left undisturbed, can be stored almost indefinitely. However, if air enters into the mass, refermentation and spoilage can occur.

During refermentation, microorganisms become active again in the silage, converting the remaining water-soluble carbohydrates and lactic acid to butyric acid, which significantly reduces palatability. Decay-type microorganisms also increase, changing proteins to ammonia, carbohydrates to carbon dioxide, and generating heat. Energy and protein losses during refermentation are excessive and palatability is greatly reduced. Refermentation can be avoided by keeping the silage mass covered to exclude air and by exposing the smallest area possible when feeding out the silage.

Forage with low levels of water-soluble carbohydrates (as with nutrient deficient or overmature plants) does not support high levels of anaerobic microorganisms and acid production. Also high moisture levels (15 to 25 percent dry matter) found in direct-cut forages dilute the level of water-soluble carbohydrates and do not support a good fermentation. Legumes especially should not be used for direct-cut silage as they are lower in water-soluble carbohydrates than grasses. High-moisture or direct-cut forage produces a foul smelling silage that is high in butyric acid. Seepage from the silage mass is higher than with medium-moisture and low-moisture silage. The seepage obviously reduces weight of the silage (shrink) and allows valuable nutrients to escape.

Making High-Quality Silage

Here are some tips for producing high-quality silage.

- **Cut at the proper stage of maturity. For grasses and legumes, this is early bloom; for corn, it is when the kernels are at the hard dent stage.**

- **Ensile at the optimum moisture level. Corn is at the optimum moisture/dry matter level when cut at the hard dent stage. Forages should be cut and wilted to 30 to 45 percent dry matter for a good fermentation and minimum seepage. Use a forage moisture tester to gauge moisture levels. (See Appendix C.)**

- **Finely chop to improve packing. Plant material to be ensiled must be packed tightly in the storage structure to exclude as much air as possible. Fine, uniform chopping aids in packing and excluding air. The recommended length of cut is ⅜ inch.**

- **Pack continuously while filling horizontal (bunker) silos. Use a tractor to pack the pile continuously during filling and periodically after filling for 2 to 3 days. Horizontal silos should be filled with wedges of material (like books leaning over on the shelf) rather than layered (like a sandwich) to reduce the exposed surface area.**

- **Fill the silo rapidly. The less time the silage mass is exposed to oxygen, the better. Cover the pile daily during the silo-filling period. Bunker silos should be crowned in the center to allow precipitation to run off.**

- **Top the pile with better forage. Forage in the upper third of the silo should contain 65 to 70 percent moisture to supply weight for compaction. Cover the pile with a plastic sheet weighted down at the sides and top. Many farmers use old tires to hold down the plastic. Be sure to use enough tires – they should touch each other on the pile.**

A fresh pile of chopped forage should not be fed for 3 to 5 weeks, while fermentation takes place.

CORN SILAGE

Corn silage is typically high in energy and low in protein, calcium, and other minerals. It is a very palatable feed for sheep and is often less expensive than hay with the same nutrient value. Corn silage is not transported economically over long distances due to its bulk and high (65 to 70 percent) moisture content. Therefore, it is not subject to the same market demand as hay, which is often hauled a few hundred miles. Corn silage also has an advantage over hay in that it does not contaminate the fleece as hay chaff does.

Many sheep producers do not feed corn silage due to the lack of an adequate storage structure or feeder space and the additional handling entailed. Storage requirements for silage are more critical than for hay because of a high moisture content, spoilage, and amounts fed. If the silage can be picked up daily or every other day from a nearby farm, then storage requirements are minimal.

Photo 10-2. Ewes and lambs share bagged corn silage on the Arlen Gangwish Ranch, Shelton, Nebraska. (Photograph by Chuck Savage, courtesy Ag-Bag Corporation)

Be sure to clean feed bunks each day and do not allow sheep to eat silage after it has been out of the silo for over 24 hours. Corn silage that is cut too coarsely, is too dry, or is poorly packed ferments poorly. It often spoils and can harbor the bacteria *Listeria monocytogenes*, which causes a disease of the central nervous system called listeriosis. However, this is unusual in properly made silage, and when old silage is not allowed to accumulate in feed bunks.

The maturity of the corn plant at harvest is one of the most important factors determining the total dry matter yield per acre. On the average, it takes 25 days for the dry matter to increase from 19 to 30 percent, when most corn varieties are at the proper stage for harvest as silage. With advancing maturity and as the level of dry matter exceeds 35 percent, the storage losses (of energy and protein) increase and palatability and digestibility decrease. At 30 percent dry matter, most of the leaves are still green, the kernels are hard and dented, and the corn can undergo a desirable fermentation in the silo.

Supplementing Corn Silage

Corn silage is low in protein and must be supplemented if fed to ewes in late pregnancy and lactation or to lambs. It is commonly supplemented with sulfur, ground limestone, and urea. Urea, when added to corn silage, is converted into ammonia in the rumen where the microorganisms use the nitrogen to synthesize proteins. Ammonia in excess of microbial needs escapes as gas (belched) or is absorbed into the blood where it is converted by the liver back to urea and excreted in the urine. In order to use urea efficiently in sheep rations, observe the following guidelines.

- **Do not use urea on lambs under 50 pounds or those without a functional rumen.**
- **Urea will be utilized most efficiently when fed with an energy source.**
- **Do not add urea to corn silage of less than 27 percent dry matter or above 35 percent dry matter.**
- **Allow 2 to 3 weeks for sheep to adjust to a urea-fortified feed before expecting maximum utilization.**
- **Urea can be added to corn silage at the blower or spread on the load as it is removed from a wagon according to the rates in Table 10-2.**

Table 10-2

UREA-FORTIFIED FEED	
Corn Dry Matter (%)	**Urea (lbs./ton)**
25	8
28	9
30	10
32	11
35	12

Table 10-2.   Rates at which urea may be added to corn silage.

Crude protein is an estimate of the protein in a feed. It is determined by measuring the nitrogen content of the feed and multiplying the nitrogen by a factor of 6.25 (varies depending on the feed) to obtain crude protein (CP). Urea and anhydrous ammonia both have been used to increase the crude protein content of corn silage. Urea supplementation of up to 12 pounds urea per ton of silage can increase the crude protein from an average of 8 percent in unsupplemented silage to 12 to 13 percent CP. This is an inexpensive method, adding about $3 to the cost of a ton of silage.

A major limitation to feeding corn silage is the extra amount of feed that must be handled, compared to hay. About 2.3 pounds of silage are required to supply the same amount of total digestible nutrients as 1 pound of hay.

Let's assume that you are wintering 50 ewes and plan to replace all of the hay with corn silage. At 10 pounds of silage/head/day, this is approximately 45 tons of silage for the cold months. Feeding dry hay at 4 pounds/head/day, you would handle about 18 tons of hay. Silage feeding can be mechanized and automated, but this is limited to flocks large enough to justify the added investment.

Silage is not a substitute for concentrates. Feeding silage as the only feed to ewes in late gestation may not meet their energy requirement, since the capacity of the rumen in a pregnant ewe is limited. Note that the silage rations in Table 10-3 contain shell corn to meet the energy requirements at certain stages of the production cycle. Although the table suggests daily intake of 6 to 12 pounds of silage per head, ewes will consume up to 14 pounds of silage prior to lambing and up to 30 pounds per head after lambing.

To determine the costs of feeding corn silage, ask what a 32 to 40 percent protein supplement costs, the cost of the silage, and your time. These costs can be compared to buying and feeding good-quality hay.

Photo 10–3. *Corn silage (left) and haycrop silage (right) stored in a silo bag. (Photograph by Chuck Savage, coutesy the Ag-Bag Corporation)*

Table 10-3

FEED IN POUNDS				
Type Feed	Early Gestation	Late Gestation	Lactation	Replacement Lambs and Yearlings
Corn Silage	6	8	12	6–8
Shell Corn		1	1–2	.6
Protein Supplement: 35% CP	.25	.4	7–1	.3
Alfalfa Hay	1–2			

Table 10–3. Silage rations.

HIGH-MOISTURE CORN

High-moisture shelled corn (HMSC) and high-moisture ear corn (HMEC) are high-energy, highly palatable feeds for sheep, but both require storage in an airtight or "oxygen-limiting" silo. HMSC is typically 25 to 30 percent moisture compared to dry shelled corn which is around 13.5 percent moisture. HMEC can have up to 40 percent moisture at harvest. High-moisture corn undergoes a fermentation in the silo which preserves it and maintains palatability. If stored in a conventional concrete silo or silo-bag, it is preferable to treat it at filling with an acid-type grain preservative or anhydrous ammonia. It should be fed out at a rate of at least 2 to 3 inches per day. The cost of the preservative is approximately $6 to $10 per ton of grain. Because of the extra storage requirements, high moisture corn should be considered as a feed when it can be purchased reasonably from a larger commercial livestock operation nearby and used as high-energy concentrate for lambs or ewes in late gestations and early lactation.

HAY

There are many sheep farms that do not have enough hay land to meet livestock requirements. Small and part-time farm operations may not be able to justify the expense of owning haying machinery. Labor during critical hay-making periods may not be available, or the additional management of seedbed preparation, seeding, and fertilizing a hay crop may be more trouble than it is worth for the small farm. Finally, there are many livestock producers who simply have no interest in making hay. In all of these cases, hay becomes a purchased feed, and there is less control over quality and price.

Hay of all types is one of the least expensive sources of energy for livestock. Hay can have a high nutritive value if it is high in digestible energy and protein, low in fiber, and high in palatability. These qualities are best determined by a chemical forage analysis and simple observation.

Evaluating Hay

Visual checks reveal several factors that affect the value of the hay: color, odor, coarseness of stems, type of plants, and presence of foreign matter—such as bottle caps, twigs, mice, soft drink cans, and so on. Hay should be green, indicating healthy plant material before cutting. Green color is a sign that the hay contains normal amounts of beta-carotene, the precursor of vitamin A. Loss of green color (yellow, brown, or gray hay) indicates a problem: weather damage, sun bleaching, heating after being baled, mold, or nutrient-starved forage.

Hay should have a pleasant, sweet smell, similar to dry lawn clippings. Avoid hay with a sour, tobacco-like, musty, or moldy smell. Livestock will not eat hay with an unpleasant odor. The molds also contribute to lung problems.

Photo 10–4. Small bunker silo on the Noon Family Sheep Farm, Waterville, Maine.

Photo 10–5. *Round bale silage at John Robert's farm, Shoreham, Vermont. (Courtesy AgReview Magazine, Farm Resource Center)*

Sheep prefer fine-stemmed, leafy hay over coarse, stemmy hay of low feed value. Young, immature plants are high in protein and energy and low in fiber. Early cut hay is more digestible, its rate of rumen passage is higher, and animal intake is greater than with late cut, coarse hay. When looking over a hay sample, check the size of the plant stems, leafiness, and softness of the stems. Alfalfa should be cut before it has reached 1/10 bloom (early bloom) for high yields, feed value, and palatability. Grasses, including timothy, orchardgrass, and bromegrass, should be cut as the flower heads start to emerge, in the "boot stage." Under proper rates of fertilization and by cutting at an early stage of growth, most fields can be harvested 3 or 4 times a season. Cut this frequently, the hay is high in energy and protein.

Learn to identify the forage grasses and legumes in the field and in hay. Many broadleaf weeds and grasses also make good hay; other plants may be too hairy, bitter, difficult to cure, or toxic to livestock. Often animals will not touch the poisonous species in the field but cannot distinguish the plants after they are baled as hay.

Select the type of hay based on the type of livestock, production, stage of growth, and other feeds to be used. Requirements will range from the leafiest alfalfa for lactating ewes or lambs, to poor-quality grass hay for drying ewes off. The most important point is to be specific about the type and quality of hay you want. A good place to see different kinds of hay is at your county or state fair or the winter farm show. Hay of all kinds is judged at these meetings, and the judges' comments can often give you a quick lesson in evaluating hay.

MAKE HAY OR PURCHASE ALL FEED?

Small or part-time farmers need to compare the cost and quality of purchased hay versus making it themselves. If your animals need more than 30 tons of hay a year and if family labor is available, it could be cheaper to make hay than to purchase it at $75/ton. Delivery of hay to your place could raise the price by $10/ton. Under average management, a farm with 10 acres in hay could produce 30 tons or 1500 bales a year.

SAMPLE HAY-MAKING BUDGET

Situation

1. Ten acres of average hay land, 3 ton/acre yield
2. No haying equipment ($4700 investment)*
3. Winter hay requirement of 30 tons (1500 bales)
4. Hay can be purchased at $80/ton delivered
5. Family labor is available
6. Capital is available at 15%

Options

A.	Buy hay (30 tons @ $80/ton)	$2400
B.	Make hay	
	Depreciation on equipment ($4700 over 7 years)	$670
	Interest on total investment @ 15%	705
	Fertilizer and lime @ $50/acre	500
	Gas and oil @ $15/acre	150
	Baler twine: 4 bales @ $25/bale	100
	Repairs to equipment	225
		$2350

*Second-hand equipment

Tractor, 35 pto hp	$3000
Baler	750
Mower	350
Rake	350
Wagon	250
Elevator	100
	$4700

Using the budget on page 118 as a guide, you can see that the farmer who buys 30 tons of hay at $80 a ton spends $2400. The farmer who cuts 10 acres of hay can figure on $2350 in costs for his 30 tons of hay. So, 30 tons of hay (1500 bales) seems to be a break-even point for investing in haying equipment.

Round Hay Bales

A round bale system can save up to 50 percent of the labor required to harvest and feed hay in the conventional, square hay bale system. The round baler is a more expensive piece of equipment than a square baler, but this can be offset by a greater baling capacity (tons baled per hour) and reduced labor. Feeding round bales is made easy by using wood or steel collapsible feeder panels (Figure 10–2). These may have vertical bars for the sheep to feed through and a 12-inch solid baseboard to keep hay from being pulled out and trampled. Properly designed round bale feeder panels can be used for temporary gates or turned upside down and used as creep panels for lambs.

A growing number of producers are using their round balers for haycrop silage or "balage." In this system, hay is cut and allowed to wilt for 12 to 48 hours or until it reaches 35 to 45 percent dry matter. Most round balers can be used for the high-moisture bales, which weigh the same as a bale of dry hay (85 percent dry matter), but the bale is smaller in diameter. A fork attached to the 3-point hitch or front-end loader is used to lift each bale and a tight-fitting plastic bale bag is placed over it. Finally, air is sucked out of the bag with a vacuum pump so that the bale will ferment into silage. Air exclusion in the bale, as with silage made in a silo, is extremely important for good fermentation. Once the air is drawn out of the bag, the open end is drawn tight, doubled over, and tied shut. The bales should be bagged within a few hours after baling.

The main advantage of making haycrop silage is that it is less dependent than hay on good drying weather. There is less leaf shattering from partially dried forage, and the crop can be harvested earlier in the spring to obtain higher-quality forage. More cuttings can be made in a season by harvesting early spring and fall growth as silage. Round bale silage has the additional benefits of requiring no capital investment for a forage chopper, wagon, and silo. The baler receives more use than if only used for hay, which lowers the fixed cost per bale or per ton cost of forage. Finally, the round bale silage requires only a third or a fourth the energy of conventional, chopped silage.

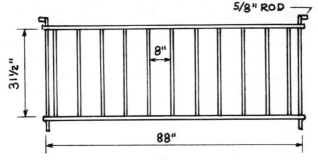

Note: All-welded construction using 1" sq tubing.

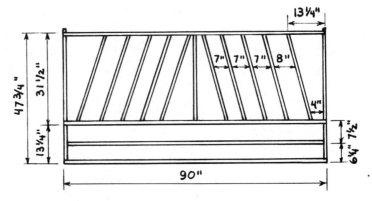

Notes: 1) Sliding panels slide along the top and bottom of side panels.
2) Drill ⅝" holes for ½" or more from ends.

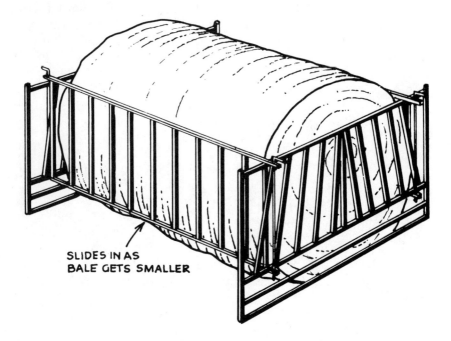

SLIDES IN AS
BALE GETS SMALLER

Figure 10–2. Collapsible round bale feeder for sheep. (Courtesy Midwest Plan
Service, Ames, Iowa)

To store round hay bales, stack them end-to-end with the ends touching and with approximately 18 inches between rows to minimize the exposed surfaces. The site should be well drained, with bale ends running up and down the slope to permit water runoff. A long pyramidal row of bales can be covered with 4-mil or 6-mil black plastic weighted with tires. Stack the bales in the order that they will be fed. Hay bales left uncovered outside may have up to 15 percent spoilage by weight due to weathering of the outside layers. Bales of silage also should be stored on a well-drained site and can be stacked in a pyramid not over 4 bales high. A typical bag will last 2 years if care is taken not to tear the plastic.

In general, a medium-sized ewe will consume approximately 8 pounds of haycrop silage (35 to 45 percent DM) per day. It is best to offer only as many silage bales as can be consumed in 1 or 2 days, to reduce spoilage. Acid-type preservatives can be sprayed onto the forage at baling to inhibit mold and spoilage. Anhydrous ammonia or urea can be sprayed onto haycrop silage at baling to inhibit mold growth (due to the preservative effect of ammonia) and to increase the nitrogen value (crude protein) of the hay—an advantage over acid-type preservatives.

FORMULATING RATIONS

Matching the nutritional requirements of sheep with the feedstuffs available is one of the most important management tasks. The nutrient requirements of sheep used to formulate rations are covered in the *Sheepman's Production Handbook* by the Sheep Industry Development Program, Inc., Denver, Colorado. This reference is used to determine the nutrient requirements and to balance the ration according to the available feeds, stage of production, body weight, and other factors. The information that is *not* adequately covered in many sheep reference books is how to determine a least-cost ration.

Forage analysis is useful for balancing a ration, monitoring crop quality, and buying and selling forages. Random samples should be taken from the forages to obtain an accurate estimate of feed quality. The sampling procedures are quite specific and will help to produce reliable test results. See your County Extension Agent for information on sampling method.

PRICING FORAGES

Forages can be compared in price on an energy and protein basis after an adjustment has been made to put all the forages on a dry matter basis. The cost of a forage per pound of dry matter is:

$$\frac{\text{Cost per ton}}{\%\ \text{DM} \times 2000} = \text{cost/lb. DM}$$

For example, hay at $80 a ton and 90 percent dry matter costs $0.044 per pound of dry matter and hay at $80 per ton and 87 percent dry matter costs $0.046 per pound of dry matter (a difference of $4.00 per ton of hay). Pricing haycrop silage or corn silage on a dry matter basis is even more important than with hay because the dry matter can vary by as much as 10 percent. In other words, 1 ton of silage may have 200 pounds more water in it than another ton, yet the 2 can have identical energy and protein values on a dry matter basis.

Most hays fall between 85 to 90 percent dry matter. Hay and silages shrink or lose weight in storage. A small percentage (2 to 5 percent) of moisture evaporates from fresh baled hay over a period of about 1 month. Silage may shrink up to 20 percent due to seepage of plant juices, molding (wasted feed) and refermentation. There is a loss in nutritional value as well as weight in improperly managed silage.

A general rule for pricing corn silage based on the price of hay is to assume that a ton of corn silage is worth a third the price of a ton of baled hay. Thus, if good-quality hay is selling for $80 per ton, the price of corn silage at the seller's farm is $27 per ton.

LEAST-COST RATIONS*

Is barley at $135 to $145 a ton and 13 percent protein a better buy than corn at $155? Is 16 percent crude protein dairy concentrate at $165 per ton a better buy than corn at $155? You must be able to answer these questions with every feed purchase to be competitive in the lamb feeding business.

The objective of a good sheep and lamb feeding program is to use the lowest cost feed that will provide adequate nutrition while still being acceptable to livestock. A good starting point is to determine the least cost sources of energy.

---

*This information originally appeared in *The New England Farmer*, October 1983, Vol. 7, No. 10.

Total digestible nutrient (TDN) values give you a measure of the energy available from common feedstuffs. TDN figures overestimate the energy value of roughages compared to concentrates in animal production, but are conveniently listed in the *Sheepman's Production Handbook*. Some of the TDN values for commonly available feedstuffs are shown in Table 10-4.

Once you know the energy values, compare the relative cost of different feeds in terms of TDN values (Table 10-5). Referring to the table, find the TDN value of the feed in question in the left column. Follow this line across to the column under the price of the feed. This is what a ton of TDN will cost in this feed at this price.

Table 10-4

ENERGY VALUES OF FEEDS

Feed	% TDN
Alfalfa, Early Bloom	57
Alfalfa, Full Bloom	53
Barley, Grain	82
Bluegrass/White Clover Pasture	70
Corn Silage, Dent Stage	69
Corn Grain, Dry	90
Corn, High-Moisture Ear, 75% DM	61
Dairy Concentrate, 16% CP	70–75
Grass Silage, 26% DM	61
Oats, Grain	74
Grass Hay, First Cut	40–50
Grass Hay, Aftermath	55
Rye, Grain	81
Soybean Meal	77–82
Turnip, Tops and Roots, 13% DM	70–90

Table 10-4. Energy value (TDN) of common feeds for sheep.

To give an example, if a ton of second-cut grass hay (55 percent TDN) costs $105 per ton, your cost for 1 ton of TDN in this form is $191. Energy from barley (82 percent TDN) that sells for $135 per ton would cost $165 per ton of Total Digestible Nutrients. Since the hay and barley are both about 13 percent crude protein, the barley represents a good buy.

A second example can be used to compare the use of a commercial dairy concentrate (16 percent protein, purchased in bulk) against a shelled corn/high protein pellet mix (16 percent protein). The dairy concentrate is assumed to cost $165 per ton and costs $230 per ton of TDN.

Table 10-5

PRICE PER TON

% TDN	$ 35	40	45	50	55	60	65	70	75	80	85	90	95	100	105	110	115
45	78	89	100	110	122	133	144	156	167	178	189	200	211	222	233	244	255
50	70	80	90	100	110	120	130	140	150	160	170	180	190	200	210	220	230
55	64	73	82	91	100	109	118	128	137	146	155	164	173	182	191	200	209
60	58	67	75	83	92	100	108	116	125	134	142	150	158	166	175	183	192
65	54	62	69	77	85	92	100	108	115	123	131	138	146	154	162	170	177
70	50	57	64	71	78	86	93	100	107	114	121	128	136	143	150	157	164
75	47	53	60	67	73	80	86	93	100	107	113	120	127	133	140	147	153
80	44	50	56	63	69	75	81	88	94	100	106	112	119	125	131	138	144
85	41	47	53	59	65	71	76	82	88	94	100	106	112	118	124	130	135

% TDN	$120	125	130	135	140	145	150	155	160	165	170	175	180	185	190	195	200
45	226	277	288	300	311	322	333	344	356	367	378	389	400	411	422	433	444
50	240	250	260	270	280	290	300	310	320	330	340	350	360	370	380	390	400
55	218	227	236	245	255	264	273	282	291	300	309	318	327	336	345	355	364
60	200	208	216	224	232	241	250	259	267	275	283	292	300	308	317	325	333
65	185	192	200	208	216	223	231	238	246	254	262	269	277	285	292	300	308
70	172	179	186	193	200	207	214	221	228	236	243	250	257	264	271	279	286
75	160	167	173	180	187	193	200	207	213	220	227	233	240	247	253	260	267
80	150	156	162	169	175	181	187	194	200	206	212	219	225	231	238	244	250
85	141	147	153	159	165	171	176	182	188	194	200	206	212	218	224	229	235

Table 10–5. Cost per ton of TDN in feeds at various prices. UVM Extension Service (1978).

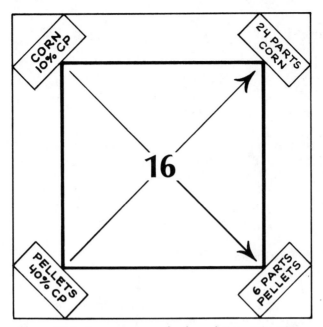

Figure 10–3. Pearson square for formulating grain mixes.

The shelled corn/high protein mixture is formulated by means of the "Pearson Square" method. The Pearson Square was used in dairies to determine how much high-fat cream and low-fat milk to blend to make a 15 percent butterfat "heavy" cream or a 10 percent coffee cream. It can be used for formulating a grain mix by following these simple steps.

- **The protein content of 1 ingredient is placed in the upper left hand corner.**
- **The protein content of the second ingredient is placed in the lower left hand corner.**
- **The desired protein level is written in the center of the square.**
- **Draw diagonal arrows to the right hand corners.**
- **Follow the arrows and subtract the smaller number from the larger one and put that number at the upper right or lower right hand corner. The answer from each subtraction gives the number of parts of each ingredient to use in the mixture (Figure 10–3).**

In our example, whole shelled corn should be mixed with a commercial 40 percent protein pellet in a 4 to 1 ratio to achieve a ration with 16 percent protein.

The 16 percent corn-protein pellet mix is easy enough to formulate, but now it must be compared to other 16 percent protein rations for price per ton and cost per ton of TDN.

Corn selling for $150 per ton is actually $168 per ton of TDN. The 40 percent protein pellet at $300 per ton costs approximately $333 per ton of TDN (extrapolating from Table 10–4 and assuming it is 82 percent TDN, or similar to that of soybean meal). Using 80 percent corn at $150 per ton and 20 percent high protein pellets at $300 per ton, the 16 percent protein mix costs $180 per ton. The cost of this mix is $201 per ton of TDN.

Incidentally, a barley/high protein pellet mixture is formulated at an 8 to 1 ratio and costs $153 per ton, or $183 per ton of TDN. These rations are compared in Table 10–6.

To summarize, the least-cost ration for sheep and lambs is based on market prices, energy and protein values, and the relative cost per unit of energy and protein. In addition, each ration must be nutritionally balanced and be palatable for good performance. In the examples used here, there were a wide range of costs per ton of Total Digestible Nutrients. While the ration is adjusted for the animal's stage of production, body condition, and so on, it should always be planned on a least-cost basis.

Table 10-6

COMPARING RATIONS		
	Cost per Ton	Cost per Ton TDN
16% Dairy Concentrate	$165	$230
16% Corn/Pellets Mix	$180	$201
16% Barley/Pellets Mix	$153	$183

Table 10–6. Sample costs of commercial and home-mixed rations containing 16 percent crude protein. The energy content of the sample 16 percent rations is quite different.

Chapter 11

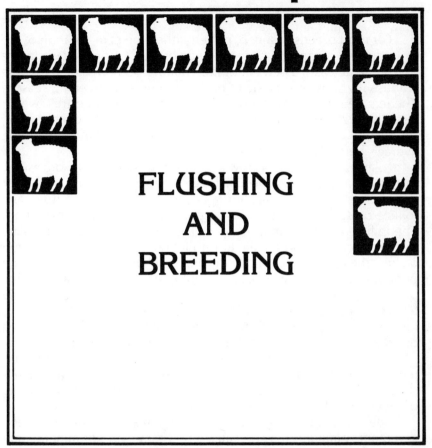

FLUSHING AND BREEDING

Good management during the breeding season, more than at any other time, determines whether you will make money or lose it in a sheep operation. Decisions about which rams to use, when to breed, what and how much to feed all affect the number of lambs born, their vigor at birth, and their genetic potential to produce meat and wool.

Your objectives at the time of mating should be to minimize the number of ewes that fail to shed eggs or show estrus and to maximize the number of eggs per ewe released, fertilized and implanted in the uterus to develop into fetuses.

ESTRUS

For most breeds of sheep, puberty (the time of maturation of the reproductive organs) comes at the age of 5 to 7 months. Ewe lambs that attain at least 70 percent of their mature body weight at this age will usually show estrus (heat) during the normal breeding season. The female is only capable of breeding at the time of estrus, which lasts about 28 hours. The ewe estrous cycle (the cyclic change in reproduction activity) occurs over a period of 14 to 21 days, with the average being 16 to 17 days.

Follicles in the ovaries grow at a rather constant rate before estrus. Just before and at estrus, the follicles grow rapidly, resulting in a higher output of estrogen, a female hormone. Toward the end of estrus, each follicle ruptures and releases an egg (ova). This is called ovulation. The follicle is transformed into a *corpus luteum*, a glandular tissue that produces another female hormone, progesterone. If fertilization occurs, the corpus luteum persists during all or most of the gestation period, and the ewe will not come into heat again until after giving birth (or aborting her lambs). Gestation lasts 144 to 152 days, or 145 to 148 days on the average. Without mating or fertilization, the corpus luteum persists for a relatively short period of time and then degenerates. The growth of the next crop of follicles begins again.

Merinos and their crosses are slow to reach sexual maturity, often not having estrus until they are 11 or 12 months of age. Finn-sheep and their crosses have earlier sexual maturity, with a majority of ewe lambs having estrus at 5 to 7 months.

Anestrus (a period of sexual inactivity) in sexually mature sheep and other ruminants may be caused by vitamin and/or mineral deficiencies, particularly a deficiency of vitamins A or E or phosphorus.

Most breeds of sheep are seasonally anestrus due to the effects of daylength on the endocrine system. Sheep normally begin cycling when the number of daylight hours drops below 14, though a high percentage of Dorset, Merino, and Tunis will cycle all year. Lactational or postpartum anestrus is common in sheep and lasts for 5 to 7 weeks after parturition (giving birth). Lactational anestrus is influenced by the season in which the lambs are born, the level of milk production (or number of lambs), and the degree of involution (return to normal size) of the uterus. Most ewes have at least 1 estrus about 2 weeks after their lambs are weaned but do not come back into heat until the following, normal breeding season.

FLUSHING

Your objectives during the breeding season most likely will be accomplished by maintaining the ewes in good body condition for several weeks before and after mating. The practice of increasing the body condition of ewes prior to breeding is called flushing, and its purpose is to increase ovulation and conception.

Flushing requires condition scoring the ewes (Chapter 9) and adjusting the ration to improve the body condition if the ewes are thin. As a general rule, the higher the body condition at breeding, the higher the ovulation rate and number of lambs that can be born. An exception is in Finnsheep or in ewes with a high proportion of Finn breeding, whose ovulation rate appears to be less influenced by body condition. The prolific Boorola Merino strain with a gene pair for multiple ovulation also would be expected to produce more lambs than most commercial breeds, irrespective of body condition.

For ewes below average in condition, it will take several weeks of supplemental feeding to put on body fat and replace tissues lost after a period of low nutrition. The usual rate of supplementation is ½ to 1 pound of concentrate above the requirements for maintenance per head per day, in addition to forage. More concentrate can be fed for a more rapid weight gain.

When flushing on grass, it is essential that the forage be of excellent quality and carry a relatively low level of infective parasite larvae or eggs. Hayfield aftermath makes an excellent flushing feed. Treat ewes for internal parasites before shifting them to clean pastures, hayfields, annual crops, or crop residues for flushing. On excellent-quality pasture, a ewe can be expected to gain from 0.2 to 0.5 pounds per day.

If you are breeding during warm weather, consider shearing prior to the flushing period to increase appetites and keep the sheep grazing instead of spending so much time in the shade. If a ewe gains 0.15 to 0.2 pounds daily on pasture alone, it will take about 4 weeks of flushing to increase her body weight by 5 pounds.

ESTROGENS IN LEGUMES

Estrogenic compounds called *coumestans* found in some forage legumes have been shown to suppress ovulation rates. Research by J. F. Smith at the Ruakura Agricultural Research Center in New Zealand indicate that disease-free and insect-free alfalfa has a low level of coumestans (0 to 5 ppm) and is an effective flushing feed. With disease or insect injury, the level of coumestans is significantly higher (25 to 100 ppm) and highly estrogenic. The effect takes place within days of grazing the affected alfalfa.

Red clover and subterranean clover also contain a fertility depressing compound called *formononetin*. This chemical can cause temporary or even permanent infertility in ewes. All red clovers contain high levels (up to 1.5 percent of leaf dry matter) of formononetin. Research by G. H. Shackell at the Invermay Research Center, New Zealand, indicates that temporary infertility can occur soon after ewes graze formononetin-rich forage. In a study at Invermay, 2 groups of 100 ewes each were given access to red clover pasture or ryegrass/white clover pasture. The group on red clover showed a significant drop in reproductive performance.

The effect is temporary depending on the length of the grazing period and amount of red clover in the stand. This was demonstrated by another experiment in which ewes grazed for 3 months on pastures containing 0 percent, 30 percent, and 80 percent red clover. One month before breeding, all the ewes were shifted to red-clover-free pasture. At low levels of red clover (30 percent), a 1-month recovery period was sufficient to restore the ewes to their normal levels of reproduction. At the high level of red clover (80 percent), returns to service, barrenness, and lamb drop were still severely affected, and a 1-month recovery period was not sufficient.

Australian workers have shown that permanent infertility occurs when ewes have long-term access to formononetin-rich subclover pastures. Similar results have been obtained after a 3½ year study at Invermay with red clover.

With this information in mind, the following points should be considered when planning to graze red clover.

- **Grazing time on red clover immediately before and during breeding should be kept to a minimum.**

- **Ewes should be kept off the pasture at least 1 month prior to mating if the stand contains over 30 percent red clover.**

- **The minimum time before red clover begins to affect reproductive performance is less than 9 days.**

- **Red clover silage contains high levels of formononetin and is not recommended as a flushing feed.**

- **Red clover hay appears to be low in formononetin and can be used as a supplemental feed for flushing and breeding.**

Workers at the Ohio Agricultural Research and Development Center in Wooster reported delayed conception when ewes were mated on ladino clover pastures. Others have reported the same effects from red clover, trefoil, and alfalfa. For these reasons, ewes should be flushed and bred on grass pastures, mixed pastures, or annual forage crops, such as turnip or rape, whenever practical.

Dr. C. Parker at the Ohio Agricultural Research and Development Center compared the effect of breeding ewes in a drylot versus breeding on pasture. Columbia and Targhee ewes of mixed ages were put in a drylot or on bluegrass, alfalfa, or ladino clover pastures approximately 2 weeks prior to the start of the breeding season. Ewes in the drylot were fed 4 pounds of alfalfa hay per head per day and 0.5 pounds of concentrate. Ewes mated in drylot produced fewer lambs per ewe lambing than ewes bred on either bluegrass or alfalfa pastures. Mature ewes responded most favorably when mated on bluegrass, though yearling ewes responded best from alfalfa pasture.

EMBRYONIC MORTALITY

Fertilization failures may be due to the death of the egg, abnormality of the sperm, or physical barriers in the female reproductive tract. Ewes exposed to high temperatures may have a high incidence of abnormal eggs. The nutrition of the ewe, hormonal imbalances, overcrowding of multiple lambs in the uterus, and environmental stress all contribute to embryonic mortality. Heredity and inbreeding have also been shown to have an effect on the number of lambs carried. Injury or infection at lambing time may lead to the formation of scar tissue and adhesions in the uterus which interfere with the movement of the egg and fertilization.

Some prenatal mortality is normal and unavoidable. Somewhere on the order of 25 to 40 percent of the embryos in sheep are lost around the time of implantation (attachment of the fertilized egg to the wall of the uterus) or in the 2-week to 3-week period following mating. These embryos are resorbed and go unnoticed, in contrast to the aborted fetuses that are lost at a much later stage of development.

To avoid large embryonic losses, maintain ewes in optimum breeding condition and on a steady or gradually rising plane of nutrition for 2 to 3 weeks after the ewes are bred. To avoid environmental stress, bring the flock under shelter if cold weather or extreme heat is forecast. Also, wait 3 weeks or so after breeding before moving ewes any distance, changing feed, or handling them. Breeding should proceed with a minimum amount of interference.

SEMEN QUALITY

Rams should be shorn prior to breeding and kept cool to minimize damage to the sperm caused by excessive heat. The scrotum should be sheared also as its function is to hold the testes away from the body's heat. The normal body temperature of the ram is about 102 degrees F. and that of the testes averages 94 degrees F. When the air temperature reaches 90 degrees F. or higher, rams may suffer temporary sterility for 4 to 6 weeks.

Semen testing and evaluation is a highly technical and complicated process. You may be able to have your veterinarian perform a semen test, although there is a simple and less expensive way of testing a ram's fertility. It involves no stress to the ram (unlike electroejaculation), no training to collect semen (as with the use of an artificial vagina), and results are almost the same. Jack Price of Price Stock Farm, Maryland, described this simple and inexpensive way of collecting a semen sample:

- **Use a marking harness on the ram to identify ewes that have been mounted.**

- **Observe ewes twice a day at the beginning of the breeding season and select a ewe that has had a recent, heavy mark.**

- **Place the ewe in a stanchion or on a trimming stand.**

- **Use a clean (preferably sterilized) plastic artificial insemination sleeve. These are used to protect straws of semen used in dairy or beef cattle insemination.**

- **Gently insert the sleeve forward and slightly upward to the cervix (about 4 inches).**

- **Withdraw the sleeve. It should be partly covered with a small amount of semen.**

- **Place the semen on a microscope slide and place a slide cover over it. A 100X to 500X microscope (found in most high school biology departments) can be used to see the sperm cells. Sperm cells are less than 1/500 inch long, tadpole-shaped, and make up a relatively small portion of the ejaculate. Low quality sperm will have broken heads and tails, low relative concentration, slow movement, and a high number of abnormal heads. On the average, a ram will ejaculate about 1 ml of semen containing 400,000,000 to 8,000,000,000 sperm.**

This method of collecting a semen sample using an AI sleeve (cost about $.30) may be preferred if some fertile rams get mistakenly culled because they fail to respond to the electrical stimulus of an ejaculator. It is generally agreed that a natural ejaculate is the most satisfactory sample for predicting ram fertility.

PREGNANCY-TESTING

Ram marking harnesses (available from Nasco, see Appendix C) are often used to detect mounts and give a reasonable idea of the number of ewes that were bred. The nylon harnesses work well because nylon doesn't rot or stretch the way leather and canvas do. But ram harnesses are not a foolproof way of detecting pregnancy or breeding activity because the crayon can get lost or become covered with manure and soil. Rams may mount unreceptive ewes. Rams may be infertile.

During the natural breeding season it is common to have 80 percent of the ewes conceive at the first breeding interval, with 96 percent of the ewes bred by the end of a second breeding interval. Pregnancy testing can help identify open or barren ewes not bred as a result of poor ram performance or ewe infertility.

Palpation Rods

There are several proven methods of pregnancy detection available to commercial producers. The palpation rod method, developed by Dr. Clarence Hulet at the USDA Sheep Experiment Station in Dubois, Idaho, has an accuracy of about 65 to 95 percent when the fetus is 65 days or older. The ewe is strapped to a table on her back and a blunt rod is inserted about 14 inches into the ewe's rectum. By gently raising the rod and holding a hand on the ewe's belly, you can lift the fetus with the rod and feel it with the other hand. The ewe is deprived of food and water for 24 hours prior to palpation to eliminate any fecal matter.

Ultrasonic Pregnancy Testers

The ultrasonic Doppler instrument uses a rectal probe and an electronic device to pick up the sound of the uterine artery and fetal heartbeat—it is the same monitoring instrument used in hospitals on pregnant women. Accuracy is about 70 to 95 percent depending on the operator's ability to locate the heartbeat (which is around 160 beats per minute).

Several ultrasonic pregnancy testers are available to detect the presence of fetal fluids rather than to amplify the fetal heartbeat. Ultrasonic devices for detecting pregnancy, backfat, and loin eye muscle respond to the different densities of these tissues and feature external probes. A full bladder in a ewe can trigger a false reading and the probe needs to have skin contact for greatest accuracy. Many operators can obtain a 90 to 95 percent accuracy on a 60-day to 120-day fetus.

The use of rectal instruments or probes to detect pregnancy may result in some losses (in the order of 3 percent) of lambs due to peritonitis, abortion, or other injury caused by the operator. There has been no evidence of injury to the ewe or fetus from the use of pregnancy testers with external probes. See Appendix C for a listing of manufacturers of ultrasonic pregnancy devices.

Chapter 12

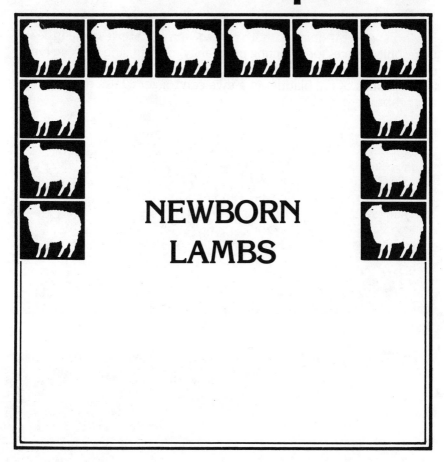

NEWBORN
LAMBS

NORMAL LAMBING*

A ewe's gestation period is 144 to 152 days (average 147). About 10 days before she is ready to lamb, her teats become firm and full of colostrum. Her vulva slackens and becomes slightly swollen.

The lamb in her uterus lies with its spine upwards toward the ewe's spine; its front legs point toward the ewe's vagina, and its head rests between its front legs.

---

*This section on "Normal Lambing" was written by James R. Wadsworth, V.M.D., Department of Animal Health, UVM, and is reprinted here with permission.

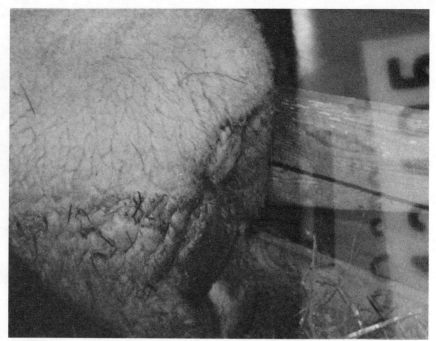

Photo 12-1. Thick mucus (the cervical plug) appears when the ewe is close to lambing.

Photo 12-2. The lamb's front feet appear within an hour or two after the water bag has broken.

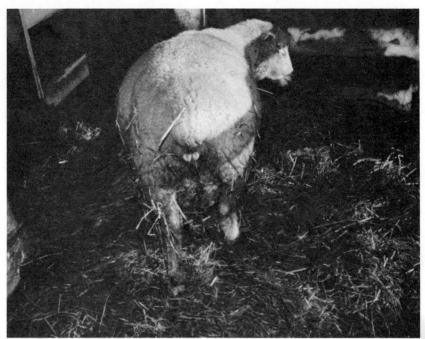

Photo 12–3. Normal presentation with the lamb's two front feet and head coming out first. The ewe lies down and strains to push the head out.

Photo 12–4. Place the lamb up by the ewe's head so she can identify it and lick it clean.

Changes in hormone balances in the ewe's blood stream stimulate uterine contraction, moving the lamb toward the cervix. The ewe's cervical seal passes from the vulva as a thick, creamy, white mucus. Increasing uterine contractions stimulate further dilation of the cervix. The ewe becomes anxious, uneasy, switches her tail, bleats often, and gets up and down. She may strain. This period of cervical dilation lasts 3 to 4 hours.

As uterine contractions become stronger and more frequent, the lamb and its waterbags are pushed toward the dilated cervix. Both waterbags burst as the ewe strains; the second waterbag releases a thicker fluid. This phenomenon serves to lubricate the birth canal. Continued straining by the ewe gradually expels the lamb's front feet first, followed by its head. Delivery is fast after the ewe passes the lamb's head and shoulders through the birth canal.

A single-lamb birth is usually completed within an hour after the rupture of the first waterbag. Ewes lambing for the first time, or multiple births, may require a longer time to deliver.

The fetal membranes (afterbirth) pass 2 to 3 hours after lambing. Separate membranes are passed for twins or triplets.

Most ewes need no help at lambing. Their lambs are born front feet first and delivery takes about 2 hours.

Delayed delivery is evident by continued straining with no sign of the waterbags. Also, continued straining after rupture of the first waterbag may occur, with no appearance of the lamb. Partial expulsion of the lamb or abnormal delivery require immediate assistance.

DYSTOCIA

Dystocia, or difficult birth, may be due to a big lamb, a lamb in an abnormal position, lambs with large heads and shoulders, excessive fat in the ewe's pelvic area, hormonal deficiencies, or failure of the cervix to dilate. Dystocia is fairly common in sheep lambing for the first time and in small ewes bred to big rams.

The general rule is to examine a ewe if she has made no progress after 3 hours of labor. The ewe may be lying down and relaxed (or tired) enough to let you examine her. Using a clean hand and disinfected forearm, examine the birth canal to check if the lamb is in a normal position for delivery. A partially dilated cervix can be dilated further by gently stretching it out with your fingers or by using hormone injections.

The sheep producer can obtain oxytocin (a hormone) from a veterinarian for treating the ewe during a difficult birth. Oxytocin may speed up the delivery and assist in the involution (contraction and expelling the contents and return to normal size) of the uterus. However, if there is any doubt about a lambing problem, the veterinarian should be called for advice. The veterinarian should be called if the shepherd does not feel competent or if the ewe is very weak.

Difficult births and sheep obstetrics are illustrated and discussed in *The Beginning Shepherd's Manual*, and practically every other book available on raising sheep.

Routine sheep obstetrics are part of the fun and frustration at lambing, but there is a point where we are interfering too much with the natural process. Ewes that require assistance at lambing should be recorded as such and are not as desirable as ewes that lamb without trouble and are good mothers. A reasonable goal would be a maximum of 5 assists in every 100 ewes, but some producers have to assist in 2 or 3 out of every 10 births.

Photo 12-5. Tools to have at lambing include (left to right): elastrator for castrating and docking, eartag pliers, 60 cc syringe with French catheter for stomach feeding.

CARE OF NEWBORN LAMBS

Within a few hours, the lamb has gone from complete protection inside the ewe to complete exposure on the floor of the lambing pen. The young lamb is wet, and probably cold and hungry. Mucus should be removed from the mouth and nose with a towel so that the lamb can breathe. A wet, slightly bloody navel cord may still be attached to the lamb. It should be cut to a length of about 2 inches and immediately dipped in 7% tincture of iodine to disinfect the navel area. The lamb should be placed near the mother's head to let the ewe lick it clean. Help her to dry the lamb by rubbing it with cloth towels.

A stong maternal bond starts to form in these first few hours after birth. Sometimes a ewe won't accept its lamb or lambs, refusing to let them nurse or butting them away. She may have to be constrained in a stanchion so the lambs can nurse unassisted, or you may have to graft the orphan lambs onto another ewe. If these measures fail, the lambs will have to be reared artificially.

Sometimes it helps to massage the ewe's udder for 30 seconds to stimulate milk let-down. Milk out a stream or 2 of colostrum (the first milk) to work out the mucus plugs in the teats and to make sure that there is milk. You may need to assist the lamb to nurse by placing its mouth onto the teat. Usually the ewe will nudge the lamb from behind and the lamb responds by lurching forward and mouthing around for a teat. To encourage a new lamb to keep nursing, you can also nudge or tickle the base of the lamb's tail.

The lamb should be weighed soon after birth. Record the weight to within a tenth of a pound. Check newborn lambs every 4 to 6 hours to see that they have nursed (you can feel a full belly under the navel on lambs that have nursed successfully). If they have not nursed within an hour, go ahead and tube feed the lamb with a catheter, esophageal probe, or use a baby bottle.

If the ewe was not in a lambing pen or "jug," move her now to a clean, dry pen. Small ewes will need a 4-foot by 4-foot area and large ewes will need a 4-foot by 5-foot or 5-foot by 5-foot area. The ewe and her lambs should be kept in the jug for 2 to 3 days, or until her lambs are strong enough to keep up with her.

For the first 2 days the ewe should be fed good-quality roughage and water, but no grain. Feeding concentrates to her may produce a surplus of milk, over and above what her lambs can handle. After the third or fourth day, the ewe can have her full requirement of concentrate, which meets her needs for lactation. A ewe nursing twins will have approximately a 30 percent greater nutrient requirement and a ewe nursing triplets will have a 50 percent greater nutrient requirement than a ewe nursing a single lamb.

PENS AND CUBICLES

Ewes generally go off by themselves to an area farthest from the feeders and waterers to deliver their lambs. Restraining the ewe before lambing is seldom done because of the number of ewes and difficulty in predicting the time of birth with any accuracy. Ewes that are within a few days of lambing can be grouped together in a clean, well-bedded "drop area" and observed more closely. There may still be some losses of baby lambs in the drop area due to trampling and mismothering (ewes adopting lambs other than their own). It is best to limit the number of ewes in the drop area to 50. Individual lambing pens (jugs, jails) can virtually eliminate these losses, but the ewe usually is not penned until she is in labor or the lambs are born.

H. Gonyou and J. Stookey at the University of Illinois' Dixon Springs Research Facility have had success with lambing "cubicles"—4-foot by 6-foot, 3-sided pens accessible to ewes about to lamb. The open side has a 10-inch threshold to keep newborn lambs inside the cubicle. They recommend that the cubicles be located in far corners and along the wall farthest from the shepherd's work area, although any area favored by the sheep is suitable. They allowed 1 cubicle for every 10 ewes. During the first year, 40 to 45 percent of the ewes lambed in the cubicles instead of the usual drop area. There were no incidents of mismothering among the ewes that used cubicles and over 80 percent of the ewes using cubicles had no interference from other ewes while caring for their lambs. Less than 30 percent of the ewes lambing outside the cubicles were left alone. Cubicles also reduced lamb stealing and appeared to improve the maternal bonding process. Ewes lambing in cubicles were more inclined to use them again in subsequent lambings.

STANCHIONS

Trevor Jones, commercial sheep producer and former faculty member at Fairview College in Alberta, has used stanchions for lambing since 1973. Stanchions did away with all problems of mismothering and trampling that occurred with the use of a drop area and reduced the amount of labor required for lambing checks. The barn at Fairview College was constructed with a slatted floor and manure pit located underneath the stanchion pens, insulation, and a feed alley (Figure 12–1). These features eliminated daily manure cleaning, reduced the need for supplemental heat, and allowed plenty of individual care for the ewes

Ewes were synchronized to breed as a group using progestogen sponges (see Chapter 19). This hormone treatment gave control over the number of ewes that would be lambing at the same time, and

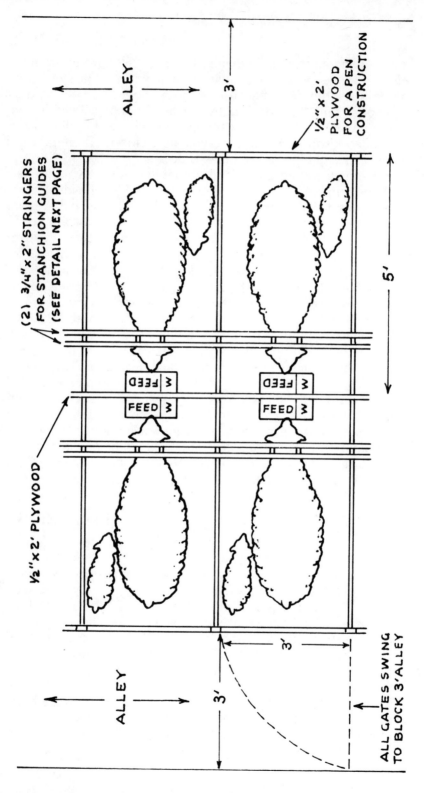

Figure 12-1. *Stanchion lambing pens at Fairview College, Alberta, Canada.*

permitted all of the stanchions to be used. The ewes were placed in stanchions 2 to 3 days prior to the anticipated lambing date of 147 days after breeding.

Ewes in stanchions usually lie down and give birth unassisted to 1 lamb. The ewe stands, turns her head in the stanchion, and softly calls her lamb up to her front. The newborn works its way forward and then is licked off and urged to stand. The lamb then reverses direction and eventually finds a teat and begins nursing. If more than one lamb is born, each one is licked off or begins nursing. When all the lambs are licked dry and nursed, they curl up under the ewe's nose. This sequence of events generally runs true for all the lambs. Most of the ewes adapted to the confinement of stanchions within a day's time and none suffered from the temporary restraint. The barn was kept warm (50 degrees F.) to minimize the risk of chilling the newborn lambs. Shorn ewes in a well-insulated barn in adequate numbers generate enough body heat to maintain 45 to 50 degrees F. inside without supplemental heat, even in the Northern states and Canada.

The stanchion pens take up 19.25 square feet compared to the 25 square feet of the conventional 5-foot by 5-foot lambing jugs. Grafts of quadruplet lambs onto ewes with twins, or twins onto ewes with singles, was relatively easy to accomplish since the synchronized group of ewes lambed within a few days of each other and the stanchions facilitated adoption of the bonus lambs. Trevor Jones obtained a death loss of less than 1 percent using mostly student help and stanchions.

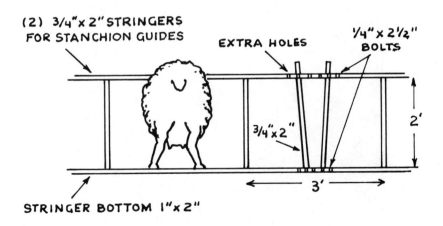

(2) 3/4" x 2" STRINGERS FOR STANCHION GUIDES

EXTRA HOLES

1/4" x 2 1/2" BOLTS

3/4" x 2"

2'

3'

STRINGER BOTTOM 1" x 2"

COLOSTRUM

Probably no other factor is more important to baby lamb survival than the first feeding of colostrum. This first milk is rich in antibodies and large proteins (immunoglobulins) which protect the lamb against disease, at least for the first few critical weeks of life. Unlike with a human fetus, antibodies from the ewe's blood stream do not cross the placental barrier, and a newborn lamb is completely dependent on colostrum for its first level of immunity.

At birth the lamb's intestines are lined with specialized cells that permit antibodies from the colostrum to pass directly into the bloodstream. The cells are replaced by normal epithelial cells within 24 to 48 hours after birth. Even though the ewe secretes a significant amount of antibodies in her milk for 3 to 5 days after lambing, the lamb's capacity to absorb the antibodies decreases steadily after birth.

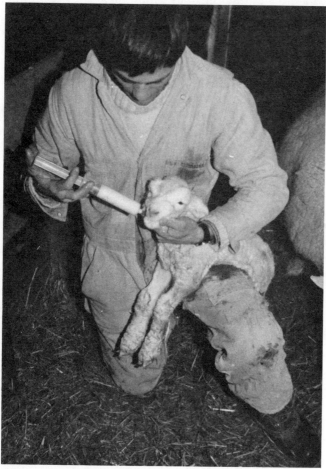

Photo 12–6. Lambs should receive 10 cc of colostrum per pound of body weight; administer with a stomach tube if the lamb is weak or chilled.

This is why colostrum should be fed within 30 minutes of birth for maximum absorption of antibodies and no later than 6 to 12 hours after birth. After that, feeding colostrum will provide a high level of energy and protein to the lamb but most of the benefit of the antibodies will have been lost.

Excess colostrum can be taken from the older ewes in the flock who have more to spare than the young ewes and have a broader immunity to diseases due to more years of exposure. The colostrum may be placed in ice cube trays or plastic containers and frozen. Later it can be thawed out at room temperature and fed warm (at body temperature) to weak or orphan lambs.

A next best substitute for ewe colostrum and ewe milk is goat's colostrum or milk. Cow colostrum is the next best substitute for ewe colostrum and is available in large quantities.

Whenever possible, ensure that the lamb receives colostrum. There should be enough frozen colostrum on hand to take care of 2 to 5 percent of the lambs, at a level of 4 to 6 ounces per lamb. (One ounce equals 29.5 cc.) If none is available, use a human baby formula, such as Infamil or Similac, for the first few feedings before switching to lamb milk replacer. Some producers have fed newborn lambs warmed, canned evaporated milk diluted 1 to 1 by volume with water or a "kitchen remedy" consisting of 1⅓ pints homogenized milk, 1 beaten egg, 1 teaspoon sugar, and a few drops of baby formula vitamins.

Weak lambs that will not or cannot nurse should be stomach fed with a rubber catheter (¼-inch diameter or less), 12 to 16 inches long. Attach it to a rubber bulb or a 60 cc syringe. To use the stomach tube, lay the lamb on its side or have it straddle your knee, wet the end of the catheter and gently slide it down the throat. As you slide the catheter down, the lamb will swallow once or twice. Keep pushing the catheter gently down to the stomach (or until the catheter is down 10 to 12 inches). Attach a filled syringe or rubber bulb and pump the colostrum slowly into the stomach. When the syringe is empty, pinch the upper section of the catheter (to prevent any milk from dripping into the trachea or lungs) and withdraw it. The current recommendation is to feed 20 cc of colostrum per pound of lamb birth weight at its first feeding. A 10-pound lamb would require 200 cc of colostrum for its first feeding. If the lamb seems vigorous, it may only need one 60 cc dose of colostrum and then be allowed to nurse on its own. However, there is a danger that a small feeding of warm colostrum will make the lamb drowsy; then it falls asleep and does not get up to nurse again until its gut has closed down to further absorption of antibodies.

BROWN FAT

The healthy lamb at birth has fat reserves to draw upon. According to work by Dr. John Robinson at the Rowett Research Institute in Scotland, the only difference between a small lamb and a large lamb at birth is that the small lamb is a thin lamb. Instead of the normal body fat of 3 to 3½ percent, the small lamb has only 1 to 1½ percent fat at birth. Approximately 60 percent of this fat is "brown fat" located over the back and neck. (The brown fat has a tremendous blood supply which gives it a brown color). This fat is metabolized in place and the energy is released into the blood passing through the fat. The blood transports energy metabolites to other parts of the body, keeping the lamb warm. The brown fat is used up within 20 minutes of birth, after which the lamb becomes increasingly dependent on milk for survival.

CONSTIPATION

Despite your best efforts to get the lamb to nurse, or to feed it colostrum, some lambs will show a weak, limp, and bloated appearance about 12 hours after feeding. They may hold their head down and be cold around the mouth. Often these are the lambs that failed to expel their meconium, a dark black material that occupies their gut at birth. If the fecal material remains in the gut it dehydrates and constipates the lamb. A catheter similar to the one used for stomach feeding and a 20 cc syringe can be used to give a soapy water enema to these lambs. Approximately 20 cc of soapy water at body temperature can be flushed slowly into the rectum. The meconium should be expelled immediately; if not, a second enema may be needed.

IMMUNITY

Immunity is the ability of an animal's system to fight off a disease to which it has been exposed. At several points along the lamb's development, vaccinations are given to develop immunities and protect the lamb against specific diseases. Colostrum imparts a level of passive immunity; that is, it contains antibodies which provide the lamb with short-term but immediate protection. In passive immunity, the lamb itself plays no part in the production of antibodies.

In active immunity the animal produces the protective antibodies from its own immune system. This is triggered by exposure to the disease or to a vaccine. In a vaccine we give the animal a disease-causing organism that has been killed or modified so it does not produce the disease, in order to stimulate the production of antibodies in the animal. The first vaccination primes the animal's immune system, but does not produce immunity. A second, booster vaccination given 2 weeks later stimulates the immune response to a higher level. In 1 week following a booster vaccination, the animal is considered to have immunity to the disease. Even then, an annual booster may be needed to restimulate the production of sufficient antibodies to prevent the disease.

DIAGNOSTIC LABS

Lambs that die unexpectedly or without a clear diagnosis need to be examined by a veterinarian, who may perform a postmortem examination. The veterinarian may submit the entire lamb or samples of the organs to an animal disease diagnostic laboratory for further tests to identify the disease causing organism. The postmortem and laboratory test results can be a valuable educational opportunity for new and experienced shepherds. Sheep producers can work with the laboratory, the state Extension Animal Pathologist, and the local veterinarian as a team to detect health problems at an early stage.

The lab may perform one or more of the following services.

- **Necropsy or postmortem exam. This is used to detect gross lesions in the carcass and to select adequate specimens for more specialized tests.**

- **Histalogic exam. Performed under the microscope, this test uses processed thin sections of diseased animal organs. A pathologist can examine characteristic damage, lesions, or cells from these sections.**

- **Microbiologic exam. Detects the presence of microbial pathogens (bacteria, virus, fungi, mycoplasma, etc.).**

- **Chemical analysis. Detects nutritional deficiencies, toxicities, effects of mycotoxins, pesticides, industrial poisons, and feed and water problems.**

- **Other examinations. These include the detection and identification of internal and external parasites, serology, urine chemistry, etc.**

After the laboratory results have been completed and interpreted, it may be necessary to make field investigations. It is the diagnostician's task to detect or define the problem; then the sheep producer and a local veterinarian can implement control measures. The real value of an accurate diagnosis is to establish preventive measures to control the disease.

For a complete list with addresses of the animal diagnostic laboratories in the United States, write: USDA—APHIS Division, Federal Building, Hyattsville, Maryland 20782.

Chapter 13

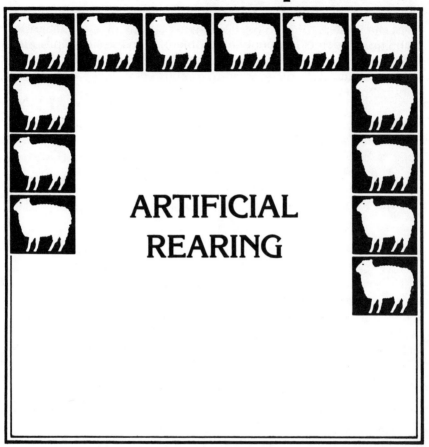

ARTIFICIAL REARING

In order to wean a 200 percent lamb crop, sheep must produce more triplet and quadruplet lambs. Some of the triplet lambs will have to be "grafted" onto different mothers who have enough milk or be raised artificially on milk replacer. The majority of producers in this country don't achieve anywhere near a 200 percent lamb crop, and starvation is still their number one cause of baby lamb mortality. Artificial rearing may save some of those lambs when grafting techniques fail, but the costs are much greater. Whenever possible, it is cheaper and there is less labor involved if the lambs are grafted onto ewes with extra milk.

Ewes recognize their lambs by smell, which is important for successful grafting. Most grafting techniques work fairly well for large flocks, which have dozens of ewes lambing within hours of each other.

The best time to trick a ewe into accepting an orphan is at the moment she is giving birth to her own lambs. There are several grafting techniques you can use, depending on how quickly you can manage to match an orphan with a ewe that just lambed.

SLIME GRAFTING

Slime grafting is most successful when it is done immediately after birth while the natural newborn is still wet and there are fresh placental fluids to rub onto the orphan. As soon as the natural lamb is born, the orphan (usually less than a few days old) is rubbed against the newborn and any of the birth fluids. With a little luck, the ewe will recognize both lambs as her own. This is a fairly successful technique.

WET GRAFTING

Wet grafting is practiced after the ewe's own lamb has been licked and is less successful than slime grafting. The orphan and the natural lamb are dunked up to their eyes in warm, salty water, rubbed together, and left with the ewe in a maternity pen for several days until — perhaps — a bond is formed. During the confinement in the pen, the lambs will pick up similar odors from the ewe and from the environment, sometimes fooling the ewe into accepting them.

SKIN GRAFTING

Skin grafting is used when a newborn lamb dies at birth. It is skinned and the pelt slipped onto the orphan. The head and tail of the orphan are smeared with any body fluids that are available from the dead lamb.

Stockinettes take advantage of synthetics to accomplish the same thing as a skin graft. Edward Price and his co-workers at the University of California at Davis developed a system of transferring cloth jackets after absorbing the smell of the natural lamb to an orphan. In their experiments, lambs were fitted with nylon Stretchtex orthopedic stockinettes within 3 hours of birth (Figure 13–1). The tubular stockinette covered the back of the head, neck, body, and much of the tail. Slits were made for the legs and around the anus before being put on the lambs, then openings were made for the ears, sheath, and naval cord (Figure 13–2). Stockinettes were immediately removed, turned inside out and placed on the orphan. Finally, the ewe and both lambs were isolated in a pen for 48 hours. The stockinette was removed from the orphan after 48 hours. Using this simple technique, 88 percent of all the attempted grafts were successful.

Price suggests that it is the presence of the natural lamb's odor rather than the absence of the orphan lamb's odor that is used for identification. That would explain why slime grafting often works and wet grafting often fails. Using stockinettes, lambs up to 12 days old were successfully grafted. The researchers emphasize that the stockinette should cover the back of the head and the base of the tail (since that is where the ewe will be sniffing).

Stretchtex nylon is light, tear resistant, and conforms to the lamb's body. A 25-yard roll will produce 30 stockinettes at a cost of about $.50 each. You can buy the material at medical supply stores.

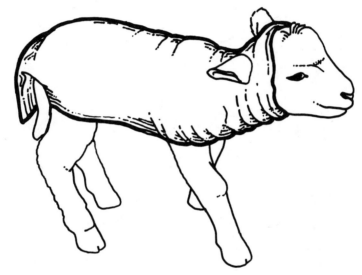

Figure 13-1. Lamb wearing tubular stockinette made from Stretchtex orthopedic stockinettes.

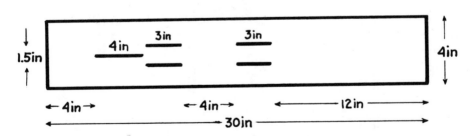

Figure 13-2. Before placing the stockinette on the lamb, slits are made for the legs, ears, sheath, navel cord, and around the anus.

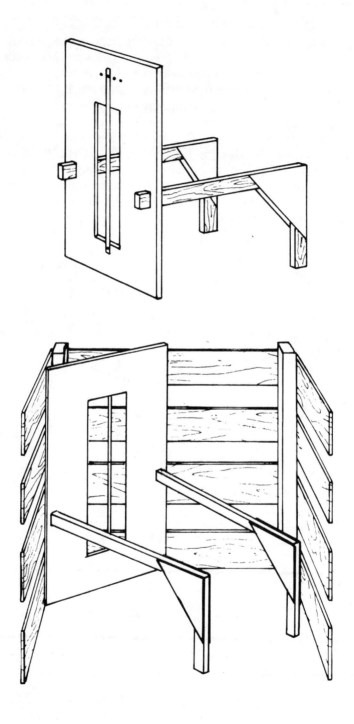

Figure 13-3. Wooden adoption stanchion.

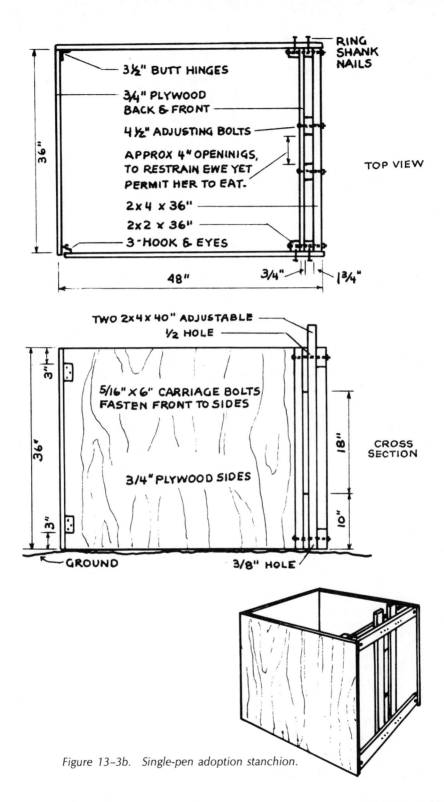

RING SHANK NAILS

3½" BUTT HINGES

3/4" PLYWOOD BACK & FRONT

4½" ADJUSTING BOLTS

APPROX 4" OPENINIGS, TO RESTRAIN EWE YET PERMIT HER TO EAT.

2 x 4 x 36"

2 x 2 x 36"

3 HOOK & EYES

36"

48"

3/4"   1¾"

TOP VIEW

TWO 2x4x40" ADJUSTABLE

½ HOLE

5/16" X 6" CARRIAGE BOLTS FASTEN FRONT TO SIDES

3/4" PLYWOOD SIDES

3"

36"

3"

GROUND

18"

10"

CROSS SECTION

3/8" HOLE

Figure 13–3b. Single-pen adoption stanchion.

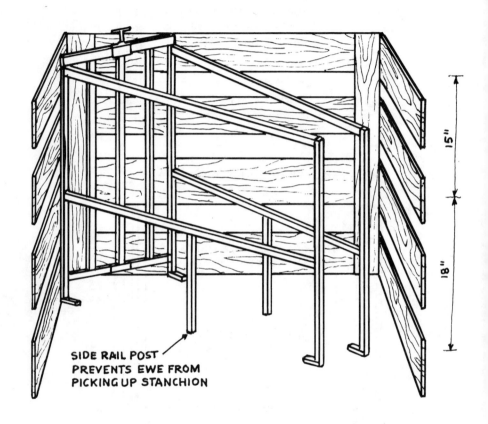

15"

18"

SIDE RAIL POST
PREVENTS EWE FROM
PICKING UP STANCHION

Figure 13–4. A metal adoption stanchion placed in a lambing pen.
(Courtesy of Midwest Plan Service, Ames, Iowa)

The ewe may have to be restrained in a head stanchion to allow the orphan adequate opportunity to nurse without your assistance. Eventually, the ewe will accept the orphan by default. Adoption crates such as those pictured in Figures 13–4 and 13–5 are devices to restrain the ewe so that she can get up or down but cannot look back to identify the lambs that are nursing on her. The ewe is placed in the stanchion for 4 days with the orphan lambs (or her own lambs that she refuses to nurse). She is then released from the stanchion but remains in her pen with the lambs for another 4 days. Researchers at Oklahoma State University reported an 83 percent success rate for lambs grafted with the help of an adoption crate. At the USDA Sheep Experiment Station in Dubois, Idaho, an 85 percent success rate (102 grafts out of 120 attempts) was realized with the crates. Incidentally, of the grafts which were not successful, 4 percent were due to ewes without sufficient milk and 11 percent were due to lamb deaths and other failures. The average time to make a successful graft was 4.8 days.

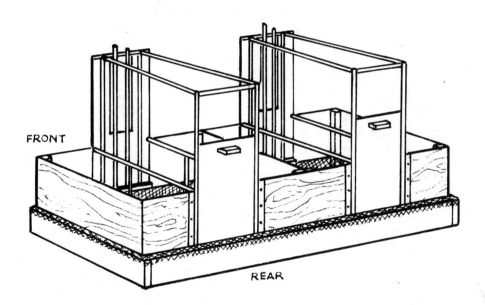

FRONT

REAR

Figure 13–5. Wooden adoption crate. (Courtesy of Midwest Plan Service, Ames, Iowa)

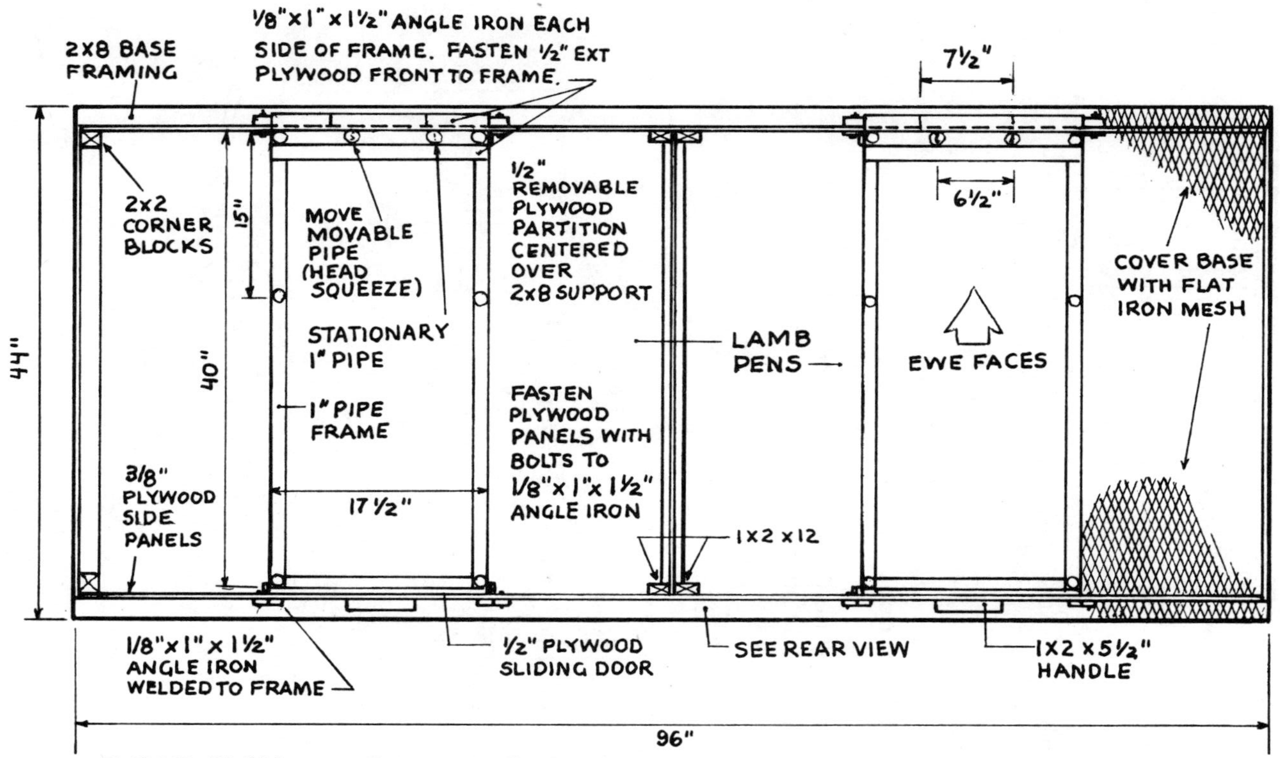

FLOOR PLAN: ADOPT-A-LAMB CRATE

Figure 13-6. Floor plan of adopt-a-lamb ewe crate. (Courtesy of Midwest Plan Service, Ames, Iowa)

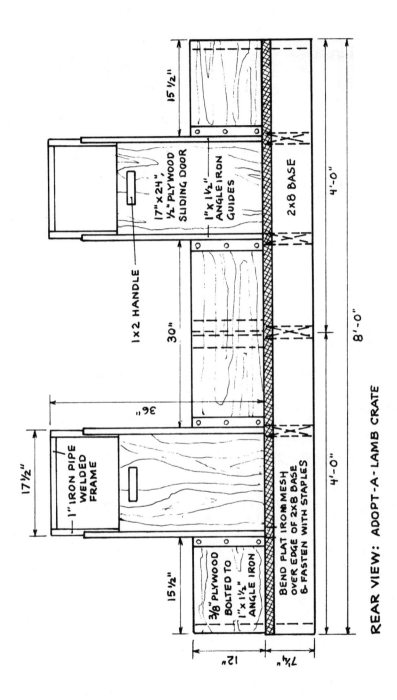

15 1/2"

17"x24"
1/2" PLYWOOD
SLIDING DOOR

1"x 1 1/2"
ANGLE IRON
GUIDES

2x8 BASE

1x2 HANDLE

30"

4'-0"

8'-0"

36"

1" IRON PIPE
WELDED
FRAME

17 1/2"

4'-0"

BEND FLAT IRON MESH
OVER EDGE OF 2x8 BASE
& FASTEN WITH STAPLES

15 1/2"

3/8" PLYWOOD
BOLTED TO
1"x 1 1/2"
ANGLE IRON

12"

7 1/4"

REAR VIEW: ADOPT-A-LAMB CRATE

WHICH LAMBS TO RAISE ARTIFICIALLY

Candidates for artificial rearing include orphans that could not be grafted, obviously weak lambs, and any other lambs over and above your supply of lactating ewes. Lambs to be reared artificially should be selected within a few hours of birth and removed from the ewes before the lamb gets too attached. Some producers argue that the best lamb to take away is the weakest one and others recommend that the largest lamb be reared artificially. The first group say that small lambs may not survive anyway. If these lambs can be raised artificially they will be a bonus. The second group says that the largest lambs can adapt to a self-feeder and don't need the mothering that small and weak lambs require. Joe Stookey, shepherd at the University of Illinois' Dixon Springs Research Center, suggests the early removal of a ewe's natural lamb, in order to graft 2 orphans onto her. Thus, 2 ewes with singles exchange their lambs and receive an extra orphan for grafting. No matter which way you lean, be flexible. Ram lambs are often the ones to be reared artificially—they will not be kept anyway for breeding stock and make acceptable gains even on milk replacer.

Make sure the lambs have the benefits of colostrum within an hour of birth. Feed at least 8 ounces in 2 feedings using a bottle and rubber lamb nipple. The hole in the nipple should be enlarged slightly if the colostrum is very thick and the lamb has difficulty sucking it out. Move the lambs to a warm, dry training pen and leave them for a few hours, until they are hungry again. Training pens should hold up to 10 lambs for a few days while they are taught how to nurse from the nipples on a self-feeder. Be on hand every 4 to 6 hours to assist the lambs, by moving each up to a nipple, placing its mouth on the nipple, and keeping a hand in back of its rump to prevent the lamb from backing away. Adding an older, trained lamb to the pen sometimes saves you time. The lambs may need an artificial source of heat, such as an infrared lamp, during the training period to prevent getting chilled. More ingenuity is needed to come up with some simple solar or alternative heat sources for the lamb training pens.

SELF-SUFFICIENCY PENS

Once lambs have been trained to nurse, they can be moved to the self-sufficiency pen. (Lambs that are still weak should be left in the training pen where there will be less competition at the nipples from the vigorous lambs and you can keep a better eye on them.) Space requirements in the self-sufficiency pen will vary from 2 square feet per lamb on slatted flooring to 6 square feet per lamb on bedded floors. The lambs should stay there until they are weaned.

The design of the self-feeders is basically the same for the training pen and the self-sufficiency pen. Feeder nipples in both areas should be 14 to 15 inches above floor level with shields around each nipple to prevent lambs from standing to the side and chewing on them. Allow 1 nipple spaced 2.5 inches apart, for every 3 to 5 lambs. Up to 50 lambs can be reared in 1 pen; but for most flocks, this pen need only be large enough for 15. Self-feeder nipples (such as Lam-Bar nipples) have plastic tubes that drop into the milk reservoir. The nipples should be 7 to 8 inches above the bottom of the milk container; most lambs can draw the milk up this far.

The milk reservoirs can be made out of insulated picnic chests, plastic tool boxes, plastic buckets, and PVC pipe. Keep the milk cold (40 to 50 degrees F.) Plastic milk jugs can be filled with water, frozen, and placed in the milk to chill it. These jugs of ice can be used over and over. Lambs will not overeat on cold milk. Spoilage is also reduced. Self-feeders can be located outside the pen with the nipples jutting into the pen. The milk reservoirs should be covered to keep dust and other contaminants out.

From the day they enter a self-sufficiency pen, lambs should have access to fresh water and a high-protein (24 percent CP) creep feed. Creep feed is a high-energy, high-protein concentrate for lambs. It is formulated for acceptability by young lambs as their first dry feed. Lambs will start to eat small amounts of creep feed as early as 1 to 2 weeks of age. Access to the creep and water can be through 5-inch to 6-inch diameter holes cut in 1 wall of the pen, 12 to 14 inches from the floor.

Ewe's milk contains about 20 percent solids of which 40 percent is fat (thus 40 percent fat on a dry basis). By comparison, a typical lamb milk replacer contains less than 25 percent fat on a dry basis. Mixing the replacer in the proper amount of water is important for maximum feed efficiency and economy. Avoid calf milk replacers since they have high levels of lactose (milk sugar) which cause lambs to get diarrhea and bloat. A premium quality veal milk replacer (about 20 percent fat on a dry basis) has been mixed in equal proportions with lamb milk replacer with the same performance as the lamb milk replacer and is about 10 percent less expensive.

Most milk replacers contain antibiotics for preventing diseases, such as infectious diarrhea or enterotoxemia (overeating disease, a gut infection). They should not be fed less than 30 days before slaughter (or according to the label) to prevent drug residues in the meat. This is a potential problem if artifically reared lambs are sold at weaning to ethnic lamb markets which desire a 35-pound to 40-pound milk-fed lamb.

Cleanliness around the floor and feeders is very important in artificial rearing as diseases from a dirty environment can spread quickly among lambs in close confinement. Artificially reared lambs are more susceptible to internal parasites and gut infections than lambs raised on ewe's milk. Antibiotics in milk replacer help prevent disease but cannot control an outbreak when it occurs.

To clean utensils used for the milk replacer, follow the same procedures a dairy farmer follows to clean milking equipment.

- **Rinse utensils in cold water.**
- **Wash in hot water and detergent.**
- **Rinse in a bleach and warm water solution.**
- **Rinse again in cold water.**

There is no reason why a dairy goat can't be kept on the farm just for producing milk for orphan lambs. A good doe will produce about 2500 to 3000 pounds of milk in a lactation, or enough for 3 to 5 lambs per day during the first 100 days of her lactation. There is no risk of antibiotic residues in the lambs either.

COSTS OF ARTIFICIAL REARING

At the time the lambs are born, you have already spent 70 percent of the total cost to raise a lamb. The costs include housing and maintaining the ewe, health care, breeding, and many other annual costs involved in the sheep operation. The additional costs of rearing a lamb artificially include milk replacer, the annual fixed or overhead costs on feeders and facilities, and 1 to 2 hours of labor per lamb for a 4-week to 6-week milk-feeding period. It may take 10 minutes to an hour just to train the lamb to use self-feeder nipples. Once the lamb reaches 25 to 30 pounds, it can be reared for nearly the same expense as lambs raised naturally with the ewe.

From day 1 until weaning at 5 weeks, an artificially reared lamb typically will consume ½ to 1 pound of milk replacer or 2 to 4 pints of milk per day. The average daily gain averages 0.5 to 0.7 pounds, slightly less than lambs reared by the ewe (Table 13–1). Once on a solid diet, they will consume 1.5 to 2.0 pounds of concentrate per head per day, gradually increasing their intake with further weight gains. Under the conventional system of artificial rearing, lambs are weaned abruptly from their milk replacer diet at 4 to 5 weeks of age or when they reach 25 to 30 pounds.

Research by J. K. Judy, F. F. Guenther, and C. F. Parker at the Ohio State University found the average lamb reared artificially (and weaned at 4 to 5 weeks) consumed a total of 20 pounds of milk replacer (15½ gallons of milk) and 143 pounds of dry feed from birth to 90 days of age. They also found that the practice of restricting milk intake for 1 week prior to weaning resulted in lamb performance that was superior to performance after an abrupt weaning.

Table 13-1

Item	Milk Feeding			Weaned on Dry Feed	
	1st 2 weeks	2nd 2 weeks	5th week	6th week	7th week
Number of Lambs	28	25	25	25	25
Number of Days	14	14	7	7	7
Initial Weight	4.8	8.2	12.9	12.7	14.7
Final Weight	8.2	12.9	12.7	14.7	17.5
Weight Change	3.4	4.7	.2	2.0	2.8
Average Daily Gain	.243 kg	.336 kg	.029 kg	.286 kg	.400 kg
Daily Dry Matter Intake*					
Milk Powder	224.8 g	464.4 g	– –	– –	– –
Creep Feed	5.0 g	27.8 g	165.8 g	475.5 g	853.7 g
Protein	82.8 g	116.0 g	36.3 g	104.5 g	187.8 g

*Milk powder contained 24 percent protein; creep feed, 22 percent protein.
Note: Kg × 2.2 = lbs; g × .0022 = lbs.

Table 13–1. Performance of lambs during the milk-feeding period and the first 3 weeks of post-weaning (University of Minnesota, 1978).

Table 13-2

LAMB STARTER DIET (2 TO 6 WEEKS OF AGE)

Feed	%
Soybean Meal	40
Alfalfa Meal	15
Corn Meal	27
Cerelose (glucose)	10
Profat (50% tallow, 50% skimmed milk)	10
Salt Trace Mineral	.5
Limestone	2.0
Vitamin A 1000 USP Units per lb. Finished Ration	
Vitamin D 1000 USP Units per lb. Finished Ration	
Vitamin E 1.0 Int. Unit per lb. Finished Ration	

Table 13–2.   Cornell lamb starter diet for lambs 2 to 3 weeks of age.
(From: Sheep! magazine, May, 1983.)

Table 13-3

17% PROTEIN FATTENING DIET

Feed	%
Corn	67
Alfalfa Meal	15
Soybean	14
Fish Meal	1
Limestone	2
Di Calcium Phosphate	.5
Gypsum	.25
Salt	.25

Table 13–3.   Cornell lamb-fattening diet for weaned lambs.
(From: Sheep! magazine, May, 1983.)

EARLY WEANING

Lambs can be weaned as early as 2 weeks of age to lower the costs of artificial rearing. Brian Magee, the shepherd for the Cornell University flock, has been successful at weaning lambs at 2 weeks of age by increasing the concentration of the milk replacer to make lambs thirsty enough to start drinking water. During the first week, the concentration fed is 1 part powder to 4 parts water (by weight); the standard dilution is 1 part powder to 2½ parts water. During the second week, the milk is gradually concentrated to the standard mix of 1 part powder to 2½ parts water just before weaning. Again, water and dry feed are offered at all times.

The starter diet that Brian Magee uses is a pre-ruminant diet, which meets the nutritional requirements of a lamb that cannot yet chew its cud and whose rumen is not ready to ferment carbohydrates. The Cornell starter is finely ground like chick feed and incorporates easily digested carbohydrates, such as lactose and glucose, and higher levels of fat and protein than conventional creep feeds (Table 13–2).

Magee suggests that coarsely ground creep rations sometimes just sit in the young lamb's rumen and cannot be digested until the lamb learns to chew its cud. Even with high-fiber pelleted creep rations, particles small enough to escape the rumen of the young lamb may get lodged in the fourth stomach (the abomasum), restricting the flow of milk through the gut. The lamb looks full but may be starving to death. The carbohydrates get partially broken down in the abomasum, causing bloat and the lamb may die. The problem of abomasal bloat in the Cornell flock has been reduced by using a system that gets lambs started drinking water as soon as they start ingesting dry feed, using a finely ground starter ration and, dropping the milk replacer abruptly.

The minimum weight to wean lambs at 2 weeks is 15 pounds (12 pounds for Finn-cross lambs) according to Cornell research. Western-type white face lambs (Rambouillet and other breeds common in the West) that grow poorly (less than 0.5 pounds per day) on milk replacer have not done well when weaned at 2 weeks of age. The lambs remain in the pen but the milk reservoir is allowed to run dry. Nipples are left in place for a few days to act as pacifiers. Lambs that have had little human affection (petting, sucking a finger, hand feeding) and that have never been left without milk will quickly find out how to satisfy their hunger and be successfully weaned.

At 5 weeks of age the early-weaned lambs are offered a conventional 17 to 19 percent crude protein ration (Table 13–3) and the starter diet is discontinued after 6 weeks. In 1983 the total feed cost to raise 1 Dorset or Finn-cross lamb from birth to 100 pounds was $30. The mortality rate during the 2-week milk-feeding period was 5 to 10 percent and mortality from weaning to slaughter was less than 5 percent. These figures are about equal to those from lambs raised naturally.

Chapter 14

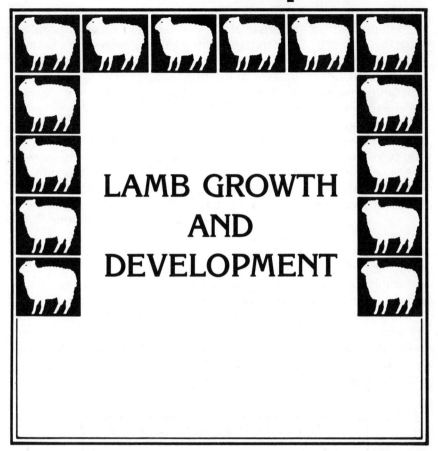

LAMB GROWTH AND DEVELOPMENT

Growth is defined as an increase in bone, muscle, and connective tissue. These tissues are differentiated from fat, which develops mainly in the fattening phase. Some fattening occurs during normal muscle and bone development, but most fattening occurs after bone development is complete, and muscle development is approaching its maximum development (Figure 14–1).

Development is the coordination of the rate and amount of growth. The two processes result in an increase in size, weight, and proportion of bone, muscle, connective tissue, and fat.

Bone matures the earliest, reaching its maximum growth before physiological maturity and before most of the fat is deposited. Muscle tissue takes longer to mature; most of the growth occurs midway through the animal's development. Maximum development of bone and muscle are considered to be fixed by genetics and age.

In the young lamb, internal fat, such as kidney, heart, and pelvic fat, is deposited first. External fat is deposited next. Finally, marbling (fat in the muscle tissue) is formed. When fat is mobilized on a mature animal, the marbling is the first to go. Some fat is necessary in lamb to ensure palatability – flavor, tenderness, and juiciness – but excess fat is largely waste that is trimmed from the carcass before it reaches the consumer.

A lamb's growth rate (Figure 14–2) accelerates in the first few months, slows down with sexual maturity, and levels off with advancing physiological maturity. Individuals differ in their rate of growth due to genetic and environmental factors. Sex and body type are examples of genetic factors that influence both the rate of growth and the point at which the animal is physiologically mature.

At any given point in their growth and development, late-maturing, large-framed animals are heavier, have less fat, have more muscle, and produce leaner, higher-yielding carcasses than early-maturing, small-framed animals. If you are producing for a market that wants a light carcass (45 pounds) with a moderate degree of finish (.15 inches of backfat), use an early-maturing, small-framed ram such as a Dorset, Cheviot, or Southdown. The trend in this country for the past 20 years has been toward a heavier carcass with the same moderate degree of finish. Lambs that yield a heavy (60-pound) carcass with 0.1 to 0.3 inches of back fat are produced by a large-framed, late-maturing ram, such as a Suffolk, Hampshire, or Columbia.

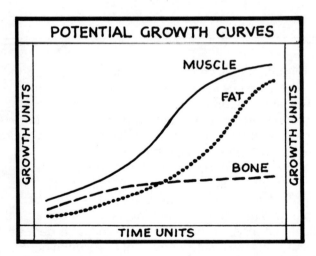

Figure 14–1. Typical lamb growth curves for bone, muscle, and fat.

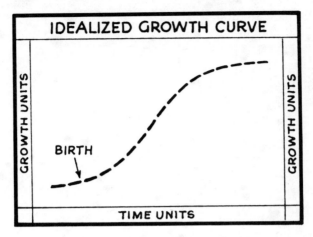

Figure 14–2. Typical lamb growth curve.

FACTORS INFLUENCING GROWTH

The principal nutritional factor affecting weight gain is the proportion of energy in the ration. During the lamb's rapid growth stage from 45 to 90 pounds liveweight, high levels of energy in the ration increase average daily gain and feed conversion efficiency (pounds of feed required for each pound of liveweight gain). However, the economic advantage depends on the cost per unit of energy in the ration. The ration will be cheap even though it has a high cost per unit of energy if it allows the lamb to grow quickly and be sold when prices are high. A slow rate of gain or an apparently poor feed conversion efficiency (as with lambs on pasture) may be perfectly acceptable if the feed is low-cost and plentiful, and lamb prices are low. Lambs fed on a high-energy, high-protein ration grow faster and fatten (are finished) at lighter weights than lambs fed on a low-energy ration. Lambs that grow slowly must be slaughtered at heavier weights to achieve the same amount of finish since the point at which they reach physiological maturity is delayed by a lower level of nutrition.

The sex of the animal influences growth. Rams are typically heavier, leaner, and physiologically less mature than castrated males (wethers), who are less mature than ewes born at the same time.

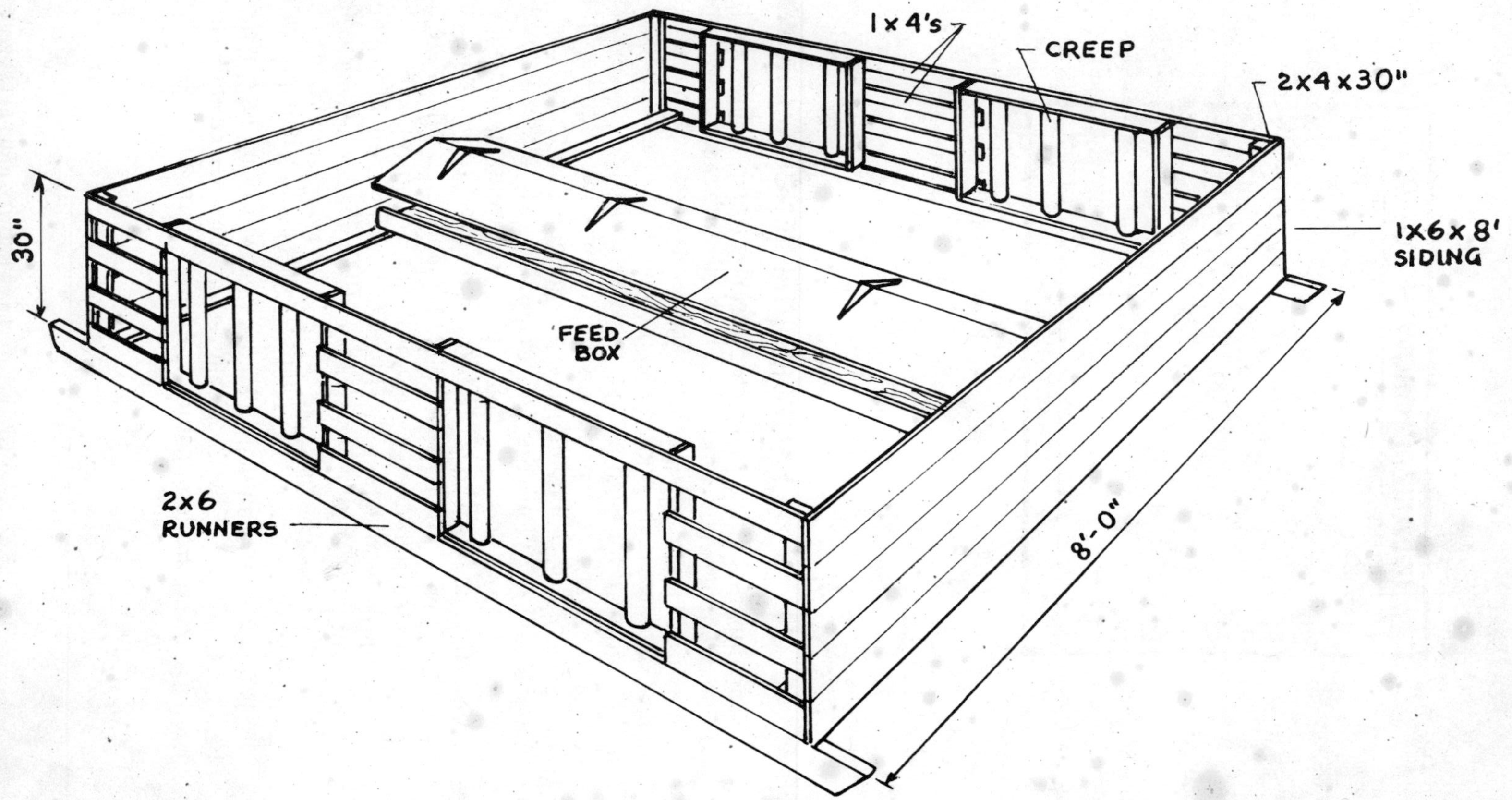

Figure 14-2. Movable lamb creep. (Courtesy of Midwest Plan Service, Ames, Iowa)

Labels on figure:
1×6×8' SIDING
2×4×30"
CREEP
1×4's
8'-0"
FEED BOX
2×6 RUNNERS
30"

Therefore, ram lambs can be expected to give faster, more economical gains, and produce a leaner carcass. However, ram lambs past the age of 6 or 7 months develop more of the secondary sexual characteristics (heavier necks and shoulders, larger testes, etc.), which lowers the value of the carcass. They become sexually active at this time and create a nuisance in mixed groups of lambs assembled at feedlots and slaughter plants.

Daylength also affects growth and development. Research by B. D. Schanbacher and others at the U.S. Meat Animal Research Center at Clay Center, Nebraska, evaluated the effect of short (8-hour) and long (16-hour) days on the growth of ram lambs, wethers, and ewe lambs. Ram lambs under the 16-hour days had higher average daily gains (0.83 pounds per head) compared to ram lambs under the short-day regimen (0.7 pounds). Long daylength lambs had slightly better feed efficiency and heavier slaughter weights than short-day lambs. Similar effects were obtained with wethers and ewe lambs. The effect of daylength on average daily gain was greater than the effect of the sex of the animals on weight gains. It appears that extending the natural daylength to 16 hours (using electric lights in the barn) to obtain a 10% increase in average daily gain will definitely pay if lamb is sold somewhere near $.50 to $.70 per pound and electricity is $.04 to $.08 per kilowatt hour.

CREEP FEEDING

Lambs in early stages of growth can make extremely efficient weight gains on high-concentrate rations. If high-grain or high-concentrate rations are to be economical with sheep, they must be fed during this stage unless you have a source of cheap grain. Most sheep producers can take advantage of the lamb's high feed conversion phase by creep feeding.

Creep feeding gives preweaned lambs access to a high-concentrate ration while excluding the ewes. The feed should be a highly palatable concentrate that will maximize the energy and protein intake of young lambs.

The creep area should be warm, dry, well-lit, uncrowded, and within sight of the dams. A creep area can be set up in the barn or on pasture, using portable panels that let small lambs through but keep the ewes out (Figure 14–3). A well-designed creep will get lambs started on solid feed at an early age, often when they are just a week to 10 days old.

By the time the lambs are 6 to 8 weeks old, they will be eating 1.5 to 2 pounds of creep feed per lamb per day. Before weaning, the conversion from dry feed to weight gain is 2 to 1 to 2.5 to 1, high enough so that it is economical to feed concentrates even in a grass-fed lamb program. Dry meal or small pellets are the most acceptable form for the youngest lambs; though once they are on solid feed, the lambs will prefer pellets or whole grains. Creep feeding is usually advantageous for the following reasons:

- **To reach an early market and bring a higher price**
- **To take advantage of extremely good feed conversion during the early life of the lamb**
- **To maintain the finish of nursing lambs**
- **To avoid added handling of older lambs**

RUMEN DIGESTION

Mature sheep and other ruminants have a 4-chambered stomach (Figure 14–4). The young lamb, however, functions essentially as a monogastric or simple-stomached animal. At birth, the abomasum is the largest of the 4 chambers and is the principal site of digestion for milk. As the lamb grows, the rumen increases in capacity and the abomasum decreases in relative capacity. The function of the rumen is to provide a suitable environment for the growth of microorganisms which utilize roughages such as cellulose (plant fiber). It takes 8 to 12 weeks for the young lamb to develop a functional rumen and to be able to utilize roughages.

The only carbohydrate that the young lamb can use efficiently is lactose (milk sugar) or its components, glucose and galactose. The enzyme lactase is produced by young lambs to aid in the digestion of lactose. As the lamb develops, the activity of lactase declines. There is an increase in maltase and amylase, enzymes which break down starch, the main carbohydrate in grain.

The establishment of the microbial population in the rumen occurs naturally as the lamb is exposed to the environment and ingests solid feed. While the lamb relies on milk, there is little development of the rumen. However, the ingestion of roughages and grain stimulates the growth of the papillae (fingerlike projections) along the wall of the rumen which increases its surface area and stimulates the growth of muscles that cause rumen contraction and regurgitation of the cud.

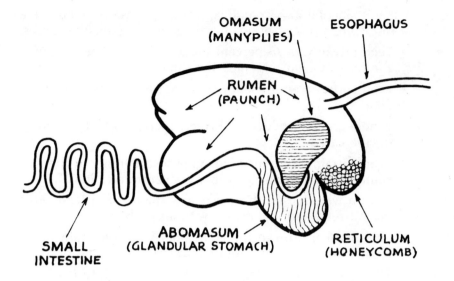

OMASUM (MANYPLIES)

Figure 14-4. The 4 chambers of a sheep stomach.

Once the microbial population is established, roughages in the rumen can be fermented by bacteria and protozoa. The carbohydrates are converted into volatile fatty acids – acetic, propionic, and butyric acid. These get absorbed through the rumen wall into the bloodstream to be metabolized as energy. Large numbers of papillae improve the absorptive capacity of the rumen by increasing the surface area. The rumen pH is normally in the range of 5.5 to 7.0 in order to support the desirable microorganisms. Saliva, secreted while the animal is eating and chewing its cud, contains buffering compounds which help neutralize excess volatile fatty acids in the rumen. Wild ruminants and sheep on all forage-based rations seldom develop acidosis.

WHOLE GRAINS

A ground or crumbled creep feed is best for the first dry feed offered to young lambs. Whole grains may be offered at the same time in a separate feeder. The lambs generally prefer a whole grain or pelleted ration after they have become accustomed to dry feed and are weighing 25 pounds or more.

There is no apparent advantage to grinding, rolling, or pelleting grain to increase its digestibility for lambs. In research by Dr. M. Talt at the University of British Columbia, whole grains consistently gave better results than processed grain rations in raising market lambs.

- **Feed intake was 25 percent higher while the percent of the feed utilized remained the same**
- **Feed conversion efficiency was improved by 5 to 10 percent**
- **Whole grains produced a firmer, more desirable finish on the carcass**
- **Whole grains were less damaging to the lining of the rumen than ground, low-fiber concentrate rations**
- **With a whole grain there was less chance of a lamb going off feed and less grain overload problems**
- **The physical form of the grain fiber in whole grain results in a different kind of fermentation in the rumen**
- **There was no advantage to feeding roughage to lambs on a whole grain ration**

In conclusion, lambs are very efficient at chewing their feed and can process the grain themselves. Table 14–1 shows typical market lamb rations used in Canada based on whole barley and a 32 percent crude protein, commercial protein/vitamin/mineral supplement. Use a high-calcium mineral mix that contains no more than 20 ppm (0.002 percent) copper. Barley and other small grains are low in calcium, and higher levels of copper are toxic to sheep.

Table 14-1

LAMB RATIONS

Lamb Weight (pounds)	Protein Level in Total Ration (%)	Ration Ingredient Barley: 32% Pellet (by weight)
Less Than 30	18	2:1
30 to 60	16	3:1
Greater Than 60	14	4:1

Table 14-1. Recommended market lamb rations based on whole barley and a commercial 32 percent protein supplement. For example, 2 parts barley is mixed with 1 part 32 percent protein pellet to make an 18 percent protein feed.

REARING AND FINISHING SYSTEMS

Most sheep producers in the United States lamb in late winter or early spring and use spring and summer pasture and range for ewes and lambs. They market lightweight feeder lambs and finished market lambs under a variety of management systems. The systems vary by the degree to which they utilize pasture or range for feeding lambs.

- **Option 1. Lambs are raised entirely in a drylot or in confinement from birth to market.**
- **Option 2. Lambs are raised in a drylot while lactating ewes are given access to pasture.**
- **Option 3. Lambs are raised entirely on pasture with the ewes.**
- **Option 4. Lambs are raised on pasture and creep fed grain or other concentrate.**
- **Option 5. Lambs are weaned from ewes on pasture and finished in a drylot. This system includes finishing feeder lambs.**

Milk production in the ewe peaks at 21 to 35 days, during which time milk is the main source of nutrition for the lamb. Starting within the first 2 weeks after birth, the lamb will start eating grain, hay and/or grass, after which there is a linear increase in the lamb's consumption of dry feed. The relationships between milk production, lamb weight, and dry feed intake are shown in Figure 14–5. Lamb weights could be more or less than those shown. Dry feed intake and milk production also could be different than this example. However, the relationships will be approximately the same.

The optimum time to wean the lamb to a drylot or different pasture is at the point when milk becomes less important than other feeds in supplying nutrition to the lamb. This occurs around 56 days after birth. The earliest age to wean lambs is when they are fully able to utilize dry feed at or about 40 days after birth.

One advantage of drylot feeding (Option 1) is that you will have greater control over the quality and quantity of feed for the lambs than with pasture rearing. Drylot lambs are raised in a more predictable length of time and with a more predictable degree of finish than pasture lambs. Exposure of drylot lambs to internal parasites can be reduced drastically with well-designed feed bunks and waterers that do not allow the lambs to get their feet in to contaminate everything. It can produce fast and economical gains in early-weaned lambs and is rapidly replacing the system of letting ewes and lambs run together on pasture (Option 3).

E. Morgan and others at the University of Missouri studied the option of giving ewes access to pasture while restricting their lambs to a drylot for the first 56 days of lactation (Option 2). A control group of ewes remained with the lambs all day in the drylot. They found that the ewes fed with the lambs in a drylot lost an average of 5 pounds of bodyweight, while ewes with access to pasture lost only 1.7 pounds per head. Over the same period, lambs nursing off the drylot ewes gained 28 pounds each and had an average daily gain (ADG) of 0.5 pounds per head. Lambs nursing ewes which had access to pasture gained approximately 34 pounds with an ADG of 0.6 pounds. This system achieves the good rates of gain of drylot conditions with the lowest feed cost per ewe because the ewe's increased nutritional needs are partly met by cheap pasture. Labor demands are high because ewes and lambs must be sorted every day.

Where drylot feeding is impractical because of the high cost of concentrates or lack of facilities, the lambing season should coincide with the period when the best natural grazing is available. However, ewes on pasture with their lambs consume approximately two-thirds of the available feed, which is justifiable when the lambs are young

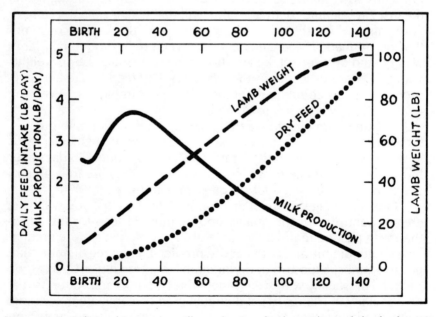

Figure 14–5. Relationship among milk production, lamb weight, and dry feed intake.

and dependent on the milk supply for their growth. Lambs to be weaned onto their own, separate pasture should have a sufficiently well-developed rumen to take advantage of a high-forage ration. This occurs at a liveweight of about 60 pounds. Early-weaned lambs raised on pasture without a grain supplement do poorly compared to lambs that remain with the ewes on pasture.

Raising early-weaned lambs on pasture and creep feeding a high-enèrgy concentrate or grain (Option 4) has the potential to be the lowest-cost lamb-rearing system. This is discussed in greater detail in Chapter 15, "Lambs on Grass."

Photo 14–1. Weigh lambs at weaning using a 60-pound hanging scale.

Option 5 is essentially a feeder lamb rearing system where pasture lambs weighing over 75 pounds are finished in a drylot. Feeder lambs have unique problems in their growth and development. They go through changes in feed, environment, and exposure to other animals. The first 2 to 3 weeks in the feedlot have been shown to be the critical period of adjustment for lambs and the time to minimize death losses.

Preconditioning lambs before they leave the home farm helps to reduce shrink (weight loss) and mortality. Shrink in feeder lambs is due to fat being used up and the rumen being emptied as the lamb is fasted prior to and during shipment. Preconditioning consists of starting feeders on the ration that will be used in the feedlot a week or 10 days prior to delivery. Feeders should be vaccinated to prevent shipping fever and pneumonia, treated for internal parasites, shorn, and sorted by weight. Lightweight feeder lambs should be at least 75 pounds; lighter weight lambs suffer excessive weight loss (over 5 percent) when moved to the feedlot.

Upon arrival, feeder lambs should be put on average-quality hay and water for a few days. They can be given ¼ pound of grain per head per day from the start, working up gradually over the next 10 to 14 days until they are on a level of 90 to 95 percent concentrates. Some groups of feeder lambs may take as long as 30 days to adjust to this full level of concentrate. Research has shown that the highest average daily gains for feeder lambs occurs during the first 2 weeks the lambs are in the feedlot and on the full level of concentrate. However, this weight gain is mostly due to regaining the fat tissue and fluids lost during the adjustment period. This brief but dramatic weight gain is compensatory gain. As the feeding period progresses, there is a definite decline in rate of gain and feed efficiency as the animal reaches physiological maturity and begins to accumulate external fat.

GROWTH PROMOTING SUBSTANCES

Zeranol (brand name Ralgro) is a growth promoter with a low estrogenic or feminizing effect (about 1/2500th the activity of DES, diethylstilbestrol, a synthetic estrogen). Unlike DES, it leaves no residue in the meat. Zeranol has been used to increase rate of gain in lambs (Table 14–2). Its effect is due to an increase in the weight of the pituitary and adrenal glands. The pituitary gland is the source of growth hormone in the body; thus, Zeranol increases the growth hormone levels in cattle and sheep. Zeranol also depresses thyroid activity to give a tranquilizing effect on implanted steers.

DES and related compounds have been criticized because of their estrogenic side effects. This has led to the development of growth promoting compounds from testosterone, the predominant male hormone. One of these compounds, Trenbolone acetate or TBA, has increased weight gains in livestock.

An alternative to steroid-growth promoting drugs are compounds which act on the microorganisms in the rumen, altering the fermentation (digestion), feed conversion efficiency, and feed utilization. Two of these products are *monensin* (Rumensin by Eli Lilly) and *lasalocid* (Bovatec by Hoffman-LaRoche). These two products have a similar chemical composition.

Monensin was originally developed as a medication to treat coccidiosis, an intestinal parasitic disease in swine and poultry. Studies with lambs have shown that this chemical, when added to the grain mix at a level of 10 to 30 grams of monensin per ton of feed, practically eliminated coccidial infections. This rate of feed supplementation was sufficient to improve feed efficiency as well (Table 14–4)

Monensin is available as a premix (to be added to concentrate feeds), salt mix, liquid supplement, and as a molasses-based mineral

Table 14-2

ZERANOL IMPLANTATION AND LAMB GROWTH

Item	Control	Zeranol (12 mg)
Number of Lambs	28	28
Initial Weight, lbs.	66.60	67.70
14-day ADG, lbs.	0.82	0.86
28-day ADG, lbs.	0.71[a]	0.77[b]
46-day ADG, lbs.	0.62[a]	0.71[b]
Final Weight, lbs.	95.00[a]	99.90[b]
Daily Feed Intake, lbs.	3.44	3.40
Feed/Gain Ratio	5.64	4.85

[a, b]Means in the same row with different letters are statistically significant (P less than .05).

Table 14–2. Effect of zeranol implantation on lamb growth. (From: J. P. Wiggins, "Growth Promotants" in Sheep! magazine, Vol. 3 No. 2, February 1982.)

Table 14-3

	Additive	Percent Barley in Ration 30	50	70	Mean for All Rations
Intake, lb./day	None	3.57	3.86	3.79	3.73
	Rumensin	3.97	3.57	3.40	3.64
Daily Gain, lb.	None	0.61	0.80	0.81	0.72
	Rumensin	0.88	0.99	0.91	0.97
Lb. Feed/lb. Gain	None	5.98	4.80	4.99	5.19
	Rumensin	4.48	3.49	3.52	3.76

Table 14-3. Performance of lambs fed Rumensin and different levels of barley.

Table 14-4

	Rumensin Level, grams/ton 0	10	20	30
Intake, lb./day	2.91	2.89	3.09	2.76
Daily Gain, lb.	0.76	0.83	0.82	0.75
Lb. Feed/lb. Gain	3.83	3.49	3.77	3.70

Table 14-4. Effect of Rumensin level on the performance of lambs.

Table 14-5

	Nonmedicated Control	Rumensin	Bovatec Level, grams/ton 11	22	45	90
Intake, lb./day	3.44	3.20	3.42	3.31	3.31	3.26
Daily Gain, lb.	0.69	0.70	0.75	0.74	0.74	0.73
Lb. Feed/lb. Gain	4.92	4.56	4.59	4.45	4.45	4.47

Table 14-5. Performance of lambs fed Bovatec and Rumensin.

block. It is not very palatable, and animals may show reduced feed intake when first introduced to it. One major drawback, unrelated to sheep feeding, is that monensin is deadly to horses. Many feed mills will not use it in their batch mixers for this reason alone. Although it has not been approved by the Food and Drug Administration for sheep feeding, this may change soon, as it is approved in several foreign countries.

Both monensin and lasalocid have therapeutic properties against coccidiosis and improve weight gains and feed efficiency in lambs. On high-grain rations both compounds can be expected to reduce the amount of feed required per pound of gain without affecting the rate of gain (Table 14–5). On a high-roughage ration, both compounds increase rate of gain and feed efficiency in lambs. The net result is that the use of these products increases the proportion of energy in the feed that is available to the animal for maintenance and gain. Furthermore, due to a protein-sparing effect of these compounds, rations containing approximately 2 to 3 percent less crude protein can be fed without adversely affecting performance.

ANTIBIOTICS AND PROBIOTICS

A wide variety of antibiotics has been used to stimulate lamb growth. Their main role has been to reduce the number of harmful bacteria that the animal usually has to combat. Benefits to the animal from the use of antibiotic feed additives may be forfeited, however, if they adversely affect the normal population of beneficial bacteria in the rumen.

Feed additives containing live bacteria are called *probiotics*. Feeding specific bacteria to livestock seems like an unnatural thing, until we consider that all fresh forages and silage contain live bacteria. Of course, bacterial innoculants are used to ensure nodulation on legumes, to convert milk into yogurt, and to give cheese its characteristic flavors. Yeasts, bacteria, and their fermentation products have been fed to livestock in various attempts to improve health, feed efficiency, and/or rate of gain.

The organisms usually found in these products are essential to proper digestion and, under normal conditions, exist in healthy numbers in the stomach and intestines. When the digestive tract loses these bacteria due to a disease or the use of antibiotics, they must be restored sooner or later. The manufacturers say that probiotics help get the digestive system working again by introducing the right organisms. Under natural conditions, the sheep's rumen is inoculated by ingesting bits of feces of other sheep, the pasture grasses, etc.

A major ingredient in most probiotics is lactobacillus. This group of bacteria is known to positively influence the ecology and microbial balance in the digestive tract by destroying or crowding out harmful bacteria. The bacteria also can influence the healing of the intestinal lining, modify the pH of the digestive tract, and produce natural antibiotics. They also produce a variety of nutrients in excess of their own needs, which is then made available to the host. While some of these products are viewed with some skepticism in comparison with conventional antibiotics, it seems they may have a place when the normal bacteria in the gut are missing, such as after a case of lactic acidosis, scours, the overuse of an antibiotic, or in artificially reared lambs.

K. Cheng at the Lethbridge, Alberta, Agricultural Research Center inoculated newborn lambs with 29 different kinds of harmless bacteria, 16 of which were isolated from the rumen and 13 from the intestinal lining. Lambs were removed from the ewe at birth and artificially reared on milk replacer. Cheng found that after 120 days, the inoculated lambs weighed 13.5 pounds more than uninoculated controls. His work is aimed at understanding more about the importance and function of bacteria in the gut.

Chapter 15

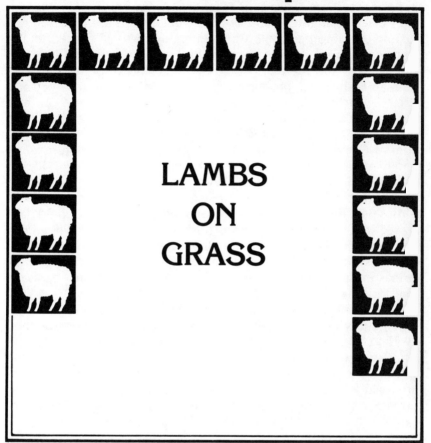

LAMBS ON GRASS

Pasture is the most natural and least expensive feed for lambs. Unfortunately, there are sheep producers who feel that raising lambs on pasture is obsolete, and that better results are obtained from feeding concentrates to lambs in a drylot. Lambs will grow to market weight faster when fed a high-concentrate ration, but the cost is 2 to 3 times higher than raising lambs on grass. Raising lambs on grass is not old-fashioned; what is old-fashioned is the way we manage our lambs to take advantage of this low-cost feed.

Most of the lamb produced in the United States and Canada is raised on grass. Lambs are born in March and April, weaned while on pasture, and marketed in October weighing 80 to 100 pounds.

Many of these lambs are sold as feeder lambs, finished on concentrates before slaughter. Most of their weight gains are made on forage and their mother's milk. Approximately 20 to 30 percent of the lambs coming off range or pasture in the fall will reach a grade of U.S. Choice, and the rest will go into feed lots to be fattened.

Many farm flock producers prefer to lamb in February or early March, wean the lambs in late April, and raise the lambs on their best spring pastures. Their objective is to have the lambs make their earliest and most efficient gains on milk and creep feed to a minimum of 60 pounds. At this size, the lambs have a fully functional rumen and a larger gut capacity for roughages than younger, lighter lambs born in March and April. With a larger gut capacity, the older lambs can consume enough roughage to make satisfactory weight gains. Thus, the lambs usually are weaned between 60 and 90 days of age. Rather than use the spring flush of grass to feed ewes whose nutritional needs in late lactation are in decline, the producers prefer to feed it just to the growing lambs. Because the weaned lambs are pastured separately, they are not exposed to internal parasites from the ewes.

Unfortunately, this system has its drawbacks. Pasture and other fresh forages are not converted into rapid weight gains because they are 75 to 80 percent water. Fresh forages simply do not have the accumulation or density of energy that is needed for the fastest rates of gain. Other factors associated with poor lamb performance on pasture include infection from internal parasites, heat stress during the summer months, low intake due to poor-quality forage, and overstocking of pastures. All of these drawbacks can be reversed with good pasture management.

GAINS ON PASTURE

Investigations by Dr. R. W. Van Keuren, agronomist at the Ohio Agricultural Research and Development Center, have shown average daily gains as high as 0.84 pounds per head per day for lambs with ewes on excellent-quality pasture (Table 15–1). These gains were obtained with February-born wether lambs on pasture with the ewes from April 27 until June 30. In his study, Dr. Van Keuren found a period of 140 days was necessary for February-born lambs to reach an average grade of U.S. Low Choice. By lambing early, the lambs were large enough (60 pounds) to utilize pasture by late April. They could be marketed as finished lambs before the end of June, while spring prices were still high.

Van Keuren cited Virginia studies where early-born lambs (average birth date about February 1) averaged 0.36 to 0.38 pounds of gain per day on Ladino clover/orchardgrass pastures. The same study reported 0.44 pounds of gain on rotationally grazed bluegrass pasture and 0.52 pounds of gain on continuously grazed bluegrass pasture. Slaughter grades on the grass-fed lambs ranged from Low Good to Low Choice.

Research from Minnesota showed gains of 0.31 to 0.35 pounds per animal per day for lambs with the ewes on rotationally grazed alfalfa/bromegrass pasture. From these studies it would be safe to assume that most sheep producers could obtain average daily gains around 0.35 pounds per head from their February-born and early-March-born lambs.

In order to plan out a successful grass-rearing system for lambs, you must choose the target marketing date and know the productivity of your pastures and the distribution of that productivity throughout the season, plan the lambing season accordingly, and control the factors affecting animal productivity on pasture.

Table 15-1

AVERAGE DAILY GAINS (lbs.) LAMBS ON PASTURE

	1955	1956	1958	1959 Wether Lambs	1959 Ewe Lambs	1960	Ave.
Alfalfa	0.47	0.54	0.64	0.84	0.71	0.49	0.62
Alfalfa/Orchardgrass	0.38	0.50	0.62	0.74	0.50	0.47	0.54
Ladino clover	0.46	--	0.70	0.71	0.72	0.43	0.60
Ladino/Orchardgrass	0.36	0.54	0.56	0.63	0.68	0.42	0.53
Orchardgrass	0.28	0.52	0.48	0.58	0.48	0.47	0.47
Average	0.39	0.52	0.60	0.70	0.62	0.46	

Table 15-1.   Average daily gains for May and June of February-born lambs on pasture with ewes (From: R. W. Van Keuren and Heinemann, Washington Agricultural Experiment Station, Bulletin 641, 1962; and Van Keuren and Heinemann, Agronomy Journal 50, 189.92, 1958).

FACTORS AFFECTING PASTURE UTILIZATION

Full utilization of pasture involves many management steps to increase pasture productivity. Under favorable conditions, production may exceed 5 tons of forage dry matter per acre, which makes sheep pasture comparable to a high-yielding hay crop. However, much of our pasture is not utilized at this level of production due to the lack of a few essential inputs such as lime, fertilizer, seed, and fencing to control grazing.

Quality of the Pasture. The efficiency of feed utilization of lambs on grass depends primarily on a high level of forage intake and a high nutrient content (quality) of the pasture. The most important factor affecting intake is probably the maturity of the forage. While sheep may browse on some tall plants or weeds, and even strip leaves off the lower branches of trees, their preference is still for a short pasture with 3 to 5 inches of growth. Vegetative growth also happens to be higher in energy and protein than growth in the bloom or seed stage.

Temperature. Temperature also affects forage intake and pasture utilization. Summer heat causes lambs to graze less. Shorn lambs are more comfortable so they graze later in the morning and resume grazing earlier in the afternoon. Be sure to provide shade if the weather will be very hot for the 2 to 3 weeks after shearing since the lambs will be more susceptible to heat prostration (the fleece insulates the body from extreme heat and cold) and sunburn. If the weather is unusually cool and rainy, shelter is necessary to avoid chilling.

Lambs not going to market within 50 days of shearing will have sufficient time to grow a "No. 1 pelt," a fleece with ½ inch of wool. This is worth more than a freshly shorn lamb's pelt. Shorn lambs with at least ¼ inch of wool are sold at most markets for higher prices than lamb in long fleeces because they appear younger and will yield a higher dressing percentage (see Chapter 16).

Time Spent on Grazing. Forage intake also is affected by the time spent on grazing. When plenty of pasture is available, a ewe or lamb will graze for about 7 hours per day and consume grass at a rate of about 1.2 to 1.4 pounds of green material per hour. On the other hand, lactating ewes or ewes and lambs deprived of feed may graze for 10 to 11 hours, no matter how short the feed supply is. Less energy is wasted by grazing when there is plenty of forage available.

Stocking Rates. Stocking rates have a marked affect on pasture productivity since they affect plant vigor as well as individual animal performance. Continuous grazing at high stocking rates defoliates the plant so that it does not have enough leaf area left for photosynthesis. Continuous grazing at low stocking rates permits an accumulation of overmature, less acceptable plant growth due to selective grazing. Individual animal performance usually is highest under this situation, but the yield of lamb, wool, or forage dry matter per unit of land is low. Close grazing at a high stocking rate with frequent rest periods is not harmful to the pasture stand as the plants are allowed to recover from their defoliation. Short-growing pasture grasses and legumes are better adapted to close grazing than tall species because of their adaptability to spread their leaf surface horizontally so only a small portion of the plant is removed at a time.

Parasites. Internal parasites can be the most limiting factor affecting lamb gains on pastures. For this reason, lambs should be pastured separately from the ewes on land that has not been grazed by sheep during the previous 12 months (clean grazing system). If lambs become moderately to severely infected on pasture, they should be moved to the barn or drylot, treated with a worming medication, and fed harvested forage and concentrate until they have recovered.

CREEP FEEDING

High-quality pasture has been shown to have levels of 20 to 25 percent crude protein on a dry basis, so it would be unusual to have protein as a limiting factor to lamb growth on pasture. Supplemental protein is necessary only in situations where the forage is overmature and low in digestible protein.

Research by Dr. D. Ely at the University of Kentucky shows a significant advantage to supplementing spring pasture in order to grow out early-weaned lambs. In his study, a group of lambs was self-fed a 13 percent protein concentrate on pasture as an energy supplement. Another group was fed either a 13 percent or 16 percent protein concentrate in a drylot. A third group of lambs grazed on a 50:50 bluegrass and ladino clover stand without supplement. The results of this experiment are shown in Table 15–2. Supplemented pasture produced slightly lower gains, and the lambs needed an average of 1 week longer to reach slaughter weight than the drylot lambs. However, the pasture-reared lambs consumed 45 percent less concentrate. Lambs on pasture alone had significantly slower gains and took longer to reach market weight than the other lambs. The amount of feed required per pound of gain was 4.4 pounds for lambs on supplemented pasture, 7.2 pounds for lambs fed 13 percent protein ration in a drylot, and 6.7 pounds for drylot lambs with 16 percent protein ration. Lambs on pasture alone had lower carcass quality (less finish), lower yield grades, and dressing percentages than lambs on supplemented pasture or drylot lambs (Table 15–3).

In a second trial, Ely switched the 13 percent crude protein concentrate to 100 percent shelled corn to supplement the lambs on a bluegrass/ladino clover pasture and stocked at 5 lambs per acre. The results were practically the same as with the 13 percent protein ration. However, the lambs on pasture supplemented with corn most

Table 15-2

Lamb Weight, lb.	Pasture Only	Pasture and 13% CP Concentrate	Drylot and 13% CP Concentrate	Drylot and 16% CP Concentrate
Daily Gain, lb.				
70–90	.39	.51	.66	.63
70–110	.34	.58	.59	.54
Average	.37	.55	.62	.59
Daily Feed Intake, lb.				
70–90	––	2.4	4.1	3.9
70–110	––	2.2	4.6	3.8
Average	––	2.3	4.3	3.9
Days to Slaughter				
70–90	44.6	36.8	26.4	27.4
70–110	70.4	67.5	64.8	64.3
Average	57.5	52.5	45.6	45.9

Table 15-2. Daily liveweight gain, daily dry feed intake, and days to slaughter of lambs fed on bluegrass/clover pasture or drylot, and slaughtered at 2 weights. (From: Don Ely, University of Kentucky. In Sheepbreeder Magazine, December 1980.)

nearly approached the quality of an ideal market lamb with a lean but well-finished carcass.

In following experiments, Ely compared orchardgrass, orchardgrass/ladino clover, and tall fescue pastures with and without a supplement for lambs. For the fescue he used the new "Kenhy" fescue cultivar, a tall fescue × annual ryegrass hybrid developed at the University of Kentucky for improved forage quality. In all of the trials, the lambs were approximately 65 to 70 days of age at the start of the experiments. Lambs were rotated between 2 pastures within each forage group at 2-week intervals, at a stocking rate of 13 lambs per acre, from April 5 to July 5. Shelled corn was limit-fed at 1 percent of body weight daily, or about 0.6 pounds per head at the start, increasing to 0.8 pounds per head in late June.

Table 15-3

Slaughter Weight, lb.	Pasture Only	Pasture and 13% CP Concentrate	Drylot and 13% CP Concentrate	Drylot and 16% CP Concentrate
Dressing %				
90	45.5	48.0	48.6	48.9
110	47.3	49.6	50.1	50.3
Average	46.4	48.8	49.4	49.5
Quality Grade*				
90	12.5	13.4	13.5	13.6
110	13.9	14.4	13.6	14.0
Average	13.2	14.1	13.6	13.8
Yield Grade				
90	1.9	2.4	2.6	2.6
110	2.4	2.7	3.5	3.7
Average	2.2	2.5	3.1	3.1

*Quality grades are broken down as follows: Prime⁺ = 15, Prime⁰ = 14, Prime⁻ = 13, Choice⁺ = 12, etc. For more on lamb grading, see Chapter 16.

Table 15–3. Carcass quality factors of lambs managed in 4 systems and slaughtered at 2 weights. (From: Don Ely, University of Kentucky. In Sheepbreeder Magazine, December 1980.)

The performance of the lambs in this experiment is summarized in Tables 15–4 and 15–5. There was little difference in rate of gain between the orchardgrass or fescue pastures, and the level of energy supplementation proved inadequate to support maximum growth. Dr. Ely concluded that early-weaned lambs could be finished properly on orchardgrass, tall fescue, and mixed pasture, but that it must be supplemented with concentrates. Shelled corn fed at a level somewhere between 1 percent of body weight and self-fed appeared to be adequate to support maximum gains on pasture with the least cost. He emphasized that lambs must be stocked heavily on orchardgrass or fescue to keep the grass short, tender, and high quality.

Table 15-4

Measurement	No Corn		Corn	
	Orchard-grass/ Clover	Fescue/ Clover	Orchard-grass/ Clover	Fescue/ Clover
Initial Weight (4/23), lb.	53.6	53.2	52.5	53.0
Final Weight (7/17), lb.	76.2	71.9	80.7	83.5
Gain/Lamb, lb.	22.6	18.7	28.2	30.5
Gain/Acre/Day, lb.	3.5	2.9	4.3	4.4
Corn/Lamb, lb.	––	––	48.1	48.1
Extra Gain/Lamb for Corn, lb.*	––	––	5.6	11.8

*28.2 minus 22.6; 30.5 minus 18.7, respectively. In other words, the pounds of gain per lamb minus pounds of corn fed per lamb equals the extra gain per lamb attributable to feeding corn.

Table 15–4. Performance of lambs grazing grass/legume pasture with or without supplemental corn. (From: Don Ely, University of Kentucky. In Sheepbreeder Magazine, December 1980.)

Table 15-5

| Measurement | No Corn | | Corn* | |
	Orchard-grass	Kenhy/Fescue	Orchard-grass	Kenhy/Fescue
Initial Weight (4/5), lb.	59.1	60.3	62.2	60.6
Final Weight (7/5), lb.	74.5	77.6	83.9	87.1
Gain/Lamb, lb.	16.3	17.3	21.7	26.5
Gain/Acre/Day, lb.	2.3	2.5	3.1	3.8
Corn/Lamb, lb.	--	--	60.6	60.6
Extra Gain/Lamb for Corn, lb.**	--	--	5.4	9.2

*Corn fed at rate of 1% of body weight daily.
**21.7 minus 16.3; 26.5 minus 17.3, respectively.

Table 15-5. Performance of lambs grazing pure strands of orchardgrass or Kenhy tall fescue with or without supplemental corn. (From: Don Ely, University of Kentucky. In Sheepbreeder Magazine, December 1980.)

RECOMMENDATIONS FOR LAMBS ON GRASS

To summarize, raising lambs on grass requires an understanding of the factors limiting the lambs' rate of gain. These factors include the weight of the lamb when put on pasture, the quality and management of the pasture, the level of parasite contamination, and the amount of supplemental feed offered.

High rates of gain from pasture alone are possible. The lambs should be 60 pounds or heavier before pasture is made their main source of protein and energy. The lambs should graze clean pasture that is relatively free of parasites. They should have a salt/mineral mix, fresh water, and shade. Shearing prior to hot weather will keep lambs more comfortable, and they will spend more time grazing. The pasture should be kept in a short, vegetative stage throughout the feeding period. Highest weight gains per animal are obtained with a low to moderate stocking rate of 4 to 5 lambs per acre, which allows some selective grazing. Under low stocking rates some plants will become overmature and will not be grazed by the lambs. Mowing the pasture to maintain a height of no more than 6 inches will provide high-quality forage. Alternatively, beef or dairy cattle can follow lambs in a pasture rotation, cleaning up taller growth that the lambs leave behind.

Research at the University of Kentucky has shown that the fastest gains with the least cost are made on grass/clover pasture supplemented with corn fed daily at a rate of 1 percent of body weight. Barley, milo, wheat, or other energy supplements could be used in place of corn.

Chapter 16

LAMB GRADING

Consumers today prefer lean meat – whether it is beef, pork, or lamb. The sheep industry has responded to consumer demands by increasing the average weight and lean meat yield of a lamb carcass. The average liveweight of lambs slaughtered also has increased steadily for the last 60 years.

The increase in slaughter weight has a major influence on the choice of sheep breeds, with a steady trend toward heavier rams that can sire a fast-growing, trimly finished 110-pound lamb. Through improved genetic selection, nutrition, and management, sheep producers have been able to increase weight while improving muscling and reducing fatness. This has been accomplished in spite of selection pressure for both lamb and wool production.

Your objective as a commercial lamb producer is to raise a properly finished lamb that grades U.S. Choice or better, with a yield grade of 2. The carcass should have a high percentage of closely trimmed, boneless, retail cuts. The modern market lamb should be large-framed, fast-gaining, thickly muscled, trim, and weigh between 100 and 125 pounds at slaughter.

QUALITY GRADES

The USDA quality grades serve as guides to the eating quality of the meat—its tenderness, juiciness, and flavor. The quality grades for lamb and lamb carcasses are: Prime, Choice, Good, Utility, and Cull. The specific characteristics that determine quality grade in lamb are the amounts of fat and muscling.

At the present time, two-thirds of the lambs slaughtered in this country are quality graded, and 98 to 99 percent of them fall into the Prime and Choice categories. The quality grade standards permit any breed or type of lamb to grade Choice, if it has sufficient finish or fat cover. Yearling and mutton sheep can qualify for any of the quality grades except Prime.

Dressing Percentages

The dressing percentage is positively correlated with the quality grade. The dressing percentage relates the carcass or dressed weight to liveweight. It is expressed by the formula:

$$\frac{\text{Chilled Carcass Weight}}{\text{Liveweight}} \times 100 = \text{Dressing Percentage}$$

A normal range for dressing percentages is 45 to 58 percent, and the average is 53 percent for shorn, Choice-grade lambs. The portions normally removed at slaughter include the pelt and contents of the gut, head, kidneys, kidney fat, testicles, and blood. In the average lamb, these comprise approximately half the liveweight. Low dressing percentages are undesirable and reflect a larger amount of waste from the animal. Factors that lower the dressing percentage include rumen and gut fill; wool; manure, mud, and moisture in the fleece; testicles; tails; and fetuses. Lambs in full fleece have a 1 to 5 percent lower dressing percentage (average 2 to 3 percent) than shorn lambs. In other words, 3 pounds of wool on a 110-pound lamb reduce the carcass yield by about 3 percent.

Lambs with a short pelt (½-inch to 1-inch fibers) sell for a higher price per hundredweight than lambs in full fleeces. A short pelt is classified as a No. 1 pelt and is the most desirable for shearling garment manufacture. Pelts with only ¼ to ½ inch of wool are classed as No. 2 and are worth less. Lambs to be sold before they are 5 months old or having less than an inch of wool generally do not need to be shorn to obtain the highest pelt premiums.

Maturity

Maturity is an estimation of the chronological age of the lamb and is a factor in quality grading live lambs and carcasses. Older lambs have longer fleeces, heavier bones, and larger heads and secondary sex characteristics, such as enlarged testicles. Older ram lambs tend to have heavier neck and shoulder muscles, giving them what is called a "bucky" appearance, which lowers the value of the live lamb and the carcass. Sheep older than about 14 months will develop their first pair of permanent incisor teeth, which positively identifies them as yearlings and not lambs.

Maturity also can be estimated by the bone and muscle characteristics in the carcass. Bone, for example, matures in a definite pattern changing from a soft, reddish, porous tissue to white, flinty, dense bone. This can be seen easily in the ribs of a lamb carcass, where the ribs of older lambs appear flat and white compared to the narrow, red, and closely spaced ribs of younger lambs. The color of the muscle or lean and presence of a break joint also are used to assess maturity. As the lamb gets older, the lean changes from a light pink color to a deep red. Lambs are classified as sheep under 1 year of age with a break joint in the foreleg. As the animal gets older, the break joint develops into a spool joint which cannot be snapped apart easily, and the animal becomes a yearling or mutton sheep.

It is useful to have some idea of lamb *liveweight* as well as to handle and view the lambs for fat cover, muscling, and maturity. The normal range of liveweights for market lambs in the United States is 90 to 130 pounds, and 110 pounds is average. These weights apply to wether, ewe, and ram lambs of intermediate to large size breeds and crossbreeds. Weighing the lambs helps to show the relationships between quality and carcass yield. However, relying only on liveweight to estimate quality and yield is not sufficient, as some lambs are properly finished at 90 pounds, whereas others are not finished until they weigh 120 pounds. You need to be able to determine the market readiness of your lambs by knowing the actual weights and by estimating maturity and fat cover.

An accurate liveweight can be obtained by weighing lambs with empty stomachs or approximately 12 hours after their last feeding. Otherwise, there will be misleading measurements due to the amount of feed and water in the animals, which is eliminated while the animals are being trucked and held at the packing house prior to slaughter.

LIVE ANIMAL EVALUATION

Sheep producers need to evaluate live lambs to determine which lambs are at the correct weight and have the optimum amount of fat for market. Lambs that are too light or lack finish must be fed for a longer period of time before they reach the Choice grade. Lambs with the slowest rates of gain, who are unthrifty, or have very little muscle should be sold as culls. Live animal evaluation allows you to quickly identify overfat, properly finished, and thin lambs to make better feeding and marketing decisions. Your live evaluation should be followed up by a carcass evaluation to confirm what you saw and felt on the live lamb.

The major components of the live animal evaluation are amount of muscling and fatness. You can subjectively evaluate overall conformation by determining the relative distribution of the muscle and general appearance of the animal. Look not only at the proportions of each part but the desirability of the individual parts. A greater proportion of weight or muscling in the leg and loin is desirable because of its high value as a retail cut, compared to muscling in the neck or shoulder. Conformation includes length of body, length of loin and rump, width of back, width of loin, depth of body, height and length of leg, and the relationships of these to each other.

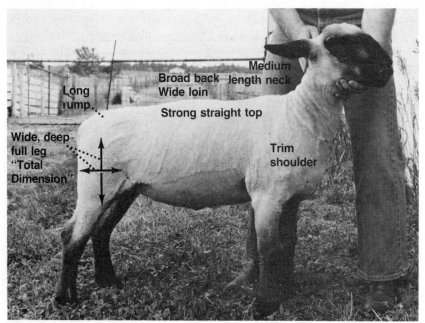

Photo 16-1. A properly finished, well-muscled market lamb. (Courtesy of Gene Hettel, Iowa State University)

Lambs with good conformation are wide and thick in relation to their length and have a plump, well-rounded appearance due to an acceptable amount of muscling and fat. Lambs with poor conformation are narrow in relation to their length and have a thin, angular appearance. Overall conformation on the live animal and carcass are expressed in the same terms as quality grades: Prime, Choice, Good, etc. Therefore, most lambs have average conformation and grade "average Choice."

Making Your Evaluation

When evaluating lambs as individuals or as a group, view them first from a distance of 25 feet. Study them first from the side, then from the rear, and finally from the front.

From the side, look at the length of body and rump. A good market lamb is long in the loin and rump, with a greater proportion of valuable cuts from these areas than a short-bodied lamb. There should be good width in the rear leg. The lamb should have a medium to large frame, which generally indicates a medium to late maturing animal that will not be overly fat at 110 to 115 pounds.

Study the lamb from the rear to evaluate width across the loin area, width of rump and rear leg, depth of muscling from top of the rump to the twist or crotch area, and muscling through the center of the rear leg. Correctly finished lambs will appear wider through the rump and shoulder than in the back and loin. They will have a natural curve over the back. Thin lambs, particularly lightly muscled lambs, are angular and narrow over the back. Overfinished lambs are flat-sided and flat and wide over the back. Fatness adds depth to the twist and width to the rump. A better estimation of fat is made by handling the lambs.

From the front, look for moderate width between the legs and moderate depth in the breast area. Overfat lambs will be full in the breast or brisket area.

After studying the animals from a distance, you can gather them tightly in a pen or have someone hold each lamb as you handle them to determine the amount of finish and muscling. The best place to feel fat cover is where bone lies just under the skin; for example, along the backbone or over the ribs. Fat is easy to detect because it is soft and does not retain shape. Bone, of course, feels hard and muscle is firm and rounded.

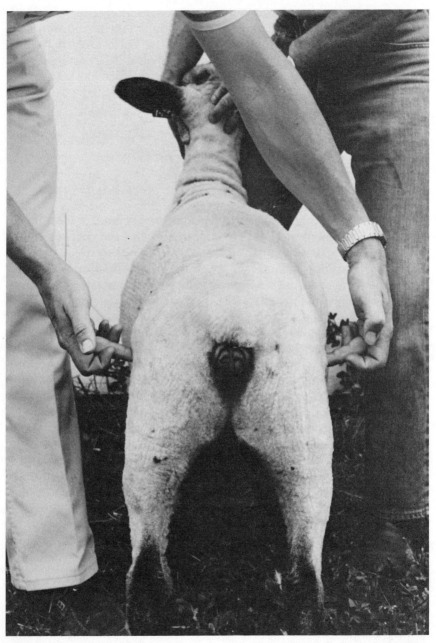

Photo 16-2. Measuring the width of the leg muscle. (Courtesy of Gene Hettel, Iowa State University)

With your fingers together, feel the fat cover along the back. Start from the shoulder and feel down the back toward the tail. Press firmly with the fingertips at several points along the back. Determine the backfat between the twelfth and thirteenth rib to help estimate the quality grade and yield grade. Correctly finished lambs have 0.15 inch of backfat and a smooth, rounded feel to the spinous processes, the bumps along the backbone. The ribs will have a slight cover of fat, which slides over the ribs and gives them a smooth feel.

Underfinished lambs with under 0.10 inch of backfat have a sharp, prominent backbone, which feels like the back of your knuckles. The ribs are sharp and it is easy to feel the individual ribs. Underfinished lamb carcasses tend to dry out in the cooler and are less juicy and flavorful than properly finished lamb.

Overfinished lambs (with over 0.3 inch of backfat between the twelfth and thirteenth rib) have a smooth feel over the backbone and the spinous processes barely can be felt with firm pressure. Excessive fat can be felt as soft areas in the fore flank, rear flank, in the twist, and around the tail. If the ribs cannot be felt, the lamb is grossly overfat.

Muscling is the second major component used to evaluate market lambs. The leg and loin are given special emphasis as they are the most valuable cuts. Length of leg can be seen from a side view and a good leg extends down well into the hock. The thickness and depth of the leg muscle can be felt by grasping the leg at its thickest point with 2 hands. A thick, bulging leg can be felt between the thumb and fingers and compared to a light or thinly muscled leg. Measure the length of the loin by stretching your hand from the last rib to the hip. To estimate depth of loin, push your fingers toward the body cavity (between the last rib and the hip); the tubular "loin eye" muscle and fat cover is measured by the depth found between the thumb and fingers.

Leg muscling is used to help determine yield grade. Research indicates that leg muscle is correlated fairly well with total muscling. Lambs with heavy leg muscles are considered to have high Choice or Prime leg scores.

The *ribeye area* is used as an indicator of the total muscling in the carcass because it can be measured objectively with a grid. The ribeye area is the average area in square inches of the right and left ribeye or longissimus muscle. In the loin, the same muscle is measured by its *loineye area*. The ribeye is the largest and one of the most valuable muscles in the carcass. It is measured after the carcass is cut between the twelfth and thirteenth rib. The normal range in ribeye muscle area is 1.5 to 3.2 square inches; 2.4 square inches is average. Clear plastic ribeye/loineye area grids are available for a nominal cost from the Cooperative Extension Service of Iowa State University (see Appendix C).

YIELD GRADES

Yield grades for lamb and their carcasses are used to identify difference in "cutability" or the yield of closely trimmed, boneless retail cuts from the leg, loin, rack, and shoulder. The main wholesale cuts of lamb are shown in Figure 16-1. A No. 1 yield grade carcass has a higher percent cutability than yield grade No. 5 as shown in Table 16-1.

Low-fat, heavily muscled carcasses are high in percent cutability and fall into yield grades 1 or 2. High-fat, lightly muscled carcasses are low in percent cutability and fall into yield grades 4 or 5. Carcasses that are average in muscling and finish fall into yield grade 3.

The factors used to estimate yield grade on the live lamb are fat thickness over the twelfth rib, percentage of kidney-pelvic (KP) fat, and leg conformation. The major factor affecting yield grade is the amount of external fat. Muscling as determined from leg conformation has little effect on yield grade. One full grade difference in leg muscling — for example, from low Choice to low Prime — only affects the yield grade by .15. The amount of internal or KP fat has an intermediate effect on yield grade.

Table 16-1

YIELD OF RETAIL CUTS	
Yield Grade	Cutability
No. 1	49.0%
No. 2	47.2
No. 3	45.4
No. 4	43.6
No. 5	41.8

Table 16-1. Yield grades for lambs or their carcasses are used to identify yield of retail cuts.

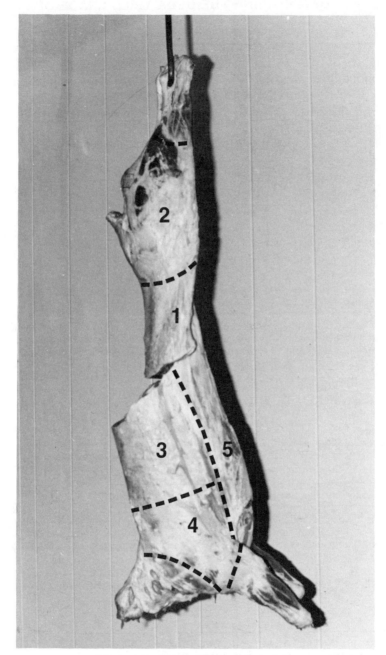

Photo 16-3. Properly finished market lamb with thick leg muscles, long rump, and wide loin. (Courtesy of Gene Hettel, Iowa State University)

DETERMINING THE USDA YIELD GRADE OF
LIVE SHEEP AND SHEEP CARCASSES

Step 1. Determine the Preliminary Yield Grade

Measure the fat thickness over the spine, at the twelfth and thirteenth rib. Use a metal backfat probe on the carcass, or feel the backbone with your fingers on the live lamb.

Fat Thickness			Preliminary Yield Grade
Inches 00	Centimeters	00	2.00
.05		.13	2.33
.10		.25	2.67
.15		.38	3.00
.20		.51	3.33
.25		.64	3.67
.30		.76	4.00
.35		.89	4.33
.40		1.02	4.67
.45		1.14	5.00
.50		1.27	5.33
.55		1.40	5.67

Step 2. Adjust for Leg Score

Leg scores are determined subjectively on the live lamb and the carcass. A thick, bulging rear leg receives a Prime leg score. An average leg with moderate amounts of muscle receives a Choice leg score. A thin rear leg muscle receives a Good leg score. The producer often has to handle a few hundred lambs before he or she is consistently accurate at grading lambs.

Leg Scores

High Prime = 15	High Choice = 12	High Good =9
Average Prime = 14	Average Choice = 11	Average Good = 8
Low Prime = 13	Low Choice = 10	Low Good = 7

a. For each leg score above 11, subtract .05 for the preliminary Yield Grade.
b. For each leg score less than 11, add .05 to the preliminary Yield Grade.

Step 3. Adjust for Percent of Kidney-Pelvic Fat (% KP Fat)

Estimate the percent Kidney-Pelvic fat on the live lamb. On the carcass, this fat can be estimated in place or removed and weighed. Remember that old lambs (9 to 12 months of age) that have been finished on a high-energy ration have higher KP fat than young lambs. Finncross lambs have higher KP fat than other commercial breeds or their crosses.

a. For each % KP Fat more than 3.5%, add .25 to the adjusted Yield Grade found in Step 2.
b. For each % KP Fat less than 3.5%, subtract .25 from the adjusted Yield Grade found in Step 2.

THE FINAL YIELD GRADE HAS BEEN DETERMINED

Step 4. Round the Final Yield Grade Down to the Nearest Tenth

Example: $\dfrac{3.33 = 3.3}{3.38 = 3.3}$

Under the USDA Yield Grade system, the final yield grade number is rounded down to the nearest tenth (3.33 and 3.38 are both rounded down to a yield grade of 3.3).

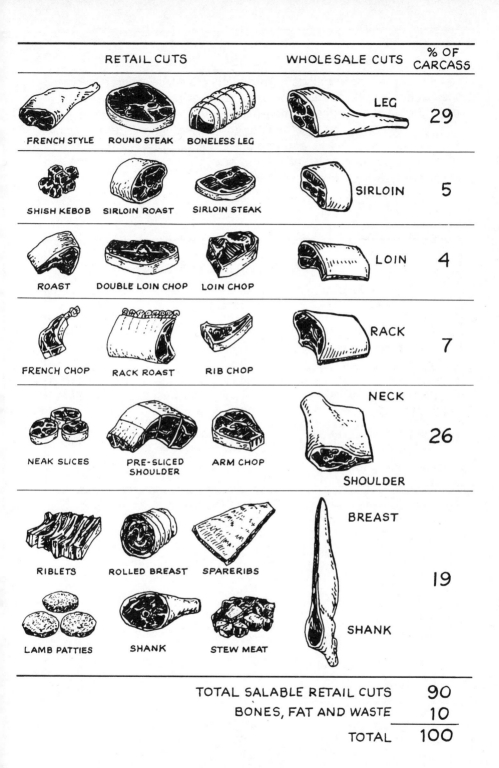

RETAIL CUTS	WHOLESALE CUTS	% OF CARCASS
FRENCH STYLE ROUND STEAK BONELESS LEG	LEG	29
SHISH KEBOB SIRLOIN ROAST SIRLOIN STEAK	SIRLOIN	5
ROAST DOUBLE LOIN CHOP LOIN CHOP	LOIN	4
FRENCH CHOP RACK ROAST RIB CHOP	RACK	7
NEAK SLICES PRE-SLICED SHOULDER ARM CHOP	NECK SHOULDER	26
RIBLETS ROLLED BREAST SPARERIBS LAMB PATTIES SHANK STEW MEAT	BREAST SHANK	19
TOTAL SALABLE RETAIL CUTS		90
BONES, FAT AND WASTE		10
TOTAL		100

Figure 16–1. Major retail cuts on a lamb carcass.

On the carcass, backfat can be objectively measured between the twelfth and thirteenth rib with a ruler or backfat probe (see Appendix C). Fat thickness is measured over the center of the ribeye.

It should be noted that the USDA is presently considering changing the basis of the live and carcass grades to place a greater emphasis on muscling. Currently, lamb prices are not adjusted for yield grade, only for quality grade.

Table 16-2

MARKET LAMB CHARACTERISTICS

Trait	Normal Range	Average
Fat Thickness, inches	0.05–0.35	0.20
Ribeye Area, sq. in.	1.90–3.2	2.40
Leg Muscling Score	Ave./Good-Ave./ Prime (8–14)	High Choice (12)
Kidney-Pelvic Fat, %	1.50–6.0	3.5
Yield Grade	1.80–4.4	3.3
Quality Grade	Good/Prime	Choice
Dressing Percentage	48–56	53
Liveweight, pounds	90–140	110

Table 16-2. A summary of characteristics of market lambs.

Chapter 17

FUNDAMENTALS OF GENETIC IMPROVEMENT

Genetic selection, production testing, inbreeding, and crossbreeding are the tools by which you can make genetic progress in your flock. Genetic improvements should mean increased profitability.

Table 17-1

HERITABILITY ESTIMATES

Trait	Average Percent of Heritability	Range of Heritability
Birth Weight	30	9–61
Weaning Weight (over 100 days at weaning)	30	18–77
Weaning Weight (60 days at weaning)	10	
Mature Body Weight	40	
Rate of Gain	30	9–58
Type Score (weaning)	10	
Type Score (yearling)	40	
Condition Score (weaning)	17	
Face Cover	56	13–78
Neck Folds (weaning)	39	6–59
Skin Folds	40	20–66
Grease Fleece Weight	38	17–61
Clean Fleece Weight	40	22–61
Clean Yield	44	39–50
Staple Length (weaning)	39	17–60
Staple Length (yearling)	47	31–73
Fleece Grade	35	29–43
Gestation Length	45	
Date of Lambing	37	
Multiple Birth	15	7–40
Milk Production	26	17–34
Number of Lambs Reared	13	
Loineye Area	53	23–93
Fat Thickness over Loineye	23	19–29
Carcass Weight/Day of Age	22	16–27
Carcass Grade	12	10–15
Carcass Length	31	9–46
Fat Weight	57	45–69
Bone Weight	30	23–32
Lean Weight	39	
Retail Cut Weight	50	41–58
Dressing Percent	10	7–13

Table 17–1. Heritability estimates for some common traits. (From: Sheepman's Production Handbook, Sheep Industry Development Program Inc., Denver, CO, 1983.)

SELECTION

In order to make any genetic improvements within a flock or breed, desirable traits must be selected for and undesirable traits selected against. The rate of genetic progress—how fast you can see results—depends on the number of traits you are selecting for, the heritabilities of these traits (see Table 17-1), and the correlations between traits. In addition, the accuracy of your production records, the number of animals you have to work with, and the generation interval (average time required for a lamb to grow, breed, and have offspring, usually 1 to 2 years) have an influence on the rate of genetic progress that can be made.

The heritabilities of the most important traits of sheep are well known, but there is some uncertainty about the genetic correlations or interrelationships among the various traits. For example, it is known that rate of gain and feed efficiency in sheep are positively correlated: as rate of gain increases so does feed efficiency, both due to genetics. Traits in sheep that appear to have a negative correlation are fleece weight and crimp, staple (wool fiber) length and fineness of fiber.

The more sheep you have, the more intensive the selection you can practice, and therefore the more rapid genetic improvement you can make. With large numbers of sheep, there is more opportunity for the genes to be expressed. You can then cull more thoroughly and with a greater degree of accuracy—a very important part of genetic selection. Shortening the generation interval with an accelerated lambing program (Chapter 18) speeds up progress even more.

If the amount of heritable variation in a trait is very small, as with birth weights, genetic improvement will not be as rapid as with a trait with a wide variation to select from. For example, there is usually only a few pounds difference in birth weights among a group of single-born or twin-born lambs. Faster progress is achieved by selecting on the basis of the 120-day weights of lambs, which have a much greater variation.

The most rapid genetic improvement in a specific trait can be made by concentrating all of the selection pressure of the breeding program on that single trait and ignoring all others. Selecting for 4 traits results in half as much progress in each trait than if you selected for only 1 trait. However, there are very few flocks that need improvement in only 1 trait, so this degree of selection (straight selection) is not practiced widely.

HERITABILITY

In a breeding program, any improvements due to environment should be recognized, as they can give a false impression of the amount of improvement which is supposedly due to genetics. When a trait, such as weaning weight or the number of lambs born per ewe, is measured, it is important to have as little variation due to environmental effects as possible.

Commercial sheep producers can use production records and heritability estimates (Table 17–1) to determine the economic and genetic contribution of a sire. The heritability estimate is the fraction of variation of a trait that is due to genetic effects. These estimates are used to determine the amount of genetic progress that could be expected over each generation. A trait that has a low heritability would show a slow rate of progress through selection. The heritability estimate is also expressed as a *range* of values depending on the breed, accuracy of measurement, or degree of influence from environmental effects.

The heritability estimates apply to traits contributed by the ram and the ewe at mating. However, each parent contributes one-half the genetic material so the heritability estimate is halved for the ewe or ram. The heritability estimate (halved) is multiplied by the variation that the ewe or ram shows in a trait above or below another ewe or ram, or above or below the average for a group of ewes or rams.

SELECTION INDEXES

The most common system of selection is to determine the 3 or 4 most important economic traits in your flock, then select simultaneously but independently for each character. You can do this by means of a selection index, which allows you to combine the most important traits of individual sheep into an overall value or score for each animal.

A selection index is used to rank each ewe and lamb according to its performance. It combines the economic importance of various traits, the heritability of the traits, and environmental effects, such as how the lamb was reared (as a single, twin, or triplet) and the age of the dam (older ewes produce more milk than yearlings). Ewes and lambs with the lowest selection index scores are the first to be culled if any genetic improvement is to be made. To construct an index, animal geneticists first calculate a selection factor for each trait in the index—clean fleece weight, wool, fiber diameter, staple length, face covering, skin folds, weaning weight, carcass conformation, and yearling weight. The selection factor is multiplied by the actual pounds of wool, lamb, etc. produced by the animal to give a weighted value. The weighted values are totaled for each animal to give it an overall score or index.

The selection factor is difficult to arrive at. It involves total variation (that is, variation due to environmental and genetic effects), genetic variation (standard deviation), estimated heritability, and the relative economic value for each trait. In addition, it takes into account whether there are positive or negative correlations between the traits. For example, is selection for clean fleece weight correlated in any way with wool grade (fiber diameter). The selection index formula almost requires the sheepbreeder to use a computer, especially for a large number of ewes and large amounts of data.

With so many economic traits contributing to wool and lamb production, a selection index is one of the most valuable tools a sheepbreeder can use. The index should place the right emphasis on the different traits depending on their relative economic importance and heritabilities. It should balance the strong and weak points of each animal so that the best animals overall receive the highest index values. Finally, the emphasis on each trait should not shift from year to year if continual progress is to be made. Environmental effects can cause annual variations in animal performance that cannot be attributed to genetics. It takes several generations to achieve meaningful progress in a selection program.

The disadvantage of selection indexes is that they may allow some animals with bad faults or defects to be retained in the flock because these characters were overbalanced by strong performance in the main economic traits. Thus, the index is only a partial guide for selection and should be combined with a visual evaluation and performance records from the previous years.

If you are interested in using a selection index, the easiest way to use one is to enroll in the Ohio State Sheep Production Testing System or some other computerized production testing system that ranks the important economic traits simultaneously in a selection index. The animal science department at your state university also can help you develop a selection index for the traits in which you are most interested.

PRODUCTION TESTING

Sheep producers who are involved in production testing use objective measurements and independent trials to evaluate and select their breeding stock. More emphasis is placed on records of performance and less emphasis on visual appraisal or personal opinions. The independent trials or tests used to evaluate and select animals are centralized ram performance tests. Centralized production record keeping systems for rams and ewes (such as the Ohio State Sheep Production Testing System) play an important part in production testing. The records cannot be altered, changed, or removed by the participants, and all records are handled in the same manner for all flocks. Producers enrolled in the centralized record-keeping systems use the same selection index for ranking animals in their flocks.

Production testing includes 2 components: performance testing and progeny testing.

Performance Testing

Performance testing is defined as the practice of evaluating and selecting animals on the basis of their individual merit or performance. Central performance testing facilities bring a large number of animals (especially ram lambs and yearlings) from several farms to a central place where they can be evaluated under similar conditions of feedings and management. Performance testing is particularly useful when selecting for traits with high heritabilities, such as post-weaning gain, 180-day weight, and carcass conformation.

Ram performance tests are usually sponsored by state universities or other independent organizations. Your state Extension sheep specialist can provide information and the address of the ram test station nearest you. A national sheep evaluation committee has been formed by the American Sheep Producers Council to coordinate the efforts of ram test stations and establish more uniform procedures and measurements of the rams on test.

Purebred breeders can benefit most from a production testing program by selecting breeding stock based on ram test data and centralized production records. Many commercial lamb producers are purchasing performance-tested rams as a guarantee of their rate of gain and feed efficiency. Since these traits are heritable, they can expect a ram with superior rate of gain to sire fast-growing lambs as well. Breeders are encouraged to place progeny groups of 3 lambs sired by the same ram on test every year to evaluate the sire. Promising individual ram lambs or yearlings that have not been used for breeding also can be placed in the ram test to evaluate their rate of gain, feed efficiency, muscling, and other characteristics measured in the ram test.

Progeny Testing

Progeny testing is the practice of selecting animals based on the merit of their progeny. The offspring of the animals are brought to a central station for testing. This is particularly useful when selecting for the following traits.

- **Traits with low heritability (for example: birth weight, weaning weight, and backfat thickness)**
- **Rams whose records were made in different flocks or on different farms**
- **Complementarity from crossing 2 lines or breeds**
- **Traits that cannot be observed in both sexes (such as milk production)**
- **Traits that can be expressed only in offspring (carcass merit or lamb mortality)**

Production records from close relatives — the sire, dam, brothers, or sisters — can supplement the performance testing record of an individual. This is important when traits cannot be measured in both sexes, such as fertility, prolificacy, milk production, or semen production.

INBREEDING

Inbreeding is the mating of closely related animals. It can be practiced for a number of generations to improve or eliminate certain characteristics. It is a process of intensive genetic selection and results in a larger number of individuals with the same or similar genetic material. An inbred animal is produced from parents that have 50 percent or more common ancestry in their pedigree, such as matings between half siblings, full siblings, cousins, or granddaughter to grandsire.

There are 2 types of inbreeding: closebreeding and linebreeding. The two differ mainly in the closeness of the relationships between the animals and the speed of genetic progress. Closebreeding is the mating of closely related animals, such as sire to daughter, son to dam, or full brother to sister.

Linebreeding is the mating of animals more distantly related, but it emphasizes the similarity to a highly desirable ancestor. Linebreeding utilizes the matings of half siblings, cousins, or granddaughter to grandsire. It is responsible for the extended families in the purebred livestock industry. Through many generations of linebreeding, the genetic base of a population or group becomes more uniform or homozygous, which makes it possible for a new, identifiable breed to emerge. Linebreeding has more application for the purebred sheep industry than closebreeding because it is less intensive and a more economically conservative type of inbreeding.

Unfortunately, the most common effect of an inbreeding program is a reduced reproductive rate initially. This discourages sheep breeders and increases the cost of the breeding effort. It increases the number of recessive genes appearing in the early generations of the breeding program. These are manifested as a reduction in size,

LINE BREEDING PROGRAM

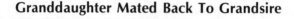

Granddaughter Mated Back To Grandsire

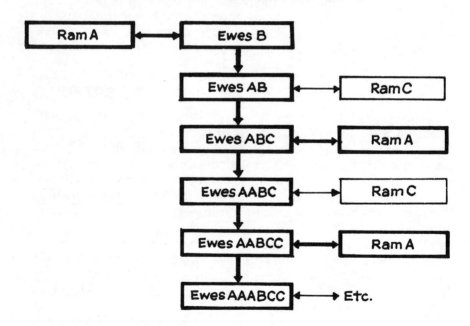

reproductive rate, and vigor, or in other abnormalities. Rigid culling is necessary to eliminate those individuals with the undesirable recessive characteristics in the process of obtaining a more uniform genetic base. This obviously is an expensive program for any breeder to undertake and requires a considerable time commitment. Also, inbreeding, particularly closebreeding, should be attempted only in flocks that already possess many superior individuals, and then only if the numbers are large enough to undergo the extensive culling program in order to obtain the resulting small number of outstanding individuals. Purebred flocks of average or below average quality will make more genetic progress by outcrossing or introducing a superior ram from another flock.

LINE BREEDING PROGRAM

Half-Siblings

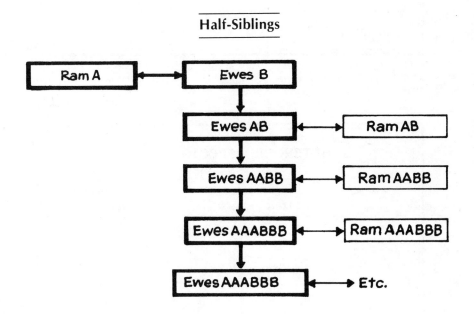

Figure 17–1. Linebreeding programs.

Table 17-2

HETEROSIS EFFECTS (LAMBS)

Trait	Level of Heterosis (%)
Birth Weight	3.2
Weaning Weight	5.0
Preweaning Daily Gain	5.3
Postweaning Daily Gain	6.6
Yearling Weight	5.2
Conception Rate	2.6
Prolificacy of the Dam	2.8
Survival Birth to Weaning	9.8
Carcass Traits	approximately 0
Lambs Born Per Ewe Exposed	5.3
Lambs Reared Per Ewe Exposed	15.2
Weight of Lamb Weaned Per Ewe Exposed	17.8

Table 17-2. Effects of Hybrid Vigor in Crossbred Lambs. (From: Breeding Programs for Profit, D.R. Notter, Department of Animal Science, Virginia Polytechnic Institute, 1981.)

Table 17-3

HETEROSIS EFFECTS (EWES)

Trait	Level of Heterosis (%)
Fertility	8.7
Prolificacy	3.2
Body Weight	5.0
Fleece Weight	13.4
Lamb Birth Weight	5.1
Lamb Weaning Weight	6.3
Lamb Survival Birth to Weaning	2.7
Lambs Born Per Ewe Exposed	11.5
Lambs Reared Per Ewe Exposed	14.7
Weight of Lamb Weaned Per Ewe Exposed	18.0

Table 17-3. Effects of Hybrid Vigor in crossbred ewes. (From: Breeding Programs for Profit, D.R. Notter, Department of Animal Science, Virginia Polytechnic Institute, 1981.)

A program of genetic selection is complicated by the fact that some genes are expressed by the appearance of the animal, such as hair color or horns, and some are not. Dominant genes cover up recessive genes for the same character. To further complicate matters, recessive genes (especially an undesirable recessive) may not show until after several generations. Recessive genes can appear only when 2 animals that both carry them happen to mate. Even then, on the average, only 1 out of 4 of their offspring will be homozygous for the recessive gene and thus show it.

Cryptorchidism (when only 1 testicle descends into the scrotum) and black wool are examples of recessive genes. When these traits appear, you can be certain that both the sire and the dam contributed to the condition, and that each parent carries the recessive gene. You can prevent that recessive from showing up by using an unrelated ram of the same breed (outcrossing) or by crossbreeding with a ram of a different breed. Producers who strive for genetic quality in purebred flocks must try to eliminate undesirable recessive genes by culling any rams or ewes known to carry the recessives. You must cull all the normal, as well as abnormal, offspring of these rams and ewes because they also could be carrying the undesirable recessive genes.

Inbreeding increases the genetic uniformity of the lines or families. It increases the degree of homozygosity within the group so that the offspring are more homozygous or pure for the desirable traits. Two inbred lines when outcrossed will give superior results.

It is estimated that purebreds normally become more homozygous by .5 to .25 percent per animal per generation. Animals that have been inbred as a means of fixing and perpetuating certain desirable characteristics, are said to have *prepotency*. A prepotent animal possesses genetic dominance and homozygosity in its genetic makeup, and there is a fairly predictable genetic outcome in its offspring. The offspring of a prepotent ram resemble both their sire and each other more closely than the offspring of an average ram. Wide variation among offspring illustrates a more heterozygous condition in the ram and/or ewes. This illustrates the point that any purchase of purebred stock should be based on the production records of all the siblings of the stock under consideration and not on the records of just a few exceptional individuals.

Purebreeding usually is desirable only in a commercial sheep operation where only one breed is well adapted to the specific environmental conditions. An example of this is the large Rambouillet flocks in Texas, which are well-adapted to a hot arid environment.

CROSSBREEDING AND HETEROSIS (HYBRID VIGOR)

Crossbreeding is the mating of animals of different breeds. It allows the producer to combine the strengths of 2 or more breeds to create individuals who are superior to the average of 1 or both parents. Crossbreeding may be done to mate individuals whose traits complement each other. The increase in performance that is usually found in crossbred animals over the average of the purebred parents is called *heterosis*, or hybrid vigor.

The effects of heterosis are very broad and are important in the performance of rams, ewes, and lambs. Heterosis is usually the largest for the traits that are least heritable (the traits that are least likely to respond well to genetic selection). For example, in Table 17-2, heterosis for carcass traits (which are highly heritable) is about 0, while heterosis for survival from birth to weaning (which has low heritability) is 9.8 percent.

From Tables 17-2 and 17-3 it can be seen that the effects of heterosis are cumulative and multiplicative. In Table 17-2, the heterosis values for weaning weight, survival rate, and lambing rate have a combined effect to increase the weight of lamb weaned by 17.8 percent. In the crossbred ewe (Table 17-3), the heterosis values for fertility, prolificacy, lamb survival, and weaning weight combine to give increased heterosis values for number of lambs born, number of lambs weaned, and weight of lamb weaned. When a crossbred ewe raising a crossbred lamb is compared to a purebred ewe raising a purebred lamb, the weight of lamb weaned per ewe in the crossbreeding system is 35 percent greater than purebred production due to the cumulative effect of heterosis. The greatest heterosis effect is obtained with 3-way crossbred ewes mated to a fourth breed of ram for market lamb production.

A composite breed such as the Polypay (developed from a 4-way cross of the Rambouillet, Targhee, Finn, and Dorset) exhibits breed complementarity which is essentially fixed or maintained by inbreeding. This has the advantage that a single flock raising its own ewe replacements can have the advantages of crossbred ewes without having to maintain several distinct breeds. Two-way and three-way composite breeds include the Columbia, Corriedale, Montadale, Coopworth, and Perendale.

Chapter 18

ACCELERATED LAMBING

Accelerated lambing is the most promising approach to maximizing income from a sheep flock because reproductive efficiency has the greatest impact on profitability. Cutting costs is also a key to profitability; but in many sheep operations, there is little opportunity to reduce costs further. The sheep producer must pay competitive wages and has the same fuel cost, property taxes, and interest rates as any other livestock farmer. Low lamb prices and the high cost of farmland have slowed expansion of individual flocks, thereby reducing the opportunity to achieve greater economies of scale. The best option to improve profitability in many sheep operations is to increase the number of lambs born per ewe and/or accelerate the frequency of lambing from the usual 12 months to 7 or 8 months.

BENEFITS OF
ACCELERATED LAMBING

Accelerated lambing has the potential to do the following:

- **Provide a more uniform supply of lamb and cash flow throughout the year**
- **Make more efficient use of existing facilities**
- **Reduce the risk of harsh weather or disease outbreaks affecting the entire lamb crop**
- **Even out seasonal peaks in required labor**
- **Permit reinvestment from the sale of 1 lamb crop into another in the same year**
- **Increase the total pounds of lamb produced per ewe per year**

The primary obstacle to accelerated lambing is the seasonal breeding habit of most sheep breeds. While there may be some individuals in all breeds that will breed out of season, the majority will not. Sheep breeds and individuals must be selected for their out-of-season breeding ability, or they have to be induced to breed by means of hormones and/or controlled daylengths (discussed in Chapter 19). Most sheep, unlike dairy cows, will not breed during lactation.

FACTORS AFFECTING SUCCESS

A successful accelerated lambing scheme depends on:

- **Selecting breeds or strains within a breed**
- **Selecting the best breeding and lambing dates for your area to take advantage of seasonal forage growth**
- **Using a breed with a long breeding season**
- **Ability of ewes to breed during lactation (rare)**
- **Maintaining a short interval between lambing and the next breeding date**

The economic success of accelerated lambing depends primarily on the availability of low-cost feedstuffs at times of high feed demand.

The latitude or geographical location affects the time of the breeding season for ewes under natural daylength. Table 18–1 shows the percentage of ewes in estrus and the ovulation rate in mature Rambouillet sheep in Dubois, Idaho, and at McGregor, Texas, by month. This data clearly shows that geographic location – latitude and perhaps altitude – affects the time of the breeding season. Differences in daylength (with the change in latitude) are believed to be the main factor influencing the breeding season in sheep. Note that as we move towards a more constant daylength, the seasonal effect on fertility is much less. Native sheep from areas close to the equator which have relatively constant 12-hour daylengths have a long breeding season.

Selecting nonadapted sheep to breed out of season can be a long and fruitless experience. For example, the Morlam sheep, developed by the USDA in Beltsville, Maryland, were genetically selected for over 15 years in an attempt to obtain a group that would breed out of season. While selecting heavily for this characteristic, the selection program inadvertently disregarded milking ability. The sheep that would breed and lamb out of season did not have enough milk to make it a worthwhile practice.

Table 18-1

Month	% Ewes in Estrus		% Ewes Ovulating	
	Idaho	Texas	Idaho	Texas
January	100	100	100	100
February	100	100	100	94
March	89	40	94	52
April	26	38	32	32
May	2	31	2	31
June	7	44	7	75
July	6	94	6	94
August	12	86	41	100
September	88	94	100	94
October	100	94	94	100
November	100	97	100	91
December	100	100	100	100

Table 18-1.   The effect of time of breeding on estrus and ovulation in mature Rambouillet ewes in Idaho and Texas. Each statistic based on 30 to 32 observations.

Table 18-2

Lambing Periods Per Year	Lambing Interval		Lambings/Ewe/Year		Time Spent Lambing/Year	Common Name
	First Breeding Opportunity	Second Breeding Opportunity	Bred at First Opportunity	Bred at Second Opportunity		
	(mo)	(mo)	%	%	(days)	
1	12	24	1.0	.5	60+	Normal
2	6	12	2.0	1.0	120	Twice a Year
3	8	12	1.5	1.0	90	3 Lambings in 2 Years
5	7.2	9.7	1.67	1.25	140	STAR
6	6 or 8	10	2.0 or 1.5	1.20	180	CAMAL

Table 18–2. Comparison of accelerated lambing schemes and once a year lambing.

ACCELERATED LAMBING SCHEMES

Research on accelerated lambing schemes started in the 1960s, when a "3 lambings in 2 years" or 3-in-2 system was developed and promoted to sheep producers. This is the oldest and probably the most popular accelerated lambing scheme in use today.

3-in-2 System. In a 3-in-2 scheme, sheep are bred at 8-month intervals with breeding periods occurring in April, August, and December. The lambing periods are in January, May, and September. Usually the flock is split into 2 groups, each with an 8-month breeding interval. Ewes not bred on one 8-month interval can be switched to the next group, which results in a 12-month breeding interval for them.

Under a 3-in-2 scheme, Finn, Rambouillet, and Dorset and their crosses perform satisfactorily without hormone or controlled light treatments. Polypays have also performed satisfactorily on a 3-in-2 accelerated lambing scheme. The main advantage of a 3-in-2 scheme is that the ewes can be bred in the normal spring and fall breeding seasons, and there is no breeding in June or July when the percentage of ewes in estrus is very low.

The ewe has a gestation period of around 146 days, and a practical minimum age to wean her lambs is about 30 days. Thus, the theoretical maximum reproductive performance of an individual ewe would be to lamb twice in 1 year. Research has shown that the average lambing interval of ewes lambing in 2 consecutive intervals is around 200 days. A 200-day lambing interval allows no more than 50 to 55 days for weaning and breeding. Few ewes will be able to maintain a 200-day or 7-month lambing interval for more than 3 consecutive breedings before falling into a longer rebreeding period. A really productive ewe might lamb on a 7-7-9-month, 7-7-10-month, or 7-7-7-9-month interval breeding program.

At the Southwest Livestock and Forage Research Center in Ft. Reno, Texas, groups of Dorset, Rambouillet, and Dorset × Rambouillet sheep were lambed at 6-month and 8-month intervals. From the beginning, only 35 percent of the ewes exposed actually lambed in the fall. Of these, 80 to 85 percent bred for a spring lambing. Only 23 percent of the ewes lambing in the fall and spring got bred for another fall lambing. The average period from lambing to conception was 66 days for ewes lambing in 3 consecutive intervals. Weaning spring-born lambs at 30 days improved the number of ewes conceiving for fall lambing. However, the work at the Southwest Research Center showed that under practical conditions, these breeds cannot maintain a 6-month interval because of poor conception rates in spring-lambing ewes.

The Beltsville accelerated lambing scheme uses a 9-month interval, with 4 lambings in 3 years. Under this system, the ram is put with the ewes 4 months after lambing and every 3 months thereafter. Breeding occurs in May, August, November, and February for January, April, July, and October lambings. Two more intensive accelerated lambing schemes have been developed since the invention of the Beltsville system. These are the CAMAL system and STAR (Magee) system developed at Cornell University by Dr. Douglas Hogue and Brian Magee (Table 18-2).

CAMAL (Cornell Alternate Month Accelerated Lambing). This scheme strives for a 6-month lambing interval. Ewes are exposed every other month, giving them the opportunity to lamb on a 6-month, 8-month, or 10-month interval. The ewes may have a 6-10-8, 8-8-6, 10-6-8 interval, or any combination of these. Very few ewes actually achieve 3 consecutive 6-month intervals, but all the sheep have the opportunity to do so.

The CAMAL system requires exceptional management and accurate, economical group feeding to be successful. In practice, it is difficult to predict stages of pregnancy for proper feeding without separating out many groups of ewes and maintaining each as a breeding unit. It is also difficult to judge which ewes should be flushed, since any ewe could be flushed at the 6-month or 8-month interval and not actually get bred until 10 months.

Another problem with the CAMAL system is the need to wean the lambs at 30 days if a 6-month lambing interval is the objective. Under the CAMAL system, ewes in lactation for the typical 56-day period have to be exposed to the ram during lactation to obtain a 6-month interval. Lactating ewes exposed to the ram are at a nutritional disadvantage compared to ewes that are flushed and bred after weaning.

The STAR System. Brian Magee's revision of his original CAMAL system works on a 7.3-month interval. The year is divided into units consisting of half the average gestation period of 146 days. Half of 146 is 73 days and there are exactly five 73-day periods in a year. Three of these units make up the optimum reproductive cycle with the first two for gestation. The third 73-day period makes a comfortable lactation, weaning, and breeding period, an improvement over the 50 to 55 day period required in the CAMAL system. Under the STAR system, ewes have the opportunity to lamb at 7.3-month, 9.7-month, or 12-month intervals. Lactating ewes are not exposed to a ram, but weaning at 50 to 55 days is required to stay on a 7.3-month interval.

A ewe that completes the cycle perfectly will lamb 5 times in 3 years. Otherwise she slips to exactly 3 times in 2 years (two 7.3-month intervals and one 9.7-month interval).

The STAR makes a handy breeding wheel for this system (Figure 18–1). To quickly find the lambing period for an August 8 breeding, go around the wheel clockwise past 2 star points or half gestation periods to January 1. To find the next breeding period for this group of ewes, go to the next clockwise star point at March 15, a half gestation period later. Again follow around the wheel 2 star points to find

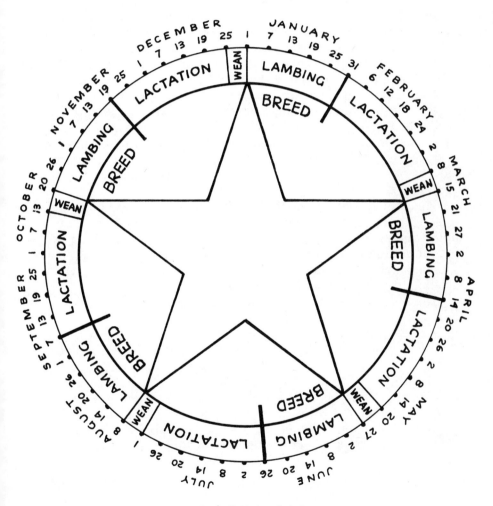

Figure 18–1. Cornell University's Star system.

the lambing period, August 8, which corresponds with a March 15 breeding. After the August lambing, these ewes will be exposed to the ram at the next star point or October 20. Continue around the star in this manner and the ewes will lamb exactly 5 times in 3 rotations.

Magee has found he needs only a 20-day breeding period during the natural peak breeding season (October to November) for high conception rates. The full 30-day breeding period is followed during the rest of the year. Currently, he is researching ways to synchronize ewes to shorten the lambing period. Since 1982 he has used a vasectomized (teaser) ram with purebred Finn ewes to synchronize them naturally. The vasectomized ram is put in with the breeding flock for 10 days prior to turning in the fertile ram. For the last 2 years, Magee reports his Finns exposed to a teaser ram in August were bred within a 3-day period and lambing in January lasted only a week.

Fertile rams that are capable of breeding out of season are essential under an accelerated lambing scheme. Magee keeps a record of a ram's potential fertility over the year with monthly measurements of the scrotal circumference. A change of ± 1 inch or more is an indication that the ram has a seasonal change in testes size and probably will not be as useful as a ram maintaining a constant scrotal circumference.

The 73-day periods in the STAR system allow lambing and breeding periods to coincide for ease of management. Most importantly, the late gestation period for bred ewes and the flushing period for unbred ewes coincide for ease in feeding. The first breeding is immediately after weaning, so ewes do not have to be bred while lactating to achieve a short lambing interval.

The sheep under the STAR system performed significantly better than those under the CAMAL system in terms of individual lambing percentages and annual lambing percentages. Much of this was due to the early weaning, which leaves the ewe in better body condition for breeding. As Magee points out, a shortened lambing interval combined with an increase in lambing percentage can be a powerful method of increasing yearly lambing rates. The system is a logical next step for breeders who are already on a 3–in–2 scheme and wish to reduce their 8-month breeding interval. They could accelerate to a 5–in–3 scheme without changing their existing breeding/weaning dates.

Chapter 19

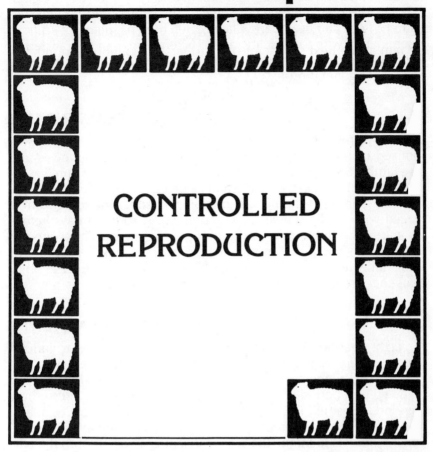

CONTROLLED REPRODUCTION

Controlling reproduction is necessary to increase the productivity and profitability of the farm flock. Inducing and synchronizing the estrous cycle in a group of ewes, as well as chemically inducing lambing, are often used to maintain an accelerated lambing program and are important in reducing labor costs at lambing time. This can be accomplished by natural means using a teaser ram or controlling daylength.

There are also chemical methods for synchronizing, as well as inducing, estrus in ewes, such as treatments with progestogen or prostaglandins. Chemical treatments to control reproduction have a greater degree of risk compared to natural methods and are recommended only when the producer has the management ability to use them properly.

Ewes also can be induced to superovulate, or release more eggs, and increase their lambing percentage. The highest performing ewes within a flock can be superovulated, then bred by means of artificial insemination with top-quality rams. The embryos can be transferred to other ewes to extend the number of genetically superior offspring in a single generation.

TEASER RAMS

Many producers regardless of the size of their flock use a vasectomized or teaser ram early in the season to encourage ewes and ewe lambs to start cycling. The sudden introduction of a ram (vasectomized or not) is often enough stimulation to induce estrus, especially at the beginning of the normal breeding season. One teaser ram is placed with 50 to 70 ewes (maximum) about 10 to 14 days before turning in the fertile rams. A majority of the ewes will get bred in the first heat cycle after using a teaser. A teaser makes good use of a cull ram who has displayed plenty of sex drive (libido) but has other traits that are undesirable.

LIGHT TREATMENTS

Light treatments can be used in small or large flocks to induce and to some extent synchronize estrus by controlling the ewes' exposure to daylength. A 4-month period of long (16-hour) days, followed by a period of short (8-hour) days is necessary. These short days induce estrus. This routine can be used to induce estrus at any time of the year and apparently works for all of our commercial breeds. The intention is to mimic the seasonal light changes prior to the natural, fall breeding season.

If sheep are to be bred during a time when the natural daylength is short (December to January), estrus may be induced by turning lights on at either or both ends of the day to give 16 hours of light per day during the fall to simulate long days. After 3 to 4 months of the long days, expose the sheep to naturally short days in December and they should start cycling. This has the advantage that any barn can be used. Otherwise a barn is needed that can be completely darkened in order to simulate the short days.

During the light period each day, the ewes can be let outside for natural light or kept under artificial lights. The natural broad spectrum of wavelengths of light can be approximated with the use of high-pressure mercury lamps or a combination of "warm" white and "cool" white fluorescent lamps. A moderate amount of light is necessary to achieve a physiological response in the ewes, specifically 247 lux measured 3 feet above the floor. Dim lights can be turned on for night-time lambing inspections with little or no disruption of the program. Long days can be simulated by turning lights on between 4:00 and 10:00 P.M. and between 6:00 and 8:00 A.M. in the northern states and Canada.

PROGESTOGEN INJECTIONS, IMPLANTS, AND SPONGES

Progesterone is a hormone secreted by ovarian tissue called the corpora lutea. It inhibits the estrous cycle. When the corporus luteum bursts at the onset of estrus, progesterone secretion stops and the ewe exhibits estrus and ovulates. Similarly, during pregnancy there is a slow but steady release of progesterone which inhibits estrus.

When progesterone or progesteronelike compounds (progestogens) are given by injection or implants or introduced through the use of intravaginal pessaries or sponges, they mimic pregnancy and ovulation stops. When the injections stop or the sponge is withdrawn, the majority of ewes will show estrus within a few days. There are 2 manufacturers of progesterone products: G. D. Searle and Co. and Tuco Pharmaceutical Co. The progestogens are more active chemically than the natural hormone.

After removing the progestogen sponges, 65 to 75 percent of the treated dry ewes will breed at the first estrus and 15 to 20 percent will breed in the second or follow-up estrus. Spring treatments, however, result in low conception rates of around 50 percent. This is due to seasonal anestrus and/or lactation anestrus in spring-lambing ewes. Also, very few spring-lambing ewes will breed in the follow-up estrus. However, these low conception rates can be partially overcome by weaning lambs early—at least 2 weeks before inserting sponges and by choosing breeds with a long breeding season.

The progestogens often are used in conjunction with an injection of Pregnant Mare Serum Gonadotropin (PMSG) which usually gives a more predictable and precise synchronization. PMSG also has a mild superovulatory effect, thus increasing the lambing percentage. It is probably not necessary to inject PMSG to ensure a fertile estrus if the ewes have been synchronized during the normal breeding season.

As a result of the use of progestogen injections or sponges, ewes can be both induced and synchronized to lamb over a 4-day to 5-day period. This saves labor, makes more efficient use of facilities if used for accelerated lambing, and produces groups of similar-aged lambs for marketing. It is essential that ewes be in good breeding condition for best results with this program.

PROSTAGLANDINS

Despite success with progestogen sponges to synchronize estrus, these products are not available to producers in the United States. In an effort to find an alternative, F. Schwulst and D. Simms at Kansas State University experimented with the use of a prostaglandin to synchronize estrus. Prostaglandins are a group of hormones and hormonelike substances that have the ability to control the length of ovulation and can stimulate contraction of uterine muscles.

In the experiment, ewes were injected intramuscularly with 3 cc of a commercial product containing 15 mg prostaglandin. During July breeding, 33 percent more ewes came into heat and were serviced by the ram during the first 4 days of breeding as a result of the treatment compared to the number of untreated ewes bred in the control group. In a September breeding, the prostaglandin treatment resulted in 30.5 percent more ewes in heat and serviced by the ram during the first 4 days of breeding. In the treated group, 46.9 percent of all ewes lambed during the first week compared to 26.3 percent of the control group. Prostaglandins are only effective at synchronizing estrus in ewes and ewe lambs that are cycling normally.

INDUCED LAMBING

Prostaglandins are also a factor in normal lambing, or parturition, but have been found to be ineffective at inducing delivery before day 140 of gestation. Experiments also have been conducted with the corticosteroids, such as flumethasone, to induce parturition. Flumethasone treatment resulted in a high percentage of ewes lambing within 72 hours of the injection when given on day 141 of gestation. Slyter and Hoppe at the South Dakota State University reported that the use of flumethasone to induce parturition resulted in 45 out of 99 ewes lambing within 24 hours of treatment. The ewes had been synchronized at breeding time with prostaglandin. Flumethasone has been more successful than the other corticosteriods, dexamethasone, and betamethosone, or prostaglandins at inducing lambing.

MAINTAINING RAM FERTILITY

Most rams do not show a restricted breeding season, but do show seasonal variations in semen production and quality, as well as sexual activity. Exposing rams to short daylengths during the normal non-breeding season results in testicular growth, increased mating activity, and improved semen quality. The ram should be exposed to 8 hours of light per day for 10 weeks before breeding in the off-season. Exposure to short daylengths also has been shown to be useful for rams that will be used for semen collection. There is some evidence that regular (every other week) exposure (within sight and smell) to ewes in estrus also helps to maintain rams in breeding condition.

ARTIFICIAL INSEMINATION

Artificial Insemination (AI) permits some of the most outstanding bulls to be available to the average dairy producer for as little as $5 per service. Currently about 50 million sheep are bred artifically every year, mostly in the Soviet Union.

AI has been difficult to develop for sheep because there are no reliable indicators or visible signs when the ewe is in heat. Secondly, the ewe has a small and highly convoluted (folded) cervix that makes it difficult to deposit the semen directly into the uterus. In cattle, the AI technician palpates through the rectum to locate the cervix and to guide the semen straw into the uterus. In sheep, the inseminator must locate the cervix visually and then can deposit semen only into the external cervical opening or, if possible, the first cervical fold.

Most AI in sheep has been done with fresh, diluted semen. There is research underway to determine the best diluents and freezing and thawing procedures to use for frozen semen. This would give producers the full benefit of AI since frozen semen can be stored for years, shipped easily, and exported. Other advantages as a result of using AI include:

- **Increased availability and use of superior sires leading to more rapid genetic improvement**
- **Reduction in the number of rams needed, and thus in the cost of ram maintenance for the flock**
- **Less venereal-type diseases**
- **Elimination of infertile rams by collecting and analyzing semen samples**

The use of AI could be an important merchandising tool for American sheep breeders. Other countries might be able to "purchase" our rams by purchasing frozen semen. Currently there are severe limits on the export of live animals because of strict quarantines.

The disadvantages of AI include:

- **Cost**
- **Difficulty in detecting ewes in heat**
- **Need for a trained inseminator**
- **Rams must be trained for semen collection**

In addition, AI results in a reduced rate of pregnancies compared to natural service. The estimated percentage of pregnancies obtained in 1 heat cycle from natural service is about 85 percent; from AI using frozen semen, 55 percent. However, the *number of pregnancies* that are possible using AI is much greater than for natural service. For example, 1 ram should be able to breed 50 ewes naturally in 1 season. Using fresh semen from 1 ram, and assuming 50 percent of the semen is utilized and a 75 percent pregnancy rate, AI could result in 350 pregnancies. With frozen semen, 100 percent utilization of the semen (no spoilage) and a 55 percent pregnancy rate, the number of potential pregnancies from 1 ram is 1344.

EMBRYO TRANSFER

Embryo transfer (ET) is a procedure where fertilized eggs or embryos are surgically removed from a donor ewe soon after mating and placed in a recipient female who then becomes pregnant and later gives birth to the young. The main advantage of ET is that it can increase the number of offspring from an exceptional ewe. Ewes can be superovulated with hormones to produce many embryos that are suitable for transfer.

For embryo transfers to be successful, the donor and recipients must come into heat on the same day. This is possible with the use of progestogen sponges or prostaglandin. Other hormones can be used to superovulate the ewe so that she releases multiple eggs instead of the usual 1 to 3 eggs released during a single heat. On the average, superovulated ewes will produce up to 9 embryos suitable for transfer. Of these, about 70 to 80 percent should survive the transfer to produce lambs.

Both donor and recipient undergo surgery 4 to 7 days after the onset of heat. The uterus of the donor and recipient is reached through an incision just in front of the udder. Tubes are placed in the uterus of the donor and the uterus is flushed with a solution to remove the eggs. The eggs are examined and if they are normal, 1 to 3 eggs are placed in the uterus of 1 or more recipients. If the transfer is successful, the recipient ewe will lamb about 138 days after surgery. If all of the eggs are removed from the donor, she will be in heat again 10 to 15 days after surgery.

Surgeons who have considerable experience in ET usually can recover embryos 3 to 5 times from the same donor. However, it takes skill to recover and evaluate the eggs and to perform surgery in the reproductive tract. Sheep breeders who are considering ET should know whether the lambs produced will be worth significantly more than the cost of the procedure.

Embryo transfer and AI are new and exotic technologies in the sheep industry. Due to the limited number of veterinarians and technicians performing these techniques, the operations are very expensive, at least in the hundreds of dollars per ewe donating the embryos for transfer. No standard fees exist for AI or ET in this country.

Chapter 20

PRODUCTION RECORDS

Genetic progress has eluded many sheep breeders because they have not used production records for their long-term planning. Few breeders can outline their "5-year plan" or say what levels of production they hope to achieve. Their livestock production and health records are used primarily at weaning and breeding and to make short-term marketing decisions. But, producers should compare their records from one year to the next to see where and how much improvement occurred and what was the economic impact of their decisions.

Unfortunately, data from other flocks often is not available for drawing comparisons. It would be helpful if producers could compare the production of their flock with others of the same size, breeds, and age distribution.

The sheep industry has lagged way behind the dairy industry in standardizing production records. Standard production records enable comparisons between herds and individuals within the herd.

Dairy farmers have found that many comparisons, estimates, and projections can be generated from a few key numbers as long as there are a sufficient number of farms providing data to average and serve as benchmark figures. The creation of standard production records requires cooperation among farmers to agree on how the measurements are made. Our central ram performance testing programs are one place to standardize production records nationally.

The production records should be used to:

- **Identify productive ewes**
- **Identify ewes to cull**
- **Evaluate lamb performance**
- **Evaluate ram performance**
- **Assess the effect of management changes**
- **Provide information about the pedigree**
- **Support subjective evaluations with objective measures**

MEASUREMENTS

Very little, if any, selection emphasis should be placed on breed type and conformation in most flocks. Instead, selection should be based on the economic traits in which your breed already excels. The most profitable genetic improvement can be made after selecting for the economically important traits, rather than following fads in fashionable breed type. You can set minimum performance levels, and these can be updated annually. For breeding stock, there are about 10 to 20 actual factors to be concerned with:

- **Identification**
- **Birthdate**
- **Birth weight**
- **Birth type (single, twin)**
- **Sire, dam**
- **Sex**
- **Breeding date**
- **Breeding weight**
- **Weaning weight**
- **Weaning date**
- **Weight at 60, 90, 120, 180 days**
- **Wool weight**
- **Shearing date**
- **Height, length at 120 days**
- **Feed conversion**

These additional factors should be noted:

- **Assisted birth**
- **Milk supply and mothering ability of dam**
- **Lamb vigor**
- **Inherited defects**
- **Conformation and soundness**
- **Scrotal circumference**
- **Fleece quality**

RECORD FORMS

To be useful, measurements should be recorded on one of the available record forms. A barn record should be kept in the lambing area to record lambing information as the lambs are born. These forms are available from many breed associations and your state Cooperative Extension Service.

In addition to a barn record, many producers keep individual ewe production records. This may be nothing more than her registration papers, or it may include data on each of her lambs and all health treatments. Many prefer to keep health records in one diary, instead of on individual record forms, since most treatments (for example, worming, vaccinations, etc.) are done on a group basis.

Another aid to record keeping is the computerized on-farm production testing programs offered by several universities and farm services. There are at least 5 of these programs, recording data on about 7000 ewes in 20 states. The programs are low cost and provide great savings in time.

COMPUTERIZED PRODUCTION RECORDS

Perhaps the most widely known records system is Ohio State University's Sheep Production Testing Program. OSU has a low-cost, time-saving program that fits most purebred and commercial operations. Entries are made on a "field record sheet" for ewe identification, lamb identification, birthdates, birth weights, 90-day lamb weights, and fleece weights. There is also a coded "remarks" column about the ewe. This data (birth weights, 90-day lamb weights, etc.) is used to rank or index the ewes and lambs in the flock based on their production. The ewe index (one of the columns on the individual ewe record form) estimates the genetic value of each ewe based on the sum performance of average adjusted lamb weights, number of lambs born and how they were reared (as single, twin, etc.), and the fleece weight of the ewe. A ewe index ratio ranks the ewe against what is average for the flock. Similar figures are developed for lambs, where each lamb index includes the adjusted 90-day weight, multiple birth and type of rearing, and the fleece weight of the dam. The ewe index and lamb index numbers are especially valuable for selecting flock replacements or culling ewes that are below average for your flock. These indices are not used to compare your sheep with another flock.

The distinguishing characteristics of the OSU program are its emphasis on adjusted 90-day lamb weights and optional entries for lamb and wool quality evaluations. For example, the OSU program allows the sheep producer to specify the muscling and fat cover of the lamb on a scale of 1 to 6, 1 being "a loin deficient in muscling" and 6 representing "ideal." Four additional columns are provided in the field record sheet for evaluating the lamb's type, again on a scale of 1 to 6, where 1 is inferior and 6 is ideal. The producer can give a type score on the correctness of feet and legs and how well the head and general appearance conform to the standards for that breed.

Wool scores or codes include the dam's fleece weight, face cover, wool grade, and staple length. The muscling, fat cover, and wool scores do not enter into the figuring of the ewe or lamb indices. They are recorded only for your information. For more complete records, the producer can use 26 codes (A to Z) to describe any condition affecting records, such as "deformed lamb," "assisted in delivering lamb," "abnormal udder," or "ewe with chronic lameness."

There are some minor problems with the Ohio State program. One can question whether average producers can accurately determine wool grades and, if they could, whether they would use the information. The muscling and fat cover scores also are very subjective in measurement and hard to define under the 1 to 6 system. Ohio State's *Bulletin 452* which describes the sheep production testing program does not elaborate enough on these scores, leaving the producer to decide what a muscle score of "2," "3," "4," or "5" should be. However, these scores can be very useful if you are informed on how to evaluate them. Of course, they are also optional.

On the whole, the OSU program provides a good evaluation of the ewe based on the most important characteristics: prolificacy, rearing abilities, wool production, and performance of her lambs. In seconds, the computer can sort data by breed and age of ewes and print out an individual ewe report with a lifetime history. If the ewe has one or more lambing records on file, the program gives you a "Predicted Producing Value," which estimates her future level of performance. The program provides a system for the producer to make genetic selection of individuals, select families with the best performance, eliminate genetic defects, and so on.

For further information on the OSU Sheep Production Testing Program, write: Richard Smith, Extension Livestock Specialist, Ohio State University, 2029 Fyffe Road, Columbus, Ohio 43210.

The University of Wyoming sponsors an on-farm ram performance testing program for white-faced rams. They are evaluated for wool production and fleece quality. On-farm testing is possible through the use of an independent wool testing laboratory which evaluates fleece samples for fiber diameter (grade) and clean wool production. Producers weigh yearling rams at their first shearing and bag each fleece separately. The fleece is identified and submitted to the university along with the birthdate, birth type, and shearing date of the ram. Body weight and clean fleece weight are adjusted to a 365-day basis, and this information with the fiber diameter measurement are provided to the breeder. These data form an objective basis for selection based on wool quality and quantity and can be incorporated into the breeder's evaluation of staple length, wool character (color, crimp, etc.), and uniformity of grade, along with wool cover over the face and conformation of the ram.

Chapter 21

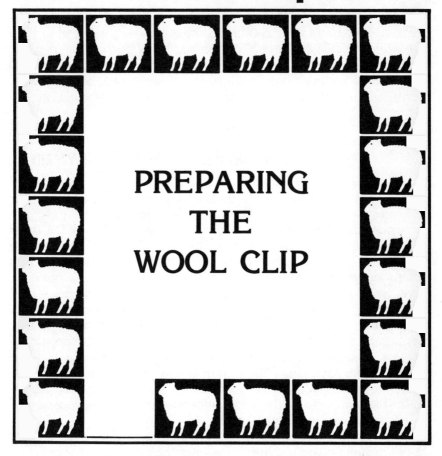

PREPARING THE WOOL CLIP

Wool is an amazing raw material which has no equal among a wide spectrum of natural and synthetic fibers. It is a renewable product with unique properties of bulk, elasticity, and absorption. Wool fibers can be stretched repeatedly, as much as 30 percent more than their normal length or compressed into a tight ball, and yet they will quickly recover to a normal size and shape.

Wool can absorb up to 30 percent of its own weight in water before it begins to feel damp. Wool garments soak up body perspiration and keep the wearer feeling warm and dry. Textile technology has produced wool clothing that is machine washable, machine dryable, permanently creased, permanently pleated, and mothproofed.

Approximately 6 billion pounds of raw wool from about 1 billion head of sheep and over 200 breeds of sheep are produced around the world. This yields about 3.7 billion pounds of clean (scoured) wool. Our domestic clip is about 110 million pounds of greasy wool annually. Farm income from wool is derived from the sale of ewes' wool, lambs' wool, pelts, and government wool incentive payments.

WOOL INCENTIVE PAYMENTS

The USDA sets an incentive price level for wool each year, based on the costs of sheep production, labor, interest, etc. Then the USDA averages the price paid for all wool sold in the United States for the previous year. To arrive at the incentive payment, the USDA takes the percentage difference between the price it set and the average price paid the previous year and applies this percent to the price that the producer received this year. For example, if the USDA incentive level is set at $1.21 per pound and the average national price paid was only $1.00 per pound, it would take $.21 per pound to bring the price up to the incentive level. The $.21 per pound is 17.4 percent of the $1.21 incentive level. Therefore, the producer would receive 17.4 percent of the price at which he or she sold the wool as the incentive payment. If the producer can sell the wool at a higher price, he or she will receive a larger incentive payment in addition to the high price. Thus, there is an incentive to improve wool quality in order to receive a higher price.

An incentive payment also is paid on unshorn lambs that are sold. Wool producers are required to submit their original receipts from any sale of wool or unshorn lambs during the previous year to the local USDA Agricultural Stabilization and Conservation Service (ASCS) office. In 1982, nearly 90,000 producers filed for wool incentive payments.

WOOL BREEDING PROGRAMS

Many small flock owners have neglected selection programs aimed at increasing wool production and quality. The main reason is that wool receipts are only a small portion of the lamb receipts. Also, annual wool production per head is inversely correlated with lamb growth rate, reproductive rate, milk production, and desirable carcass characteristics. Selecting for these latter traits has been more profitable than selecting individuals based on their wool clip. Most traits contributing to wool production are highly heritable so significant progress could be made through genetic selection.

Currently our wool breeding programs could be improved by:

- **Selectively breeding for wool** *and* **maternal traits, such as prolificacy and milk production by using a selection index (Chapter 17)**
- **Obtaining objective performance data for wool quality in rams (Chapter 19)**
- **Objectively measuring fleece characteristics**
- **Providing premiums for good wool preparation**
- **Discounting the price for poor quality wool**

WHEN TO SHEAR

Most sheep are shorn in the spring a few weeks before a March 1st/April 1st lambing. Winter-born lambs are shorn in May or June to keep them comfortable through the summer. Feeder lambs usually are shorn as they enter the feedlot in the fall. There is no rule about when to shear; it depends on the environment, lambing schedule, and, sometimes, the availability of a shearer.

Shearing ewes about 1 month prior to fall breeding can increase feed intake for ewes on pasture and may improve the flushing effect. Custom shearers usually are available in late summer, and the weather conditions are more pleasant than in late winter and early spring. The ewes will grow a protective cover of wool by winter yet will not require crutching (shearing around the vulva and udder) prior to lambing. It is also easy to treat sheep for external parasites in the late summer. In winter, the parasites often become more numerous when sheep are kept together in confinement, and it is easier for spray solutions to freeze. The ewes are in full fleece over the summer if shorn in early fall. However, the wool insulates them from extreme heat as well as extreme cold.

There are advantages to shearing a few weeks before lambing, though. You can see the ewe's body condition more easily. There are also no dirty tags of wool for lambs to suck on. Some producers even shear 3 weeks before lambing in midwinter.

Advantages of Winter Shearing

- A greater number of ewes can be housed at lambing, making better use of the facilities.
- Shorn ewes move to protected areas more readily, taking their lambs with them. They also move more readily to protected areas to lamb.
- Some sheep ticks or "keds" are eliminated with the fleece or die from exposure to winter temperatures on the shorn sheep.
- Ewes in short fleece hold less snow and moisture, keeping the barn drier.

Disadvantages of Winter Shearing

- Newly shorn sheep require 10 to 15 percent more energy than sheep with at least 2 inches of wool.
- Newly shorn sheep are more susceptible to temperature fluctuations and cold, wet weather for the first 30 days after shearing.
- Cold weather is hard on the shearer unless there's a heated shearing area.
- Wet wool (moisture content over 12 percent) dries slowly in cold weather and can mold in storage.

PREPARATIONS AT SHEARING TIME

Regardless of when you shear, you must take certain steps to enable the shearer to work efficiently, to minimize stress on the sheep, and to protect the fleece as it comes off. It is your responsibility to have adequate labor available at shearing time and to make sure the sheep are penned and dry so the shearer can work quickly. It is the shearer's responsibility to remove the fleece in 1 piece with a minimum of second shearing cuts.

If the sheep are housed and become damp, let them run out in the open for an hour or so to dry out the fleece. The holding area should not be bedded (it is preferable to have a slatted floor) if the sheep are to be in the area long enough to lie down. Keep the shearing floor clean. A rough wood floor provides good footing and is easy to sweep clean. The shearing area should be at least 8 feet wide (10 is better) from the catch pens. The shearing room or shed should permit the easy entry of sheep from catch pens to the shearing floor. Provide adequate lighting, electrical outlets, good ventilation, and wool bag stands.

The shearer should shear the black-faced and colored sheep last, to avoid contaminating white wool with black fibers on the floor. Skirting the fleeces by removing the dirty tags and belly wool can be done more effectively and economically by the shearer than by a worker at a table. Skirting usually will remove 1 to 1½ pounds of wool, approximately 1 pound of belly wool and ½ pound of crutchings or tags. Skirting can increase the yield of clean wool by 3 percent or more.

Photo 21–1. An inexpensive wool bag holder that does not take up floor space.

You or your assistant should take each fleece from the shearer and drop it skin-side down on a slatted sorting table. The table is slatted to permit second cuts to fall through. If the fleece is to be tied, roll it with the flesh side out and the shoulder wool outermost for fleece evaluation. Rolling the fleece inside-out provides a brighter, more attractive package than leaving the weathered side out. Try not to roll the fleeces too tightly. They should have a lofty appearance. At the same time, grade the fleece and place it (tied or loose) in a burlap wool sack. If the fleeces are to be tied, use only paper twine, other fibers can contaminate the wool. Do not tie lambs' fleeces or other fleeces with short-staple wool since they will not hold together.

Pack down the wool sack after every couple of fleeces to make a dense bale. A small handful of wool in the 4 corners of the wool sack can be tied off with twine to make handles. A full wool sack or bag will hold about 250 pounds of wool; a wool "bale" formed under hydraulic pressure will hold about twice as much. Bagged wool should be stored off the floor in a clean, dry area. Mark each bag using paint brands or a livestock crayon with your name, bag number, weight, and type of wool. A minimum level of grading separates the following types of wool:

- **White, clean, long-staple**
- **Lambs' wool and short-staple**
- **Burry or seedy**
- **Black and colored**
- **Tags, floor sweepings**

Small amounts of tags and floor sweepings can be composted in the manure spreader, if there is no demand for them from wool buyers.

WOOL CONTAMINATION

Protecting wool quality is an on-going process that involves practically all aspects of sheep management—nutrition, housing, pasture maintenance, breeding, identification, etc. Your main objective is to keep the wool clean; this means no weed seeds, burrs, stains, foreign fibers, or heavy manure tags in the fleece.

A major contamination problem is due to synthetic fibers— polypropylene, polyethylene, polyester, nylon, etc.—which get into raw wool. Much of the contamination comes from plastic baling twine and plastic feed bags which are common on livestock farms. These materials find their way into the fleece when the twine is left on the floor of the barn, or it gets chopped up with the hay as it is put into a feed grinder, or it is left hanging on hay feeders and fence posts. The synthetics do not absorb yarn dye and stand out in yarn or woolen cloth. When the woolen cloth is heat-pressed, the synthetics melt out, leaving holes in the fabric. A little plastic contamination can cause a significant economic loss when found in woolen fabrics worth $60 to $100 a yard.

Vegetable matter, such as weed seeds, straw, and chaff, is a contaminant that is normally removed in the scouring and combing process at the woolen mill. Combing also removes short fibers called *noils*. Separating the vegetable matter from noils requires carbonizing, where the wool is immersed in dilute sulphuric acid or an ammonium chloride solution. Carbonization is a costly process for wool processors and results in a further weight loss of about 10 percent from the raw wool.

Paint brands and livestock marking crayons contaminate the wool to varying degrees. Some formulations scour out better than others. In general, do not use paints on the best wool on the back or sides of the sheep; use paints on the nose or poll (top of the head). Large, double-sided plastic ear tags are highly visible from a distance of 30 feet and eliminate the need for paint branding. For temporary identification, use carpenter's chalk instead of livestock crayons and mark the poll instead of the back.

GRADING

Wool grading can be done on the farm, at a wool sale by a broker or marketing agent, or by an independent testing laboratory. You can separate sheep according to their wool type at shearing time and bag fleeces by type or grade. The greasy or scoured wool can be graded professionally at a later time for the woolen mill. More wool is sold by objective grade measurements than by visual appraisal; and several wool testing laboratories will perform wool grade measurements for farmers.

Wool grades depend on the diameter of the fiber. When talking about the quality of the wool, graders are discussing how clean the wool is and the feel of it—soft, dry and coarse, etc. The United States has 14 wool grades based on the average fiber diameter and variation in fiber diameter. The average diameter or thickness of wool fibers ranges from a low of 17.7 microns to 40 microns (a micron is 1/25,000 inch).

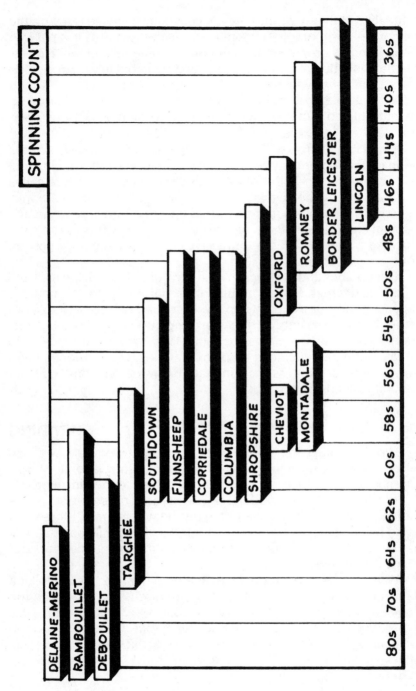

Figure 21–1. Grades of wool by sheep breeds.

Blood Grades

Under the blood grade system, wool is divided according to how far it deviates from that of a purebred Merino, which has the finest wool of any commercial breed. Thus, a ¼-blood wool is similar to that which would come from ¼ Merino sheep. Of course, with a normal variation in wool grades within the Merinos, this is not a very uniform or objective system of grading. The blood system is used very little in the wool industry now, having been replaced by the spinning count and, more recently, by micron measurement.

Spinning Count

Spinning count is based on the number of hanks (560 yards = 1 hank) of yarn that can be spun from 1 pound of scoured wool. It divides wool into 14 grades according to the thickness or diameter of the average fibers in the fleece. For example, fine wool can be spun into longer, finer yarn and has a high spinning count.

The micron measurement objectively measures fiber diameter with a testing instrument. There are 16 grades used in this system, from 18 to 39 microns in diameter. This corresponds to a spinning count of 80s to 36s. Some common breeds of sheep and their wool grades are shown in Figure 21-1.

FLEECE EVALUATION

To evaluate a fleece, obtain a sample from the shoulder or the side. The wool there should be fairly representative of the whole fleece. On a live animal, part the wool at the base of the shoulder, down to the skin, and cut off a lock of wool with hand shears. Hold the flesh end of the sample with the thumb and index finger of one hand. Hold the weathered end with thumb and index finger of the other hand. Gently straighten the wool while trying to keep the natural crimp or wave in the fiber. Measure the length of the staple. Then carefully separate some of the fibers. Ask yourself the following questions.

Do The Fibers Separate Easily Or Are They Matted? Matted fleeces are hard to comb and are worth less.

Is the Wool Soft and Springy? Softness is due primarily to fine fibers and is highly desirable. Crimp gives springiness and bulk to the wool. It is the characteristic that gives good shape retention to a knitted garment, resilience to a carpet pile, and high insulating quality to a sweater. A tight crimp is good. A uniform crimp in the fiber means easier spinning with less breakage.

Is Your Wool a True White, Yellow, Gray, or Other Color? White wool produces more consistent colors in dyed yarn. Very little scoured wool is a true white, but wool growers select towards white. Most wool is an ivory or creamy white color when scoured.

Are There Weed Seeds, Dirt, Manure Or Other Fibers Present? Contaminants may increase weight but lower the value of the fleece.

Stretch the Wool Until It Breaks. Are There Any Weak Areas in the Fiber? Some fleeces have distinct areas where the fiber thins out or is weak. Uniformity in staple length and freedom from weak areas (breaks) are desirable. A break may be due to fever or nutritional stress, often at lambing. The length of staple in a fleece with a break is determined by the length of the longest portion left from the break, not the total length. Breaks, second cuts, and short wools increase the percentage of noils (wastiness) and strength of the clip.

The most economically important wool characteristics are fineness, fineness variation, grease fleece weight, and yield of clean wool after scouring. Staple length and crimp have less effect on the value of the wool clip but are still important.

The fiber diameter varies over the areas of the body. The shoulders and sides have wool with the best length, strength, and fineness. Wool from the back usually is slightly shorter, weaker, and coarser than the sides. Wool from the britch or hind end is often coarser and stained. Belly wool is short, tender (weaker), matted, stained, and contains more vegetable matter. Leg wool (below the hocks and knees) is short and usually contains an excessive amount of hair.

Fiber diameter also varies with the sheep's nutrition. Wool produced when feed is short is finer than when feed is plentiful. The fiber diameter and standard deviation in microns can be determined by a micron test at a wool testing laboratory. They will send directions on how to obtain a representative sample from a fleece.

Fleece weights and staple length records should be maintained in both commercial and purebred flocks. Purebreed sheep producers can use micron evaluation to select prospective stud rams for their breeding programs. In the future, most rams, particularly of the fine wool breeds, will be sold with performance data that includes yearling fleece weight, staple length, micron measurement, and uniformity of grade. This will be adopted when the wool industry begins to pay a higher premium for a uniform clip.

MARKETING WOOL

You can market your wool through local dealers, wool pools, cooperative and private warehouses, and direct sales to manufacturers.

The most prestigious wool clips are the reputation clips and territory wools with characteristic yield and grade. A reputation clip granted by the wool buyers is earned by a breeder over years of sheep producing and is a mark of stability in his or her operation. Most of the reputation clips are sold as "original bag" lots because at least 85 percent of the wool falls into a single grade classification. These clips come from large flocks which follow a consistent breeding pattern. Territory wools earn a reputation for a certain quality and appearance depending on where the sheep are raised. Some territory wools are known by the color of the soil that gets into the fleece and gives it a characteristic color and yield.

Wool Prices

Wool is priced by a simple formula. The clean wool price multiplied by the percent yield equals the price for the raw or grease wool. The grease wool price less marketing charges is the net receipt to the grower. Wool marketing charges include transportation, storage, sampling and grading, and handling and commission fees. There is a trend towards marketing wool by graded lots and using micron measurement for determining grade. About 75 percent of the New Zealand wool is sold at auction pretested and graded. This way, the wool grower and buyer have a better idea of the value of the wool before it goes into the auction.

Marketing to Handspinners

Handspinners can be a rewarding market for clean, well-prepared fleeces. Select fleeces from large sheep with a long-stapled, heavy fleece. The handspinner, like the commercial mill, wants uniform grade in the fleece and clean wool. Shear carefully, skirt, roll, and tie each fleece. Label each fleece with the weight (although wool will change weight as it loses or picks up moisture), breed, and date sheared.

Favorite breeds for handspinners have medium to coarse grade wool. They prefer to spin a fleece within a few months of shearing or before the lanolin begins to harden and the fleece loses moisture. If you have to store a fleece, keep it in a cool place. Handspinning fleeces can be the basis of a mail-order business that generates many long-term customers, who depend on quality and who want wool with unusual color, luster, curl, or softness.

Chapter 22

BUSINESS MANAGEMENT

Farm management is the use of land, labor, and capital to operate the farm in the most profitable way. Even as a small, part-time farmer, you must keep accurate records, control costs, and be responsible for decisions that affect the profitability of your farm. Records on both finances and production are the basic tools of a profit-motivated manager.

USES FOR FINANCIAL RECORDS

- **To make decisions on what to buy or sell, what kind of feeding program, whether to expand the business, etc.**
- **To obtain credit**
- **To report income taxes**
- **To set up business agreements, such as partnerships, corporations, leasing, etc.**
- **To transfer the estate**

Records reveal the strong and weak points in the business and permit comparisons between similar farm operations. For records to be useful, they must be accurate and complete. It is a good idea to keep your records in a convenient spot where they are easy to pull out and use regularly.

FARM RESOURCE INVENTORY

A farm inventory is a list of what a farmer owns and what he or she owes at a given time, with values attached to each item. It is usually made at the end of the year (as close to December 31 as possible). The inventory is the basis of the Net Worth Statement, which will be described later. It is also necessary for developing depreciation schedules for buildings, machinery, and livestock.

To make an inventory, list everything of value that you own or owe with its dollar value (the value if you had to sell out or liquidate the business). This includes not only land, buildings, equipment, livestock, and supplies, but also cash (on hand and in bank accounts or securities), money owed to you (notes and accounts receivable), and what you owe (accounts payable, rent, taxes, interest, insurance).

A comprehensive farm resource inventory includes livestock registration or eartag numbers, serial numbers of equipment, automobile registration numbers, and other positive means of identification. An inventory is fairly easy to assemble and a good starting point if you have never kept business records.

ACCOUNTING METHODS

Obviously you must maintain income and expense records, although for some this is nothing more than the checkbook register. The checkbook is a very limited method for keeping track of farm accounts. For example, your checkbook will not include cash transactions, volume accounts (tons of grain, number of lambs, etc.), or totals of categorized expense items. It is useful, though, to keep separate checking accounts for your farm business and for family living because each operates under different tax rules.

Cash Accounting Method

There are 2 basic accounting methods: cash and accrual. The cash method keeps track of all income actually received and all expenses actually paid during the year. Cash receipts less cash expenses equals net operating income (or net operating loss). The net cash income figure tells you nothing about the farm's overall profitability. That requires a method of keeping track of inventory as well. Under the cash accounting method, inventories are ignored.

The advantage of cash accounting is that it is easy to maintain because only cash records need to be kept. Also, most farms report on a cash basis for income tax purposes. On the farm income tax statement, only cash income and expenses and the depreciation for that year are used to calculate net income.

The main disadvantage of cash accounting is that it does not provide a full picture of business activity because it ignores accounts receivable (money owed you as yet unpaid; for example, yarn or freezer lamb orders) and payable (bills not yet paid; for example, grain or fertilizer bills).

Accrual Accounting Method

The accrual method figures in the accounts receivable and payable and the changes in the inventory on hand with the cash receipts and expenses. It is useful for cash crop farmers who have major sources of income tied up in storable commodities (including wool). Under cash accounting, the crops in storage do not appear as income until they are actually sold. Wool brokers are inclined to use the accrual method since they may accumulate large wool inventories when prices are low.

The cash method of accounting allows great flexibility since agricultural products, such as grain or wool, can be stored and sold a year later to defer income if the farmer had a highly profitable year. Similarly, advance purchases of fertilizer, supplies, or equipment can be made to offset profits or taxable income. Other businesses have to use inventory methods when production, purchase, or sales of merchandise are the main factor of income.

Bookkeeping Methods

Both methods of accounting can be maintained under single-entry or double-entry bookkeeping. Single-entry bookkeeping is the most widely used by farmers because it closely approximates the way business is conducted and is the simpler to maintain. Single-entry systems divide all business transactions into 2 categories: income and expense. It records the flow of operating income and expenses and summarizes them on an appropriate basis (weekly, monthly, year-to-date, etc.). Single-entry systems do not keep track of assets and liabilities. This information must be kept separately to get a complete picture of the farm's financial position.

The double-entry system got its name from the process of making 2 entries for each transaction — the initial entries go into a journal where they are summarized. The totals are then entered in ledgers. Ledger accounts in the double-entry system track income, expenses, assets (or all that is owned), liabilities (or debts on all that is owned), and net worth (total assets less total liabilities). The system can show the true profit or loss since cash as well as non-cash assets and liabilities are recorded. Making entries twice — into journals and ledgers — has the advantage of building in a system of checks and balances that ensures accuracy. For the most part, farmers choose a double-entry system if they need to keep track of their net worth more accurately than is possible with a single-entry system. This is important information for lenders.

FINANCIAL RECORDS

The easiest way to keep income and expense records is with a "farm account book," a single-entry, cash accounting ledger book. These are available from the Extension Service for a few dollars. The farm account book permits a listing of all cash transactions, capital purchases, capital sales, and the totals of each income and expense category. The arithmetic has to be done by hand, which is slow, but it is a cheap and easy-to-use system.

Electronic Accounting Systems for Farmers

Most farmers find little time for keeping their financial records, which is probably the main reason they have been quick to adopt computerized record keeping services. There are several electronic farm accounting services available, such as Agrifax (offered by the Production Credit Association), Profile (Agway, a Northeast farmer's cooperative), and ELFAC (from the Cooperative Extension Service), which can have a different name in different areas of the country.

Founded in 1962, ELFAC (Electronic Farm Accounting) serves hundreds of farmers in the Northeast with monthly reports. A similar service called CAMIS is available to New York farmers through Cornell University. ELFAC is a nonprofit organization designed to help farmers keep better records and to help them use their records to make management decisions. Information from any individual farm is kept confidential, and the farmer is under no obligation – he or she can send as much or as little information as desired. ELFAC is also inexpensive, since local and state taxes help pay for the County Extension agents and Extension farm management specialists who enroll farms onto the system and help educate farmers on how to use their records.

All of the major computerized record keeping services can handle sheep enterprises, as well as field crops, Christmas trees, honey, small fruits and vegetables, etc. With some services, non-farm (home) income and expenses are included at no extra charge and a summary can be prepared for income tax purposes.

Computerized record keeping services do save time for the average farmer. Data is entered by hand using single-entries, and the data sheets are mailed away to be processed by the computer. There is no arithmetic, sorting, typing, or compiling required. The computer does all of the tedious time-consuming work, leaving the producer this extra time to devote to better management.

A farm with 100 ewes might make 25 to 50 farm entries per month, roughly equivalent to the number of checks written and receipts received each month. The annual fee for comprehensive farm computerized records on ELFAC is:

Base fee per farm	$35.00
Enterprise fee @ $ .25	
per ewe × 100 ewes	25.00
Total	$60.00

Of course the more sheep a producer has, the lower the cost per ewe since the $35 base fee is for any size farm. Assuming that a well-managed 100-ewe flock is probably grossing $8000 to $12,000 per year, allocating $60 for financial records can be justified easily. The time saved in preparing income taxes also can help justify the cost of electronic farm accounting. Another advantage to computerized records is that they are permanently on record at the data processing center. Should your records be lost, you can send for copies.

Production records should be kept on livestock and crops. Livestock records are covered in Chapter 19. Crop records should include soil test results and recommendations, fencing plans, and soil conservation service maps. Labor records also should be kept. These include a job description, hours or days worked, wages and benefits paid, and Social Security payments, if required.

ECONOMIC CONCEPTS

Understanding a couple of economic concepts is useful when putting together and analyzing financial records. These concepts are the opportunity cost of doing business and the variable versus the fixed costs of the business.

Opportunity Cost

Opportunity cost is the return that could have been received from the next most profitable use of the farm's resources (land, labor, capital). The farmer asks: "What opportunity for this land am I giving up by raising sheep?" or, "If these funds were not invested in this sheep farm, what could they be invested in and what rate could they earn in this other use?"

Here are some examples of opportunity costs to help define the concept further.

- **The opportunity cost to you of producing homegrown feed is not its cost of production but its sale value or its value for some other use (whichever is greater). Charging homegrown feed to a livestock enterprise at the cost of production gives misleading results. You may make more money by selling the feed than by marketing it through your livestock.**

- **If you grow corn on a 20-acre field, you are giving up the opportunity to grow other crops there. The opportunity cost is the income sacrificed by not growing a more profitable crop, such as strawberries.**

- **The opportunity cost of the labor you put into the farm business is the salary that could be earned in another occupation.**

- **The opportunity cost for funds tied up in operating the farm (the variable expenses) is the interest that the funds could earn if invested elsewhere, such as in a certificate of deposit. This cost is included in the 100-ewe enterprise budget on page 256 as an interest charge on operating capital. Interest is also charged against capital items such as buildings and equipment and is the opportunity cost for having funds tied up in these fixed assets.**

From these examples, it should be clear that opportunity cost is only used for planning and not as an actual cash cost to be recorded in financial records. However, it is useful to compare alternative uses for land, labor, and capital and to figure out which is the most profitable to remind you what your capital could be earning elsewhere.

Variable and Fixed Costs

Variable costs are those that change as farm production or output changes. If production does not occur, variable costs are not incurred. Variable costs are also called operating costs or operating expenses. Examples of variable costs include feed, fertilizer, seed, fuel, labor, and veterinary care. If there were no more sheep on the farm, these costs would be eliminated. On the other hand, variable expenses increase in direct proportion to the number of animals.

Fixed costs are those that are incurred whether or not production takes place. Such costs remain constant regardless of the production decisions made. Fixed costs include depreciation, interest, repairs, taxes, and insurance. Fixed costs are the costs of owning farm buildings, land, equipment, and livestock. Table 22–1 shows a good method for estimating the annual fixed costs of intermediate and long-term assets, when actual figures are not available.

Table 22-1

ANNUAL FIXED COSTS

Costs	Intermediate Assets	Long-Term Assets
Depreciation	10%	5%
Interest	6	5
Repairs	2	2
Taxes	0	.3
Insurance	.2	.2

Table 22–1. Annual fixed costs based on expected life of an asset. These rates are multiplied times the purchase price of the asset and are approximately half the normal rates, because over the useful life of an item, its value averages half of its initial cost.

DEPRECIATION

Depreciation is used to describe a loss in the value of farm equipment, breeding stock, and buildings due to age or use. Buildings begin to depreciate as soon as they are built, and some charge has to be made to account for the gradual loss in value. Farm machinery begins to depreciate as soon as it is used, and the "useful life" varies with the type of equipment. Annual depreciation is a legitimate deductible expense for federal income tax purposes. Since the entire cost of buildings, equipment, or livestock cannot be deducted in 1 year, these items are prorated and depreciated over their useful life.

For management purposes, the useful life of farm buildings is about 20 years and up to 10 years for farm equipment and machinery. Sometimes a higher depreciation or faster rate of amortization is desirable for income tax purposes.

The Internal Revenue Service (IRS) requires farmers to list new or used depreciable property purchased after 1981 by the Accelerated Cost Recovery System (ACRS), in which property is depreciated over a 3-year, 5-year, 10-year, or 15-year period. Three-year properties include pickup trucks and breeding hogs. Five-year properties include

Table 22-2

ACRS DEDUCTIONS
3-Year Property
1st year: 25% of cost or tax basis 2nd year: 38% of cost or tax basis 3rd year: 37% of cost or tax basis
5-Year Property
1st year: 15% of cost or tax basis 2nd year: 22% of cost or tax basis 3rd through 5th year: 21% of cost or tax basis

Table 22–2. *The tax basis of an asset is usually its cost when you first acquire it. This basis may be increased by improvements or alterations to the property, and may be decreased by depreciation, depletion, or amortization deductions, or by deductions for losses such as casualty or theft. This increased or decreased basis is called an "adjusted basis."*

sheep and all other livestock, most farm machinery, fences, silos, and single-purpose livestock structures. ACRS deductions have been calculated for these depreciable properties.

Straight-line depreciation is allowed under certain circumstances as well. The recovery period or useful life may be chosen by the farmer as long as it is reasonable for the item being depreciated. Straight line depreciation gives a steady annual rate of depreciation compared to Accelerated Cost Recovery in which the rate of depreciation increases as the capital item gets older. It is an easier method to use for budgeting.

To calculate depreciation by the straight-line method, the initial price paid for the capital item or property, its salvage value at the end of its useful life, and its useful life need to be found out. The salvage value is subtracted from the initial cost and the resulting value is divided by the number of years of useful life to give the depreciation per year.

DEPRECIATION ON A FARM TRACTOR, STRAIGHT-LINE METHOD

Example. Depreciation on a farm tractor figured by the straight-line method.

Cost: $16,000 new tractor
Useful life: 10 years
Salvage value: $1,000

$16,000 − $1,000 = $15,000 to be depreciated at an even rate over 10 years.

Year	Depreciation	Value Remaining
1	$1,500	$14,500
2	1,500	13,000
3	1,500	11,500
4	1,500	10,000
5	1,500	8,500
6	1,500	7,000
7	1,500	5,500
8	1,500	4,000
9	1,500	2,500
10	1,500	1,000(salvage value)

Depreciation and the Accelerated Cost Recovery system are described in the *Farmer's Tax Guide* (IRS Publication Number 225, available from county Extension Service offices or farm credit agencies). In addition, the Extension Service has depreciation record books for property purchased or in service prior to 1981 and ACRS books for items purchased or in use after 1981.

DEPRECIATION ON A FARM TRACTOR, ACRS

Example: Depreciation on a farm tractor figured under the Accelerated Cost Recovery System:

Cost: $16,000
Useful life: 5-year property

Recovery Year	ACRS Rate	Cost Recovered This Year	Unrecovered Cost Beginning of Year
1	15%	$2,400	$16,000
2	22	3,520	13,600
3	21	3,360	10,080
4	21	3,360	6,720
5	21	3,360	3,360

ENTERPRISE BUDGETS

Budgets can be used to compare the profitability of different enterprises or different management of an enterprise. A budget projects or estimates receipts, expenses, and levels of production, usually for a 1-year period. The bottom line of the budget shows the return to labor and management after all business costs have been covered. This is the figure to be compared between budgets for different enterprises—sheep, crops, dairy, etc. The budgets also can be analyzed to see how changing the costs of key inputs and outputs (such as the cost of feed and price of lamb) or changing the level of production to match the capacities of land, buildings, and/or equipment (such as number of ewes or number of lambings per year), will affect the return to labor and management. Your budget also can provide a working plan from which your operation can be managed.

Budgets are formed from the previous years' data (from the farm account book or computerized records), best estimates, and trial and error. General farm expenses such as fuel, electricity, telephone, depreciation, taxes, interest, insurance, repairs, etc. may have to be prorated between the sheep and other enterprises or home expenses. For example, a tractor may be used for the sheep enterprise as well as a small fruit enterprise, so only a portion of the total use is charged to the sheep. You can use custom machinery rates, rental rates, or a fee per hour of use of the machinery per acre. Separate electrical and gas meters for the house and barn help to reduce errors in prorating utility costs.

The sample budget is only an example of one type of budget and is not developed from actual figures in any particular sheep operation. It is more important that you know how to develop a budget than to concentrate on the bottom line or the expense figures used in the example.

I am using a 100-ewe flock in this example because it represents a serious financial commitment. It is small enough to be a part-time operation, but large enough to achieve minimum economies of scale. It is also easy to calculate in multiples of 100 ewes. The land and building requirements for a flock this size are fairly easy to meet in most parts of the country—about 2000 square feet of barn space and 30 acres of pasture. It is assumed that all of the hay and concentrate are purchased. The budget assumes a March-April lambing.

The budget does not include any receipts from the sale of registered breeding stock, although these have the potential to be high in an established breeder's flock. There would be higher marketing costs, however, if registered animals were sold, especially if showing animals was part of the marketing strategy. Marketing costs include processing freezer lambs, telephone, postage, advertising, consignment fees, health certificates, registration papers, delivery, and your guarantee.

There are many other income-generating schemes that are not reflected in these budgets. These include specialty flocks, which emphasize wool and fleeces for handspinners, freezer lambs, replacement ewe lambs, or feeder lambs. One of the nice characteristics of sheep is their suitability to a wide range of management.

SAMPLE BUDGET

100-ewe Flock Lambing in March-April

Based on: 100 ewes, 1 year old and older; 3 rams; 180 percent lamb crop; 15 percent ewe culling rate; 12 percent lamb mortality; and 15 ewe lambs kept as replacements. Lambs are raised on pasture and marketed in October and November.

Receipts

Market lambs: 180 head minus 20 head death loss minus 15 head kept as replacements = 145 lambs @ 105 lbs. or 15,225 lbs. @ $.65	$9,896.25
Cull ewes: 10 head @ 135 lbs. or 1350 lbs. @ $.15	202.50
Cull ram: 1 head @ $35	35.00
Wool: 100 ewes and 3 rams @ 8 lbs./head and 145 lambs @ 3 lbs./head or 1259 pounds @ $1.50*	1,888.50
Gross Receipts	$12,022.25

Variable Costs

Feed Costs:

Hay Equivalent @ 800 lbs./ewe, $80/ton	$3,296.00
Concentrate, ewes @ 150 lbs./head, $140/ton	1,050.00
Concentrate, lambs @ 100 lbs./head, $180/ton	1,305.00
Salt and minerals, 1000 lbs. @ $.08/lb.	80.00
Milk replacer, 100 lbs. @ $1.00/lb.	100.00
Total Feed Costs	$5,831.00

Livestock Costs:

Bedding, 2 tons straw @ $60/Ton	120.00
Veterinary and medicine	450.00
Pasture maintenance (lime, fertilizer, seed, fence repair, etc.)	700.00
Shearing @ $2/head	496.00
Supplies	150.00
Utilities	50.00
Fuel and oil	100.00
Marketing @ $4/head for 145 head	580.00
Ram (1 purchased every year)	400.00
Interest @ 12% on .5 of total operating expenses	532.62
Total Variable Costs	$ 9,409.62

Continued on next pag

SAMPLE BUDGET (Continued)

Fixed Costs

Depreciation, interest, taxes, repairs, and insurance on buildings (new cost) $8,000 × 12%	$ 960.00
Depreciation, interest, repairs on fencing and equipment (new cost) $3500 × 18%	630.00
Interest, taxes, and insurance on ewes and rams: $10,000 ewes and $1,200 rams = $11,200 × 10%	1,120.00
Interest, taxes, and insurance on land: 25 acres @ $800/acre or $20,000 × 2%	400.00
Total Fixed Costs	$ 3,110.00
Total Costs (Fixed and Variable)	$12,519.62

Summary:

Return above variable costs	$ 2,612.63
Return to labor and management**	(497.37)
Breakeven lamb price, $/cwt.***	(68.50)
Labor: 500 hours	

*Includes wool @ $.60/lb. and Wool Incentive Payment of $.90/lb. or 149 percent of the 1984 farm price.

**Return to labor and management: Total receipts less total costs (fixed and variable costs). It is your "net profit."

***Breakeven price: If lamb was $68 in our budget example, the sheep producer would cover all the costs of production (fixed and variable) but would have no return to his or her labor and management (i.e., the net profit is zero). As soon as lamb goes above $68 per cwt (per hundredweight), and if the costs stay the same, the producer makes a profit.

BUDGET ANALYSIS

From the budget, it is evident that the main source of income is the lamb receipts and the enterprise is losing money if the lamb price is $.65/lb. and input and output cannot be improved. It is a fact that individual farmers have little control over wholesale lamb prices or prices of any other farm commodities. While it would be nice to have lamb prices in the area of $.70/lb. (as they were in 1978), it is unrealistic to expect higher lamb prices will save an unprofitable enterprise. Historically, the most profitable farm operations have increased the level of output to compensate for lower prices of farm products and higher prices for farm supplies. Dairy farmers have consistently increased production per cow; crop farmers increased the bushels of grain or tons per acre; swine growers farrowed more than twice a year; all this to maintain profitability despite low farm prices.

On the other hand, many sheep producers with 140 to 170 percent annual lamb crop are at a level of production that is no better than what was achieved 30 years ago in farm flocks. The technology is available to substantially increase the number of lambs and total pounds of lamb produced per ewe per year. Low livestock productivity is the major limiting factor affecting sheep farm profitability today.

The example sheep enterprise has a number of options to increase profitability. Cost control is the first factor to improve financial success of the farm business. The farmer should pay strict attention to nonproductive expense items such as fuel, repairs, utilities, and interest. The farm is no better off for having spent money on these items. Hired labor is too often a nonproductive expense when worker productivity is low. In the example, the nonproductive expense items are minor in relation to other expenses and no changes are necessary.

Some increase in productive expense items such as fertilizer, feed, soil testing, and farm records may generate more income than the cost of the expense items. For example, every dollar spent on fertilizer can return $3 to $4 in higher yields and crop quality. Since feed costs in the example represent 62 percent of the total variable costs, anything the farmer does to reduce feed cost while maintaining animal performance will improve profitability. The farmer can consider cooperative or bulk purchase of concentrates to obtain them at a lower cost. Hay may be purchased in the field at harvest for a lower cost than when it comes out of storage later in the season. Corn silage could be a cheaper forage than hay. All of these cost-cutting measures could mean the difference between profit and loss.

Finally, farmers can't control all costs such as property taxes and insurance. While cost control is important, the greatest determinant of profit is the level of output. By crossbreeding with a prolific breed, such as the Finnsheep, the producer could achieve a 200 to 225 percent lamb crop with little additional cost or labor. Marketing an additional 20 lambs would increase gross receipts by $1365 with lamb at $.65/lb. and change the returns to labor and management to a profit.

Some farmers raise sheep to diversify a beef, dairy, or row-crop operation. Diversification may improve profitability if it minimizes some of the risks from bad weather or low market prices, makes better use of labor, or increases farm output at little extra cost. However, contrary to popular opinion, it is unusual to find a small, diversified farm that is also profitable. Large farms that have become efficient in 1 or 2 enterprises often can diversify and increase profitability. Most small-scale sheep producers would initially do better if sheep were the only enterprise and the flock was intensively managed. The example 100-ewe enterprise budget can be compared with budgets from other sized flocks—98, 115, 122 ewes, etc.—by putting all receipts and expenses on a *per ewe basis* (divide each budget item by 100).

PROFIT AND LOSS STATEMENT

The profit and loss statement (P & L) measures the actual change in profit or loss after a given period of time, usually 1 year, whereas a budget is used to estimate profitability. It shows the operating receipts, operating expenses, changes in inventory and capital assets, and adjustments for capital purchases or sales. The P & L (also called the income statement) can be used to determine strong and weak points in the farm business.

In the short term, the farmer is most interested in the net cash income or cash profit. This is defined as:

$$\begin{array}{l} \text{Operating receipts} \\ \underline{-\,\text{Operating expenses}} \\ =\text{Net cash income} \end{array}$$

Net cash income is used for debt payment, capital purchases, emergencies, and family living. However, if the farm investment changes significantly, if it expands, for example, seeking long-term financial stability, the net profit becomes more important:

$$\begin{array}{l} \quad\quad\text{Net cash income} \\ +\text{ or }-\;\underline{\text{Changes in inventory and capital items}} \\ \quad\quad =\text{Net profit (or loss)} \end{array}$$

Net profit represents the returns to the operator's labor, management, and farmer-owned capital.

The P & L is used to calculate various profitability ratios. The ratios allow financial comparisons between different sizes and types of agricultural enterprises and are becoming the standard financial indicators used by lenders. The cash expenses/cash receipts ratio provides a quick analysis of the business. If cash expenses are less than 65 percent of total cash receipts, the business is in a strong cash position. A safe margin is between 65 and 80 percent. If operating expenses are greater than 80 percent of operating receipts, the farmer may have difficulty meeting debt payments, family living expenses, and planned capital purchases.

In the sample P & L statement, taxable and insured property (under "operating expenses") includes buildings, land, and livestock. These expenses are included in the sample budget under fixed costs since they are incurred whether production takes place or not.

In general, if the end-of-year inventory values (item F in the P & L) are greater than beginning year values—for example, ewe replacements are retained to increase flock size—the net change is positive. Negative changes are appropriate if ending year values are less than beginning year values.

PROFIT AND LOSS STATEMENT

Name: _____   Period Covered: _____

Operating Receipts	Units	Total	Percent
Gross Receipts from Farming (describe)			
Miscellaneous Receipts			
A. Total Cash Operating Receipts		$ _____	100%

Cost of Goods Purchased for Resale

	Units	Total	
B. Total Cost of Goods Purchased for Resale		$ _____	
C. Total Cash Operating Receipts, Adjusted (A Minus B)		$ _____	

Operating Expenses

		Total	Percent
Hired Labor — shearing		$ _____	_____ %
Maintenance and Repairs — Machinery $3500 × 2%		_____	_____
— Buildings $8000 × 2%		_____	_____
Interest (Farm Share)		_____	_____
Rent and Leases		_____	_____
Feed Purchased		_____	_____
Seeds and Plants Purchased		_____	_____
Fertilizer and Lime (pasture maint.)		_____	_____
Pesticides		_____	_____
Machinery Hire		_____	_____
Supplies Purchased		_____	_____
Breeding Fees — ram		_____	_____
Veterinary Fees, Medicine		_____	_____
Fuel and Oil		_____	_____
Taxes (Farm Share)*		_____	_____
Insurance (Farm Share)*		_____	_____
Utilities (Farm Share)		_____	_____
Freight, Trucking		_____	_____
Other_____		_____	_____
D. Total Cash Operating Expenses		_____ $	100%
E. Net Cash Operating Income (C Minus D)		$ _____ *	

*Taxable and insured property includes buildings, land, and livestock. Taxes and insurance were covered under fixed costs in the sample enterprise budget.

PROFIT AND LOSS STATEMENT (continued)

Adjustments for Inventory and Capital Items

E. Net Cash Operating Income $ _____

Inventory Changes*
  Crops $ _____
  Supplies   _____
  Market Livestock   _____
  Other _____   _____
  _____

F. Net Inventory Change $ _____

Adjustments for Capital Items

Inventory Change of Capital Assets*
Dairy/Breeding Livestock** $ _____
Machinery and Equipment Depre-
  ciation   _____
Buildings and Improvements Depre-
  ciation   _____
Land and Improvements**   _____

Sales and Purchases of Capital Assets
Sales of Breeding Livestock,***
  Machinery, Equipment,
  Buildings and Land $+ _____
Purchases (additions) of
  Breeding Livestock, Machinery,
  Equipment, Buildings and Land $− _____

G. Net Capital Adjustments $ _____

H. PROFIT (LOSS) (Sum of E, F and G) = $ _____ *
  Returns to Operator Labor, Management and
  Equity Capital

---

*In general, if end of the year inventory values are greater than beginning year values, net change is
positive. Negative changes are appropriate if ending year values are less than beginning year values.
**It is best not to include breeding stock and land value increases or decreases due to market fluctua-
tions. These changes are not a reflection of farm earnings.
***Cull sales of breeding livestock may be listed as either sales of capital assets or operating receipts. Do
not list cull sales under both categories.

Under the "adjustments for capital items," it is best not to include breeding stock and land value increases or decreases due to market fluctuations. These changes are not a reflection of farm earnings. Cull sales of breeding livestock may be listed either as sales of capital assets or operating receipts. Do not list cull sales under both categories.

The bottom line in the P & L is the net return to operator labor, management, and equity capital. To obtain the net return to labor and management (which is the bottom line of the enterprise budget), interest is charged against the owner's equity capital.

NET WORTH STATEMENT

The net worth statement summarizes the condition of a business at a given point in time and is based on the formula:

$$\text{Assets} = \text{Liabilities} + \text{Net Worth}$$

Assets in the net worth statement are categorized according to the years of useful life. Current assets usually are sold or used in the upcoming year as a normal part of the operation. Examples of current assets are cash on hand, savings accounts, crops held for sale, feed inventory, supplies inventory, accounts receivable, prepaid expenses, and readily marketable securities. Intermediate assets support farm production and have useful lives of more than 1 year but less than 10. Many intermediate assets are depreciable. Examples include breeding livestock, machinery, and equipment. Long-term or fixed assets are permanent or have useful lives of over 10 years. Land, silos, ponds, and buildings are examples of long-term assets.

Liabilities are obligations or debts owed by the business. Current liabilities are due within a year of the net worth statement. Examples include unpaid rent, interest, taxes, and operating accounts payable. Intermediate liabilities are usually the principal payments on loans with repayment schedules for up to 10 years. Long-term liabilities include the principal balance on a farm mortgage (less the amount listed as a current liability). Assets can be valued on current market values or on original cost basis.

The net worth statement provides information for measuring the business's ability to pay its debts. The current ratio measures a farm's ability to generate enough cash within the next year to meet annual debt payments and other current liabilities. The current ratio is obtained from the net worth statement:

Current Ratio = Total Assets Divided by Total Current Liabilities

A ratio of 2 to 1 is considered good and the farmer will probably be able to pay current debts from the farm receipts. A ratio of 1 to 1 indicates a potential cash shortfall and poor debt repayment ability.

NET WORTH STATEMENT

Name: _____ Major Enterprise: _____

Address: _____ Statement Date: _____

ASSETS	LIABILITIES

Current

Cash on Hand	$ _____	
Cash on Deposit		
(Bank _____)	_____	
Notes Receivable	_____	
Accounts Receivable	_____	
Livestock Held for Sale	_____	
Crops Held for Sale and Feed	_____	
Cash Investment in Growing		
Crops (fertilizer, seed, etc.)	_____	
Securities (Marketable)	_____	
Cash Surrender Value of		
Life Insurance	_____	
Other (specify) _____	_____	
TOTAL CURRENT	$ _____	

Current (Liabilities)

Accounts Payable	$ _____
Accounts Payable	_____
Accounts Payable	_____
Portion of Intermediate Term Debt Due Within 12 Months	_____
Portion of Long-Term Debt Due Within 12 Months	_____
Rent, Taxes, and Interest Due and Unpaid	_____
Loans Against Cash Surrender Value of Life Insurance	_____
Other Debt Due Within 12 Months	_____
TOTAL CURRENT	$ _____

Intermediate

Autos and Trucks	$ _____
Machinery and Equipment	_____
Breeding and Dairy Livestock	_____
Securities (not readily marketable)	_____
Other (specify) _____	_____
TOTAL INTERMEDIATE	$ _____

Intermediate (Liabilities)

Accounts Payable to Our Bank	$ _____
Accounts Payable to Others	_____
Maturities of over 1 but under 10 years for other than seasonal needs — less portion applied to current liabilities	
TOTAL INTERMEDIATE	_____

Fixed

Farmland	$ _____
Farm Improvements	_____
Nonfarm Real Estate	_____
Household Furnishings	_____
Other (specify) _____	_____
TOTAL FIXED	$ _____
TOTAL ASSETS	$ _____

Long-term

Mortgages on Farm Real Estate (Less portion applied to current liabilities)	$ _____
Mortgages on Other Real Estate (Less portion applied to current liabilities)	_____
Other (specify) _____	_____
TOTAL LONG-TERM	$ _____
TOTAL LIABILITIES	$ _____
NET WORTH	$ _____
TOTAL LIABILITIES & NET WORTH	$ _____

CASH FLOW STATEMENT

Operating receipts and expenses in a sheep enterprise are not evenly distributed throughout the year. Even dairy farmers with relatively steady production and income have periodic cash surpluses or deficits. A cash flow statement outlines cash coming into the business and cash going out during a given period of time. Annual statements usually are broken down on a monthly or quarterly basis. Sources of cash inflow include:

- **Operating receipts**
- **Capital sales**
- **New loans**

- **Nonfarm income**
- **Interest (on savings)**
- **Cash gifts received**

Sources of cash outflow include:

- **Operating expenses**
- **Capital purchases**
- **Debt payments**

- **Family living expenses**
- **Savings account deposits**
- **Cash gifts given**

Cash flow statements are used to plan future cash needs. Realistic cash flow projections can show when to expand the business, purchase capital items, invest cash surpluses (perhaps in short-term, high-yielding certificates of deposit), or seek short-term or operating capital and what a feasible loan repayment schedule would be. It also shows potential lenders that you control the business. A cash flow statement can be as simple or as complicated as is needed.

PARTIAL BUDGETING

A partial budget can be used to estimate the effect of making a specific change in the farm operation – building a new barn, purchasing a new piece of machinery, or adding more livestock – which would have a significant impact on net income. In a partial budget, the change must be described in detail with the additional and reduced costs and returns listed. The budget estimations must be realistic and conservative, particularly when figuring what the additional returns will be. Only the costs that change with the new way of doing business should be included.

PARTIAL BUDGET (example)

Adjustment: Build a 3-ton plywood grain bin for $250 and buy commercial (16% protein) concentrate in bulk at $180/ton delivered rather than $210/ton in bags.

A. Additional Returns:
None

Total Additional Returns	$ 0

B. Reduced Costs:

Save $30 per ton of grain by buying in bulk (6 tons)	$180.00
Trucking of bagged grain @$ 6/ton	36.00
Total Reduced Costs	216.00
Total Additional Returns and Reduced Costs/Year	$216.00

C. Additional Costs:
Annual ownership costs*

Depreciation	$25.00
Interest	12.50
Repairs	0
Total Additional Costs	$ 37.50

D. Reduced Returns:
None

Total Reduced Returns	$ 0
Total Additional Returns and Reduced Costs/Year	$216.00
Total Additional Costs and Reduced Returns/Year	− $ 37.50

E. Net change in Farm income per Year — $178.50

(Total of additional costs and reduced returns subtracted from total of additional returns and reduced costs per year)

---

*Annual ownership costs are taxes, insurance, interest, depreciation, and possible storage.

In the example in the box on page 265, a farmer contemplates purchasing commercial concentrate in bulk versus purchasing the feed in bags. This partial budget illustrates a typical farm management problem.

The bottom line on the partial budget is the net change in farm income per year. However, this is not all that must be considered. The cash flow statement must be checked to see if additional debt payments can be handled. The payback period and average rate of return on the investment should be determined also as follows.

$$\text{Payback period (years)} = \frac{\text{Amount of capital required by the investment}}{\text{Additional annual earnings (after taxes)}}$$

$$\text{Average rate of return (percent)} = \frac{\text{Average annual profits from the new investment (less depreciation)}}{\text{Total capital outlay for the investment}}$$

In the example, the bulk grain bin has a payback of just over 1 year ($250 divided by $178.50 = 1.4 years). The average rate of return is approximately 71 percent ($178.50 divided by $250 = .71). Capital purchases or investments that have less than a 3-year payback could be considered priority investments well worth their initial cost. Long payback investments (7 to 10 years) include manure storage facilities, lambing barns, or silos. Intermediate payback investments (3 to 5 years) include breeding stock, pasture renovation, and handling facilities. The average rate of return is the more important figure to look at when evaluating capital purchases or investments. Obviously the shorter the payback period, the better; but the greater the return on the investment, the greater the profitability because there is more annual profit generated as a result of the investment.

Finally, when preparing a partial budget, consider convenience factors, such as reduced physical labor or reduced stress on the livestock. A farmer with a bad back may not easily justify an automatic feeding system, but it may be the only option available.

WHAT AGRICULTURE LENDERS EXPECT FROM FARM BORROWERS

While planning for major capital investments in cattle, equipment, land, and buildings, many of you will be visiting a lender to borrow additional money for your needs. Before you visit the lender you should be prepared. The lender will expect you to have the following information ready.

Provide Your Lender With an Accurate Profit and Loss and Net Worth Statement for Each Year. These should be prepared by you as of the same date each year, preferably December 31. If you are approaching a new lender and he or she has no history of financial trends in your business, be prepared to provide these records for the past 3 to 5 years.

Project a Cash Flow for Your Business, by Month, for a Year in Advance and Review It With Your Lender. If you are anticipating a major change in your farming operation, project your cash flow for a longer period of time.

Maintain a Good Set of Farm Business Records. Show your lender how you use production records in making management decisions.

Approach Your Lender in a Businesslike Manner and With a Positive Attitude. Show the lender you have confidence in your plans and in yourself. Have your plans well thought out and explain them logically. Know your costs and your benefits.

Have a Repayment Program Fully Developed. Prepare a partial budget to show the influence of the new investment on profit.

Give Your Lender Time to Review Your Plans and Make Suggestions. Don't push for an immediate credit decision on major purchases.

Always Arrange for Credit in Advance of Making Any Major Purchases. Don't inform your lender after the fact when you have made a major decision which affects you financially, and then expect him or her to provide the credit.

Maintain Good Communication With Your Lender. Tell your lender if your plans change or if unforeseen problems or circumstances arise in your operation which may affect your credit needs or interfere with making loan payments on time.

Avoid Split Lines of Credit if Possible. It is usually to your advantage that one lender has full responsibility for your line of credit. Exceptions may be in the case of short-term and intermediate-term loans with one lender and long-term loans with another lender.

Practice Good Production Management and Sound Financial Management At All Times. Use modern farming and business commitments.

Do Everything Possible to Build Confidence, Understanding, and Trust Between You and Your Lender. Exercise a high level of business integrity and always honor your commitments.

Set Long-Range Goals for Your Business and Your Family. Show your lender where you are, where you want to go, and how you plan to get there. By sharing your plans and goals with your lender, he or she can help you reach them.

See Appendix G for more sources of information on farm credit.

Appendix A

SERVICES TO SHEEP PRODUCERS

EXTENSION SERVICE

The following services are available through the Cooperative Extension Service in each state.

Soil Testing. Soil test mailer kits are available from county extension offices. Agents can give least-cost fertilizer and lime recommendations.

Forage Analysis. A complete analysis includes protein; estimated net energy; and available protein, Ca, P, K, and Mg. The cost for analysis is about $18.00. The analysis is usually done for sample hay, corn silage, or grass silage. Analyses of mixed feeds or concentrates are available also.

Farm Management. Farm account books, depreciation schedules, guides to obtaining farm credit.

ELFAC. This computerized record keeping system costs $60 a year for 100 ewes. It includes a monthly operating statement of receipts and expenses, listing every transaction and providing a financial summary. Optional records include depreciation and investment tax credit report and year-end income tax summary.

Publications. Forage seed mixtures, water supplies, fertilizing, lime, farm fences, barn ventilation, and more.

Agricultural Engineering Plans. Blueprints for barns, sheds, silos, and other farm structures.

Library. An affiliated state university will hold a large selection of farm periodicals, agricultural journals, and reference books.

Extension Agents. County agents offer assistance in the areas of home economics, youth/4-H, community development, energy, farm family rehabilitation, and agriculture. All county staff are supported by specialists at the state university. Specialists are available to individual farmers and homeowners through an initial contact with the county agent.

Appendix A (continued)

OTHER AGENCIES

Additional services are provided through other agencies.

Soil Conservation Service, USDA. Technical help on farm ponds, drainage, land clearing, sites for roads, buildings, and septic systems. SCS aerial photographs and soil survey maps are free to landowners.

Agricultural Stabilization and Conservation Service (ASCS). This USDA agency provides cost-sharing to landowners who qualify. Conservation programs include liming and fertilizing worn-out fields, manure pit construction, winter crop drop seeding, timber stand improvement, streambank protection, and wool incentive payments.

State Department of Forests and Parks. County foresters consult with forestland owners, mark trees, and so on. There is no charge for their assistance.

State Department of Agriculture. Responsible for plant and animal quarantines, pesticide regulations, meat and livestock inspection, market promotion and development.

Appendix B

TESTING LABORATORIES

See also Appendix A for testing performed by the Extension Service.

PERFORMANCE TESTING

On-Farm Performance Testing of White Face Rams
C. Leroy Johnson or M. R. Botkin
Box 3354
University Station
Laramie, WY 82071

OSU Sheep Production Testing Program
Richard Smith
Extension Livestock Specialist
Ohio State University
2029 Fyffe Road
Columbus, OH 43210

DIAGNOSTIC LABORATORIES

For a complete listing, write:
USDA-APHIS Division
Federal Building
Hyattsville, MD 20782

Appendix C

SUPPLIERS

The following suppliers all carry equipment mentioned in the text.

GRADING EQUIPMENT, SUPPLIES

Clear Plastic Ribeye/Loineye Grids (No. AS-235e)
Publications Distribution Center
Cooperative Extension Service
Iowa State University
Ames, IA 50011

Ram Marking Harness, Stainless Steel Backfat Probes, AI Equipment
NASCO
901 Janesville Ave.
Fort Atkinson, WI 53538

ULTRASONIC PREGNANCY DETECTION DEVICES

Pregsonic
Ag Electronics of Iowa, Inc.
P.O. Box 514, 5th and Broadway
Humboldt, IA 50548

Scanopreg II
Scanco
2776 N. Triphammer Road
Ithaca, NY 14850

Pregmatic II, III, and Pregnosticator
Animark Company
876 Ventura Street
Aurora, CO 80011

Pregtone and Preg Alert
Renco Corporation
116 3rd Avenue North
Minneapolis, MN 55407

Appendix D

MARKET LAMB AND WOOL PRICES

MARKET LAMB PRICE SOURCES

Lamb Market Report
American Sheep Producer's Council
200 Clayton Street
Denver, CO 80206
Wholesale and retail live and dressed lamb prices and outlook

Livestock, Meat and Wool Market News (weekly)
Agricultural Marketing Service
USDA
Washington, DC 20250

Livestock and Meat Situation (bi-monthly)
Sheep and Lamb Inventory Reports (bi-monthly)
Economic and Statistics Service
USDA
Publications Department
Washington, DC 20250
Number of lambs on feed, sheep and lamb numbers, price data and outlook

Sheep Footnotes (monthly)
Alberta Agriculture
Animal Industry Division
7000-113 Street
Edmonton, Alberta
Canada T6H5T6
Weekly slaughter lamb prices in Alberta and Toronto

Sheepman's Weekly
California Wool Growers Association
3382 El Camino Avenue
Suite 6
Sacramento, CA 95821
Dixon Livestock Auction, national sheep summary, hay market news

Western Livestock Round Up (monthly)
Available from the Extension Economist Department of Agricultural
Economics at all state universities, for producers in the Western and
Great Plains states

WOOL PRICE SOURCES

National Wool Market Weekly Review
Market News Division, USDA-ARS
Building 81, Federal Center
Box 25125
Denver, CO 80225

Commercial Bulletin (weekly)
Curtis Guild and Co.
88 Broad Street
Boston, MA 02110

British Wool Marketing Board
Oak Mills, Station Road
Clayton, Bradford
West Yorkshire
England BD146JD

Appendix E

SHEEP PERIODICALS

Black Sheep Newsletter (quarterly)
28068 Ham Road
Eugene, OR 97406

Feedlot Magazine (monthly, mostly for beef producers)
P.O. Box 1292
Minneapolis, MN 55440

The Lamb Producers Journal
Graphics 1
P.O. Box 384
Monticello, IN 47960

National Wool Grower (monthly)
600 Crandall Building
Salt Lake City, UT 84101

New England Farmer (monthly)
Box 391
St. Johnsbury, VT 05819

New Zealand Farmer (biweekly)
Box 3176
Auckland, New Zealand

Ranch Magazine (monthly)
P.O. Box 2678
San Angelo, TX 76902

Sheep! (monthly)
Box 329
Jefferson, WI 53549

Sheep and Farm Life (bimonthly)
5696 Johnston Road
New Washington, OH 44854

Sheep Breeder and Sheepman (monthly)
P.O. Box 796
Columbia, MO 65205

Sheep Canada (quarterly)
Box 777
Airdrie, Alberta TOM OBO
Canada

Sheep Farmer (bimonthly)
National Sheep Association
Tring, Herts
England HP23 6PD

Sheep Production (quarterly)
P.O. Box 185
Shoreham, VT 05770

Sheep Tales (bimonthly)
Box 146
Hadley, MI 48440

Sheep World (quarterly)
Rt. 1, Box 118
Ridgeway, WI 53582

The Shepherd (monthly)
RD 1, Box 67
Sheffield, MA 01257

Appendix F

FARM COMPUTERS

PERIODICALS

Agri Comp Magazine (bi-monthly)
103 Outdoors Building
Columbia, MO 65201
$15/year

Agricultural Computing (monthly
newsletter with reference notebook)
Doane-Western, Inc.
8900 Manchester Road
St. Louis, MO 63144
$48/year

Agricultural Microcomputing Newsletter
(monthly)
R. W. Ross, editor
Farm Economics Section
Ridgetown, Ontario
Canada NOP 2CO
Free

Compu - Farm (monthly newsletter)
Alberta Agriculture
Farm Management Branch
Box 2000
Olds, Alberta
Canada TOM 1PO
Free

Computer Farming Newsletter (monthly)
P.O. Box 17484
Memphis, TN 38187
$33/year

Farm Computer News (monthly
newsletter)
Successful Farming Magazine
1716 Loctus
Des Moines, IA 50336
$40/year

GUIDES TO AGRICULTURAL SOFTWARE

Updated Inventory of Agricultural Computer Programs, available for Extension use by J. Robert Strain and Sherry Fieser. Food and Resource Economics Department, University of Florida, Gainesville, FL 32611. A guide to public domain software from State Cooperative Extension Services. 186 pp., April 1984.

TRS-80 Agricultural Software Sourcebook, from Radio Shack retail outlets. 80 pp. February 1983. $2.95.

Appendix G

MORE SOURCES
OF INFORMATION

Here is a listing of books and publications mentioned in the text which can provide you with more information for your sheep operation.

DESIGNS FOR HAY AND GRAIN FEEDS, PANELS, BARNS, AND EQUIPMENT

Sheep Housing Handbook. Midwest Plan Service, Iowa State University, Ames, IA 50011. $5. postpaid.

DESIGNS AND PRINCIPLES FOR SHEEP HANDLING FACILITIES

Planning a Sheep Handling Facility by Bruce Brockway. FBIC Report 16, Farm Buildings Information Center, National Agricultural Center, Kenilworth, Warwickshire, England CV82LG (1976).

POISONOUS PLANTS

Poisonous Plants of the Midwest and Their Effects on Livestock by Robert Evers and Roger Link. Special Publication 24, College of Agriculture, University of Illinois at Urbana-Champaign 165 pp. with color illustrations.

FORAGES

Forages, The Science of Grassland Agriculture edited by M. E. Heath, D. S. Metcalfe, and R. F. Barnes. The Iowa University Press, Ames, IA 50011, 1973.

"Sheep Harvested Feeds for the Intermountain West," (November 6–8, 1974) Proceedings. Copies available for a nominal fee from the Sheep Industry Development Program, 200 Clayton Street, Denver, CO 80206.

HAY STORAGE SAFETY

Will Your Barn Burn This Summer? Available free from the Extension Service, University of Vermont, Burlington, VT 05401.

FORMULATING RATIONS

Sheepman's Production Handbook by the Sheep Industry Development Program, 200 Clayton Street, Denver, CO 80206.

SHEEP OBSTETRICS

Beginning Shepherd's Manual by Barbara Smith. Iowa State University Press, Ames, IA 50010. 1983.

SHEEP HEALTH

Diseases of Sheep 2nd edition, by Rue Jensen and Brinton Swift. Lea & Febiger, Philadelphia. 1982. 330 pp.

Newsom's Sheep Disease 3rd edition, by Hadleigh, Marsh, D.V.M. Robert E. Krieger Publishing Co, Huntington, New York. 1965. 456 pp.

Merck Veterinary Manual 4th edition, by O. H. Siegmund, ed. Merck & Co., Inc., Rahway, New Jersey. 1973. 1618 pp.

TV Vet Sheep Book. Farming Press Ltd., Suffolk, England. 1972, revised 1976. 178 pp.

FARM CREDIT

Credit Facts for Small Farmers. The New England Small Farmer Project, Draper Hall, University of Massachusetts, Amherst, MA 01003. 1980.

What Young Farm Families Should Know About Credit. USDA Farmer's Bulletin, Number 2135, U.S. Government Printing Office, Washington D.C. Revised September 1971.

Appendix H

SUGGESTED DATA FOR PLANNING A SHEEP ENTERPRISE

LAND

¾ to 1½ acres of improved pasture and tillage per ewe in flock. Average stocking rates vary from 3 to 7 ewes per acre of pasture.

LABOR

3 to 7.5 hours per ewe, plus 2.5 hours per lamb. Distribution of labor by months:

Jan.	Feb.	Mar.	Apr.	May	June	July	Aug.	Sep.	Oct.	Nov.	Dec.
11%	11%	19%	22%	10%	3%	3%	2%	3%	3%	4%	9%

LIVESTOCK

Culling and mortality of ewes: 20%
Lamb crop: 1.25 lambs per ewe, average. Goal of 1.8 to 2.3 lambs
Wool: 6 to 10 lbs. per sheep
Meat: Lambs (grass finish): 105 lbs. each
      Lambs (grain finish): 110 lbs. each
      Ewes: 130–180 lbs. each
      Rams: 175–325 lbs. each

Dressing Percentage: 50 to 55% usable carcass

BUILDINGS AND EQUIPMENT

Buildings

Open shed: 15 to 20 sq. ft. of floor space per ewe. Provide good ventilation, wide doorways. Provide lambing pens (4½ feet by 4½ feet) for 10 to 15 percent of total flock.

Equipment

Feed troughs and racks: 15 to 18 inches linear space per ewe. Proper height is 12 to 15 inches from the floor.

Self-feeders for lambs: 3 to 4 inches per lamb, 10 to 12 inches from the floor.

MANURE

6 lbs. per ewe, daily or 0.1 cubic foot per ewe
4 lbs. per lamb, daily

FEED REQUIREMENTS PER HEAD

Grain

Late gestation and lactation: 1 to 2 lbs./ewe; 2 to 3 lbs./feeder lamb, plus mineral supplement
Creep feeding to weaning: .5 to 1 lb./lamb

Hay

Maintenance and early gestation: 2½ to 4 lbs./ewe. Late gestation and lactation: 4 to 7 lbs/ewe, plus supplemental grain.

Corn Silage

Maintenance and early gestation: 7 to 9 lbs/ewe, plus protein and mineral supplements. Late gestation and lactation: 12 to 20 lbs./ewe, plus protein and mineral supplements; 4 to 6 lbs./feeder lamb, plus 1 to 2 lbs./day grain and protein and mineral supplement

Water

2 gallons per head daily.

PRICES AND COSTS

Ewe: $60 to $120 per head, grade
Ram: $250 to $1000
Wool: $.45 to $1.25 per pound
Pelts: $2.00 to $4.00 each, raw

Cull Sheep

$.10 to $.45 per pound liveweight

Lamb

$.60 to $.70 per pound liveweight (wholesale)
$.75 to $1.00 per pound liveweight (retail)
$1.00 to $1.50 per pound liveweight (hothouse lamb,
    30 to 45 lbs. liveweight)

Index

Grazing, 105, *105*
  costs, 44
  management, 29–46, 49, *38, 40, 41, 42*
  management system(s),
    alternate, 32–33, *41, 42*
    continuous, 30–36, *41, 42*
    rotational, 14, 17, 30, 32–37, *41, 42*
    strip, 33, 61
    three-field, three-year, 77
    12-month, 39–40, *40*
  pressure, 104–5, *105*
  season, 41–43, *41*, 59
  time, 184
Greenhouse, polyethylene, 23, *23*
Growth
  curves, *166–67*
  daylength effect, 169
  factors influencing, 167–69
  lamb, 165–80, *166, 167, 168, 171, 174, 175*
  promoting substances, 176–80

Haemonchus, 43
Hampshire, 166
Handling facilities, 27–28
Handspinners, 243–44
Hay, 44, 64, 68, 92, 93, 104–6, 111, 115–21, 122, 123. *See also* Forage(s); Grass(es)
  bales, round, 119–121, *120*
  evaluating, 116
  and grain feeders, 23–26, *24, 25, 26*
  -making budget, 118–19
  purchasing, 118–19
Haycrop silage, *114, 117,* 119–21
Hayfield, 129
Health records, 231
Heat, 189
Heat stress, 182
Herbicides, 61–63, 64, 66
Heritability estimates, 204, 206
Heritable defects, 85
Heritable estimates. *See* Heritability estimates
Heritable variation, 205
Heterosis, 212, 214. *See also* Hybrid vigor
High moisture corn, 115
Histalogic exam, 147
Holding pens, 27
Homozygosity, 210, 213
Hormonal imbalances, 131
Hormone balances, 138
Hormone treatment, 141
Horticultural crops, 107
Housing
  barns, 18–22, *19*
  confinement rearing, 18–19, *19*
  costs, 17
  floors, 20–22, *20, 21, 22*
  greenhouse, polyethylene, 23, *23*
  specifications, general, 18
  temporary, 23, *23*

Hybrid vigor, 76, 87, 212, 214

Immunity, 146–47
Inbreeding, 203, 209–14, *210–11*
Income taxes, 246–254
Income-generating schemes, 255
Induced lambing, 226
Infertility, 130–31
Inositol, 93
Intensive production system, 11, 12
Intensive rotational grazing system, 14, 34–37, *41, 42*
Interest, 44
Internal parasites. *See* Parasites
Internal Revenue Service, 252, 254
Investments, 266–68

Jug, 140–43, *142–43*
Jung, Dr. Gerald, 61–67

Kale, 59, 60, 61, 62, 64, 66, 67, 104, 107
Kale, wild, 56
Kentucky Bluegrass. *See* Bluegrass
Ketones, 97
Ketosis, 97

Labor. *See* Birth
Labor records, 249
Lactase, 170
Lactation, 92, *94*, 95, 96, 97, 102, 117, 160
Lactational anestrus, 128
Lactobacillus, 180
Lactose, 170
Ladino clover. *See* Clover
Lamb(s), 112, 117
  creep, movable, *168*
  correctly finished, *194*, 195–96, *199*
  death, 147–48
  drop, 130
  early born, 182–83
  feeder, 176, 182
  growth and development, 165–80, *166, 167, 168, 171, 174, 175*
  market, 191, 193, 202, 273–74
  milk replacer, 159–60
  mortality, 149
  newborn, care, 140, 144–48
  nipple, rubber, 158–59
  nutrition, 10, 93
  on grass, 181–90
  overfinished, 197
  rations, 172
  starter diet, *162*
  underfinished, 197
  vitamin requirements, 93
  weight, *174*
  weight gain, 182–83, 185–90